Barbara W. Hammond

STARLING

OF THE
WHITE HOUSE

*The story of the man whose Secret Service
detail guarded five presidents from Woodrow
Wilson to Franklin D. Roosevelt, as told to*

THOMAS SUGRUE
by Colonel EDMUND W. STARLING

SIMON AND SCHUSTER, NEW YORK, 1946

B
S 895 S

2817

TO MY WIFE

Contents

☆★☆

viii CONTENTS

Introduction

BY THOMAS SUGRUE

THE KENTUCKY gentleman is part of American legend, cousin alike to the Southern beauty and the Yankee trader, the Western cowboy and the city slicker. But whereas these latter have been known to deviate from the purity of their archetypes, so that on occasion Southern girls have turned out to be homely, Yankee traders have been outwitted, Western cowboys have shot themselves in the leg trying to beat dudes to the draw, and city slickers have directed innocent maidens to the YWCA, the Kentucky gentleman is true to his macrocosmic progenitor. In his own environment Kentucky horses are beaten by colts and fillies raised in other parts of the land; Kentucky beauties are outshone by the products of Montgomery and Fort Worth; but he himself, sipping his bourbon, betting his hand in a stud poker game, or pacing a lady through the infinite sprints of love, is neither equaled nor outdistanced. In any season, in any weather, his blood is red and he bows from the waist.

The late Heywood Broun was fond of the notion that nature imitates art. As a prime example he cited Dizzy Dean, the baseball pitcher, a carbon copy of Ring Lardner's Elmer the Great. There was also Tom Harmon, the Michigan halfback, who made Frank Merriwell look more like a rough sketch than a prototype. In the case of Kentucky gentlemen it was probably a desire to outdo the legend about them which prompted nature to create Colonel Edmund William Starling.

He was the sort of man who wipes his feet on the door mat before entering a house, whether it is raining or not. Sometimes he had to go and search for the mat, which had been kicked aside, but this neither disturbed nor deterred him. His voice was so soft that it seemed

ix

to come from an immaterial source, like the sounds in dreams. Yet it carried across a room without difficulty and left a memory wherever it was placed. His eyes were never without the molecular arrangement which causes a twinkle. Their centers could become hard and their lenses caught everything that moved, but the twinkle never did more than recede a little during these interruptions. His attitude was that of an ego perfectly attuned to its surroundings. He considered any man to be God's greatest handiwork, and therefore worthy of his complete attention at any and all times. In this judgment there was neither selection nor differentiation; intellect, morals, charm, were minor variations in the external mechanism; the internal part, the center and motivation, was changeless and common to all. He bowed as solemnly to a seven-year-old girl as he did to a seventy-year-old lady; he listened intently to fools; he kept wise men from stumbling when they forgot absently to step up at a curb.

Several weeks before he came to Florida to work with me on his autobiography there arrived at my house two large packing cases, heavily insured. They contained, I discovered, mementos and evidence of the Colonel's thirty-year stay at the White House—letters, diaries, photographs, newspaper clippings, souvenir menus, programs, all thrown together without arrangement or concern for the more fragile and valuable pieces. If he saved so much, I thought, why did he not preserve it with more care? Browsing through the items and separating them into categories, I found the answer. It was not he who had saved them; they had been sent to his mother, and she, in the way of women, had treasured each and given it security and refuge. That was why, from the time of her death during the Hoover administration, there was little to be found except an occasional batch of photographs with an accompanying note from Jim Farley, a man apparently as thoughtful as he is amiable. There were a few contemporary items, the oldest dated 1936, the year of his marriage. The conclusion was obvious: so long as there was a person he loved who would be pleased by such trinkets, he gathered them. When there was no such person he was indifferent even to the souvenirs of an inauguration.

His diaries had a personal inspiration; he kept them in detail and with fidelity during the second term of President Wilson, when his admiration for the great Presbyterian (and for the beauty and friendliness of his second wife) was at its height. All the programs, all the rotogravure sections, all the newspaper clippings he sent to his mother, bore jesting inscriptions in his strong, handsome calligraphy: "See your son, marching with the great men! Doesn't he look noble, or is he just hungry?" "Don't be fooled by this high-class menu. You could cook a better meal in your sleep." "See how they write up your son. Why don't you send them a letter and let them know the awful truth?" The letters themselves contained a record of his generosity and self-lessness: "I am sending you some cloth for a dress, and a silk scarf. Tell Guy I am sending him some golf balls." "I have decided to buy you a car. You need it. Look them all over and tell me which kind you would like." "You are not to do so much work. If it worries you that things are undone, then you must get more help. I will send you the money for this." Of his own worries, of his own privations, he wrote nothing. He had closed the book on himself when he was eight-een. Then, wanting to go to college, yearning to become a doctor, he had measured the sacrifice this education would cost his family and decided against it. Thenceforth he put aside all personal dreams; he did not want me to mention this lost ambition when I was setting down his story.

When he arrived to begin the work I saw the tips of his shoes for a full minute before I saw him. His feet were moving back and forth on the door mat. When the cleansing was finished he stepped inside, bowed, and took my hand. Then he sat down and said, "Let me look at you for a minute." Quietly we regarded each other. He was sub-mitting me to his personal system of character examination. Meanwhile he was reminding me of my father, probably because both of them were Christian gentlemen. When the minute was up he said, "Now we are friends. We can work together."

We went outside to sit on the beach, under the beefwood trees. There, during most of the days of that winter, we met and talked. I asked him, during the first meeting, about the letters he had received on the occasion of his resignation—there were literally thousands of them, I had heard, from senators, representatives, diplomats, judges, justices of the Supreme Court, cabinet members, and people of im-portance throughout the country, in all walks of life. He drew from his pocket a single soiled envelope. A look of tenderness and humor filled his face as he drew forth the letter. It was from an old Negro, a dining room steward in a Southern hotel. "My dear Colonel," it began. "I am filled with tears and sorrow that I shall not see you coming my way again." He did not know where the other letters were; he was never able to find more than a handful of them for me. This one he carried with him at all times.

He had been lounging in his chair while we talked. Suddenly he sat up, his body tense, his gaze on the shoreline. A flock of plovers had alighted. He was completely absorbed in watching them; the troubles of the world vanished and a country boy came forth. After a while he relaxed and turned again to me.

"Why don't you make a slingshot and get yourself a good dinner?" he asked. "They make fine eating."

I was afraid to confess to him that I was a town boy; that the only time I yearned for a slingshot was when a certain type of mammal passed by. I swung the conversation back to the troubles of the world.

"Do you think we will win the peace this time?"

Symbols of uneasiness passed through his countenance before he answered. When he did speak it was of something seemingly remote from the problem. I settled back to listen, filled with the same uneasiness, since when a man loses faith in the ability of his collective self to perform a moral deed, he has in some degree lost a portion of his own integrity, of his own sense of honesty and pride.

The Colonel felt this keenly. As he spoke, choosing his words carefully, pausing frequently, his disillusion in mankind was expressed in the form of a personal attitude: he was like a man confessing his sins, having decided after long meditation that no one is to blame but himself. He turned away from the sun, took his hat off, and held it in his hands, turning it slowly with his fingers. His head was like that of a monk, high in the region of veneration. His eyes closed as his mind gathered to the task.

Until he went to the White House in 1914 American politics was to him very much what it was to other average citizens—a complex and integral part of national life, a sort of legislative marriage in which all citizens participated, and from which all derived a small or large share of security, pleasure, irritation, and debt, along with a bountiful measure of humor. None of these had anything to do with the good of mankind in general or the morality of nations in particular. The first World War and President Wilson's attempt to establish the League of Nations initiated him, along with many other Americans, into an enlarged viewpoint, one which his Presbyterian rationalism embraced at once. The defeat of the League and the election of Harding threw him into a kind of quiet cynicism, as it did most of the people who had come to agree with Wilson. His spirit sickened at the approach of the second World War, but he saw no reason to hope it could be avoided. Once begun, it was a question of whether, when it was over, peace or an armistice would result. It depended largely, he thought, on "this fellow." (I by now had gathered that "this fellow" was President Roosevelt, and "that fellow" was President Hoover. The Chief Executives before these two he referred to by their surnames.)

He was sure that "this fellow" would be successful in negotiating with Churchill and Stalin. He had seen the idealistic Wilson snared and betrayed by Clemenceau and Lloyd George; he had also seen Wilson lose control of Congress.

"This fellow will do well for us. I would like to see him out of the White House when the war is over, and on the Peace Commission. That is what he wants himself; you can bet on that. It wasn't my business to talk with him about anything except the details of my job, but on this question of the peace I couldn't help myself.

"One day I told him that I hoped the peace this time would not be settled for several years. That would give tempers a chance to cool and common sense a chance to operate. He said to me, 'Don't worry, Ed. We won't be in a hurry this time. Mistakes like that can't be repeated.'

"The peace negotiations ought to take from three to five years, I figure, and during all that time the machinery of a new League should be getting started. I believe this fellow can do it. He has the country and Congress with him, and he is smart enough to trade with those slickers on the other side. People think he does what Churchill wants him to do. They have no need for worry. If anything, the situation is the opposite."

But although he could admire Roosevelt's diplomatic skill, and be thankful that it was available to the country, he could not love it. The political sophistication of "this fellow" was in direct contrast to the ineptness of Wilson; where Wilson had failed "this fellow" would succeed. But the coldness of that sophistication, the scientific manner in which it exploited the political immorality of the country in order to achieve ideological ends, left him with a melancholy feeling. He was capable of realizing that the immorality provoked the sophistication, but this did not comfort him. He had seen the two alternatives, the impractical idealist and the political opportunist. The political sophisticate was better than either of these, yet it did not satisfy him. He was an average citizen, and like all average citizens he longed for perfection in his leaders, though he was well aware that most of the time he got what he deserved, and the appearance now and then of a Lincoln, a Wilson, or a Roosevelt, was, in his own colloquial phrase, "pure velvet."

"This fellow handles it in the only possible way," he said to me after we had discussed for many hours the political dilemma of the country. "He is as hard and cold as steel with anyone and everyone when it comes to the things he wants done. When it is a matter of ordinary relations with people he is the nicest, kindest, friendliest person on earth. He is too easygoing, in fact. People take advantage of him."

He sat up again and looked at the shoreline. This time a fisherman had caught his eye. The man was surf casting. The Colonel watched him with the intensity of a baseball manager inspecting a rookie's batting stance. Finally he leaned back and turned to me again.

"That man can't cast," he said. "He could spit the line farther than that. Well, we'll have to write a whole book about this fellow sometime. Not now. I'm too close to him. It will take me a little time to get my sights adjusted." He sighed and smiled. "Maybe I never will be able to understand him. He's too strong a mixture for my blood. But I reckon in a country where a statesman has to be a politician in order to accomplish something for the people's good, it's the only combination that will work."

So we talked of other men and other times, poking around for anecdotes and memories. Every now and then the Colonel would get up and pace nervously back and forth. When people approached he automatically took up a position which enabled him to see clearly all of their movements. It was months before these habits began to slough off. Even then he continued to get up and leave me at intervals—to help a child mount a tricycle, to carry a neighbor lady's bundles, to get the mail and chat with the postman. One day he was gone for quite a while. When he returned he said, "I was mixing a cake for your wife."

As a human relationship our collaboration was from the beginning a success. I assumed his personality as easily as if it had been a projection of my own, a slightly previous incarnation of the psyche. The realm of friendship is undoubtedly the fourth dimension; in so far as a man accepts in himself the supernal commonness of humanity he is a participant in all existing personalities. This is a metaphysical notion which seems to reverse the natural processes of spiritual evolution, but it explains why the Colonel would have done as well with any other collaborator. He saw in every man the image of his Creator, however distorted the reflection, and he therefore considered the man identical with himself. Probably this is just another way of expressing what I have already said—that he was a Christian gentleman. It must be the rarity of such a phenomenon which brings it again and again into focus in my mind; it was a revelation, almost as in a vision, of the possibility of loving all men as brothers. Nothing he told me about the Presidents he had served was as important, in my estimation, as this ideal which his own life exemplified.

We returned, in due time, to the subject of "this fellow." By then we had covered the preceding four Presidents, and the figure of the squire of Hyde Park was clearer in the Colonel's mind. Roosevelt was a sharp break with the tradition of Presidents as the Colonel had known it. He had no awe of the office; he gave it only the ordinary respect which a man tenders to a job he has promised to fulfill. He oozed confidence; he was no more worried about his responsibilities than if he were playing a hand of cribbage. Because he was an aristocrat he could afford to be more democratic than his predecessors, who as commoners had to avoid being common. This paradox was at first a puzzle to the Colonel, but later he understood it, and admired his boss for what was obviously the only wise course he could pursue.

It may seem a lack in this book that it contains no discussion of Mrs. Roosevelt. It never occurred to us to talk about her. Early in the administration she made it clear to the Secret Service that she did not want their attention, so they let her alone. Thus the Colonel had nothing to report about her, and he probably felt, as I did, that her private life was her own business. Anyhow, her name did not come up except incidentally, and that is the only way in which she is mentioned in the story. Lest we appear too gentlemanly, however, let me say that we frequently and at length discussed the second Mrs. Wilson's pretty ankles and shapely calves.

Again and again the Colonel returned in his talk to two things. We would write a whole book about "this fellow" when he was out of the White House and when the Colonel had the tumultuous details of the New Deal straightened and arranged in his mind; and we would go fishing, when this present job was finished and ready for publication. He would teach me to cast. I protested that I was an unlikely subject. "No more unlikely than Mr. Coolidge," he said, damning me with faint praise.

The work was finished late in May. In June the Colonel went to New York to consult with Professor Allan Nevins of Columbia, the noted historian and biographer. He wanted to be sure that he had overlooked no important phases or incidents in the stream of history which had flowed through, around, and past the White House from 1914 to 1944. In July he was stricken with pneumonia. On August 3, 1944, at St. Luke's Hospital in New York City, he died. He was buried in Arlington National Cemetery, with many another soldier whose life was passed in the service of his country.

So the book about "this fellow" was not written. The story he did tell, as together we devised it from his notes, his diaries, and his memories, is hereinafter set down, without intervals for watching plovers and mixing cakes, and without the real story of the man himself, whose dreams were buried long ago in the rolling hills of western Kentucky.

In presenting the story now I wish to set down my thanks and the thanks of Colonel Starling for the help and cooperation we received from so many of his friends; from our publishers, Messers Simon and Schuster; from Mr. Mark Sullivan, Mr. Frank Morse, Mr. Herman Keller, Mrs. Calvin Coolidge; and in particular from our mutual friend Mr. David E. Kahn of New York City, himself a native Kentuckian. It was at his instigation that the work was begun, and without his enthusiasm, stimulation, aid and support, it could not have been completed.

STARLING OF
THE WHITE HOUSE

★★★

CHAPTER ONE

Kentucky Babe

CHRISTIAN COUNTY in Kentucky, rolls southward from hills dotted with coal mines to gentle farm lands that meet the Tennessee line just north of Clarksville. Its principal settlement and county seat is Hopkinsville, a quiet, old-fashioned town of some ten thousand people, in the heart of the agricultural section, where it serves as a market for the dark, rich tobacco raised by the farmers as a "money crop."

Once leaving Hopkinsville by automobile, I picked up a farmhand who was waiting for a ride. He was from another part of the county. I pretended to be a stranger.

"What kind of a place is this Hopkinsville?" I asked. "Seems like a nice town."

He cut his eyes toward me, then looked ahead at the road.

"You stop there long?"

"No, just passed through."

He nodded understandingly.

"I reckon you could call it a nice town."

"Nice people?"

"I reckon you could call them nice people."

Suddenly he snorted.

"But, they're mighty uppity!"

His voice was thick with disgust. In a gesture of confidence he turned to me.

"There ain't a single thing in the whole wide world you can tell a body in Hopkinsville. They know it all!

3

"You can't even tell 'em something that happened to yourself. They know more about it than you do!"

He turned away from me and went back to contemplating the road. "Mighty uppity!" he concluded, shaking his head.

It was in this town of uppity, know-it-all-folks that I was born on October 5, 1875, in the red brick house on North Main Street which was the home of my parents, Colonel Edmund Alexander Starling and Annie Leslie McCarroll Starling. My brother Guy was then two years old. Later my sisters, Annie Leslie and Mary Graeme Starling, were born. When I was four my father was a candidate for the office of county sheriff, and while making a speech from a public platform he was shot and killed.

An editorial published in the Hopkinsville *New Era* at the time tells of him and of his lineage:

"Colonel Edmund Alexander Starling, whose death from assassination was published last week, was descended from families of mark and distinction in Virginia and Kentucky. His relationship extended through many of the large families in both of these states, the McDowells, McClungs, Irvines, Bufords, Marshalls, Prestons, Burneys, McGavichs, Shelbys, Sullivans, et cetera, all of whom have produced men of character and position. He was no unworthy representative of his family. Born in Kentucky on the 22nd day of November, 1826, when a youth he moved to Columbus, Ohio, where in the office of his brother Colonel Lyne Starling, he acquired those exacting, comprehensive business habits which characterized him through life. From there he went to New York, where he engaged in mercantile pursuits, with eminent success, until the defalcation of a partner in the house caused him the loss of a greater part of his acquired capital. He was then appointed Indian agent and was sent to the tribes on Puget Sound, . . . After his arduous and responsible services incident to such a position, he removed to Hopkinsville where he had spent his earliest days and had received the rudiments of his education and where his mother and many of his immediate family resided. For many years he was the business partner of his brother, William Starling, now deceased, and during the war commanded the 35th regiment of Kentucky Mounted Infantry

Volunteers, in the Federal service. Since the war he married Miss Annie L., youngest daughter of the late Dr. John McCarroll of Hopkinsville, and led, with his devoted wife, in the bosom of his family that quiet and retired life which his temperament best fitted him to enjoy.

"Colonel Starling was an undemonstrative man, though strong and faithful in his friendships. He was preeminently kind-hearted and charitable, and no worthy, distressed person ever left him empty handed. There are many in this community, among the lowly, who rise up and call him blessed. . . . He was a man of the most refined tastes and exhibited the greatest fondness for books, music, paintings, and flowers. And no one who ever met him in social life or sat with him at his hospitable board, could fail to be impressed with the ease and dignity of his manners, and with the generosity and kindness of his nature. . . .

"The hand which bereft Colonel Starling of his healthy, vigorous, useful life, bereaved his wife of a fond, indulgent and faithful husband, his children of a father who would have been their guide and exemplar, his church of an Elder earnestly looking for its good, and the community of one of its kindest, most beneficent and public spirited citizens."

I remember nothing about him except that he was tall and strong and very kind to me. He had fought on the Union side in the Civil War, helping to organize and finance the regiment which he commanded. When the war ended he married and settled down in Hopkinsville.

Business was conducted at home, as my father's brickyard was behind the house. There, among the stacks of fresh bricks, I was put out to sun, and the negroes called me "Little Colonel." After my father's death they dropped the "Little" and I succeeded to his full title. It was nearly half a century before the Governor of Kentucky officially confirmed it, but that made no difference in Hopkinsville. There I was a colonel from birth.

Because the Starlings were Union sympathizers during the Civil War they attended the First, or "Northern" Presbyterian Church. The "Southern" Presbyterian Church, attended by those of the faith who had been Confederates, was nearby, its steeple within sight of ours. It had more members, but our congregation had the advantage of solidarity. We were all Starlings.

My father and Judge Landis, a cousin, had built the church, my father supplying the bricks and the labor. Our family occupied one pew; Judge Landis, his wife Mary and his daughter Anna, sat in another. In a third pew were Squire Campbell, his wife, Aunt Gamey Campbell, their daughter Graeme and their son Alec, all cousins. Louis Starling had a pew, filled to capacity by himself, his wife Fanny, and his sisters, Nannie, Lizzie and Ellis. Cousin Will Davison, his wife, Cousin Nellie, and their daughters Maria and Ellen, sat together. Cousin Walter Kelly's family took up two pews; besides Cousin Walter there were his wife Mattie, his sons McClure, Wallace and Fairleigh, and his daughters Annie Todd, Emily, and Martha. Cousin J. Matt Starling also had a pew, occupied by his wife, Cousin Jennie, his daughter Lucy, and his sons, Edmund and Lyne.

Cousin Matt himself sat in the choir, where he sang bass in the quartet. My brother Guy sang tenor, Cousin Graeme Campbell, soprano, and my sister, Mary Graeme Starling, alto. The organist and choir director was Miss Clara Bonte, who was not a relative. She held the position solely on her merits as a musician.

Matt Starling was a double first cousin of mine, a strong, quiet man, too timid to sing solos, but set in his ways and violent in his dislikes. Each Sunday before the service began he cut himself a slice of homespun tobacco, slipped it into his cheek, and took his place in the choir. Right beside him was a brass cuspidor. When the tobacco juice reached his vocal chords and soaked into them he was in good voice. It would swell out magnificently in "Rock of Ages" and "I Love to Tell the Story." Occasionally he would part his moustache with the first two fingers of his right hand and fire through the opening at the cuspidor. The "ping" resounded plainly through the church, but no one paid any attention to it except the preacher. He paused politely until the sound died away.

A much more ominous sound, also made by Cousin Matt, was the click of his hunting case watch. Services began at eleven. By twelve, thought Matt, the sermon should be over. At home Sunday dinner was waiting—broiled chicken, beaten biscuits, homemade ice cream and cake. Enough was enough. A man had to eat.

Some of the preachers agreed with him. Others, carried away by their own oratory, swept on past the deadline. In a few minutes Matt would open his watch, look at it, and snap the case shut. It was an enormous instrument, with a copper case—Matt had purchased it from one of the negroes at the brickyard, probably for this very purpose—and the sound of its closing lid rang like a pistol shot.

To the preacher it was a dismaying sound. If he had anything else to say he said it in a hurry and called for the closing hymn. Only one ever dared to defy Matt, and his was a hollow victory. He preached through two shuttings of the watch. Then, turning to the choir, he said:

"Matt, you and I seem to differ about my sermons. I think that what I have to say is important, and if it takes until after twelve o'clock, it's worth it. If you don't think so, you can leave."

Matt left. Shortly after—in a few weeks—the preacher left, too. A new man took his place, Matt returned to the choir, and services resumed their normal procedure, with an occasional snapping of the hunting case watch, but never more than one.

They sent me to school eventually, though I already knew the secret of being a Kentucky gentleman—that four things are sacred: women, religion, bird dogs, and the polls. As a student I was peaceful but not brilliant. In the third grade, Miss Brancham's room, John Ferguson laughed at the color of my tie and I punched him in the stomach. Sixty years later he remembered it, though he had forgotten the color that offended him. So had I. The strongest memory I have of my school days is the remark of Professor Charles Dietrich when he handed me my diploma from Hopkinsville High School, after I had managed to pass examinations in history, physics, Latin, Greek and trigonometry.

"I hope you make as much a success in life as you have in athletics," he said. "If you do you'll go far."

He didn't mean to slight my intelligence. At the time I was seventeen and a half years old, an even six feet in height, and a firm 170 pounds in weight. I played any and all games, and in baseball I had made a reputation as a pitcher by learning to throw a curve. Somewhere I had read about this innovation, and by practicing hours on end, day after day, throwing a ball against the brick wall of our house, I became a past master of the outcurve (now called the curve), the inshoot (now called the fast ball) and the drop. I first used them in combat during games at the insane asylum.

The Western State Hospital, as the asylum was called, was situated a few miles outside the town. One of our best players, Bill Salter, worked there as superintendent of buildings. Regularly I trudged out to see him and to play scrub games with pickup teams. Some of the best players—a few of them really skilled—were inmates. On them I tried my curve. They would drop the bat and scream at me in rage. Had I known anything then about abnormal psychology I wouldn't have teased them. Being young, strong and ignorant, I thought it was funny. So did everyone else. I hope I didn't make them any crazier than they were.

Soon I was pitching for the Hopkinsville team, and winning most of my games. Our opponents came from surrounding towns—Pembroke, Madisonville, Cadiz, Gracey, and Clarksville, Tennessee. Later we played Bowling Green and Louisville, and beat them. By the time I finished high school several colleges had offered me scholarships. Turning them down was one of the most difficult things I have ever had to do. I wanted to be a surgeon. But more than that I wanted to help out at home.

We had the brickyard for sustenance, and we had managed to live comfortably. Aunt Vina, our colored cook, had stayed with us, and now her daughter, Aunt Peggy, was carrying on in her place. We kept a horse and buggy. If I went to college things would be a little pinched. So I decided to get a job.

My brother Guy was already at work in the local bank. He was a gay, sociable lad, with a pleasant singing voice that ranged all the way from baritone to tenor, and a liking for parties and the company of girls. This latter characteristic I shared with him. I liked to sing, too, and being a bass I was allowed to fill out the quartet that consisted of Wallace Kelly, tenor; Oswin Steinhagen, baritone; and Guy, who was the lead. We performed at weddings, christenings, and parties of all kinds.

We had a small organ that was hauled in an express wagon by a colored boy. With this accompaniment we did our serenading, arriving at the home of the chosen young lady between eleven and twelve o'clock. According to custom the girl was allowed to find out beforehand that we were coming, and she invited other girls to come and spend the night with her. They prepared refreshments for us and left them on the porch. Then, at upstairs windows, they listened while we sang "Asthore," "The Girl I Left Behind," "Kentucky Babe," "Maid of the Mill," and "My Old Kentucky Home." After running through our repertoire we ate the refreshments and went home, never seeing the girls. That was real romance, standing in the darkness, harmonizing on:

> Yo' is mighty lucky,
> Babe of old Kentucky,
> Close yo' eyes and sleep!

This was in April and May. By summer we were more bold. Down in south Christian County, on Little River, there was a beautiful spring. Late in the afternoon of a hot day we would despatch two negroes to the spring in a wagon loaded with fried chicken, beaten biscuit, fresh tomatoes, freezers of homemade ice cream, cake, and demijohns of iced tea. An hour later we followed on horseback, five or six couples. At the spring we ate, then sat around, singing to the accompaniment of a mandolin or guitar, until ten or eleven o'clock. Gradually the group would melt away, two at a time, as the couples went to their horses and rode off toward home in the moonlight.

In the fall we took the girls coon hunting. Bill Walker's family had a farm about seven miles from town, and this was our headquarters. At nightfall we would gather at Captain and Mrs. Ed Walker's home on Russelville Road, where Bill and his sisters, Mattie and Mary, would be waiting with a team of mules hitched to a wagon full of straw. In this we rode to the farm—the Walkers, Guy and I, Ned Crabbe, Jim Russell, and our girls of the moment—Tony Ware, Lizzie Gaither, Bessie Dick. At the farm we formed into a hunting party—there were two hound dogs, two negroes carrying the necessary rope, ax, and lantern, and the couples. When the hunting palled we built a fire, roasted sweet potatoes, and ate them with country sausage and ham. Then, sipping coffee, we got out the mandolin and sang.

Once we caught an old, scrawny possum and put him in the chicken coop at the farm to fatten him up. A few weeks later we had a hunt, and after several hours without luck gathered in a graveyard to discuss strategy. I took Bill Walker aside and asked him if the possum was still in the chicken coop. He said it was, so we sent one of the negroes back for it, with orders to bring it to me. When he returned I gave him careful instructions; then the hunt was resumed. Within a short time one of the couples reported success. Then another fell into luck, then another. Within a few hours the scrawny old possum was treed seven times, every boy was a hero to his girl, and no one was any wiser, not even Guy.

During the winter we appeared in minstrel shows and amateur theatricals. In the minstrel shows I was allowed to sing "Kentucky Babe," as a solo. Once, when a member of the cast of a skit disappeared at the last minute, I was pressed into service as a female dancer, in a cakewalk. Hastily they dressed me in, among other things, a long pair of old-fashioned woman's drawers with lace on the bottom. They were a little tight for me. I didn't know the dance I was supposed to do, or any dance, for that matter, so I pranced. This was too much for the drawstring of the drawers, which was strained by my girth anyhow. It parted, and the drawers fell down around my ankles, trapping me. Amid tremendous applause I was dragged from the stage.

When Sam Jones, the evangelist, came to the Sam Jones Tabernacle for a series of meetings we formed an "Excelle Quartet," under the supervision of E. O. Excelle, Sam Jones' musical director and assistant, who was the author of most of the hymns we sang. This quartet was composed of Cousin Matt, Ned Crabbe, Guy, and myself. In this group I sang baritone, deferring to Cousin Matt's superiority as a bass.

We sat on the stage and had an excellent view not only of Sam, a vigorous, broad-shouldered man with a straggly black moustache, but of the audience, which reacted like a trained seal to his oratory.

He showed them no mercy. Meetings were for both men and women, but once during his stay he would lecture the sexes separately. We were present at both the men's and women's meetings, and I remember how on one occasion he greeted the women.

"Well," he said, "I've been trying to save the men. They're unfaithful and they drink liquor and it's hard to do anything with them. Now I've got you women on my hands and I've got to talk about the sins you commit.

"I'll begin with the worst one. It's gossip. I don't know of any town that has such gossips as Hopkinsville.

"Why, some of you sisters here today have tongues so long you could sit in the parlor and lick a skillet in the kitchen!

"It's the truth—and if any of you don't like it you can get up and leave!"

Nobody left. Sam had more power over those women than anyone I ever saw. Maybe it was because they were all so guilty.

By far the happiest days of my youth were spent in quail shooting. Old Uncle George Gray, a colored man, taught me to shoot with a muzzle-loading shotgun. At daybreak on cold November mornings I would be at his cabin, and we would spend all day in the fields, hunting with his two dogs, a deaf Irish setter named Nick, and Polly, a pointer bitch. No art is more lovely to watch than that of the trained bird dog moving to stand a covey of quail. How often, watching that scene, have I forgotten that I had a gun in my hand! And I never fail to take my hat off to a bird who eludes me by flying behind a tree or speeding at knee height down a slope of field.

Every winter Cousin Charles McCarroll of Owensboro and Cousin Ed Starling of Louisville came to Hopkinsville for a week of quail shooting. Cousin Matt was host, and on a few blissful occasions I was allowed to go along to help carry the game and spot fallen birds. When

I was fourteen they gave Guy and me a second-hand double-barrelled shotgun. We soon became good shots, and brought home enough rabbits and quail for the family and most of our friends.

Mine was a good and pleasant life so I did not look beyond Hopkinsville for employment. One day in late summer, about two months after my graduation, I was crossing the street to go to the courthouse. Bud Golay, Chief Deputy Sheriff for the county, stopped me.

"Decided what you're going to do?" he asked.

"No, I haven't," I said.

"Going to make it to college?"

I shook my head.

"I'm afraid not. I reckon I'll have to find something else."

He looked me over for a moment.

"How about riding deputy sheriff for Mac J. Davis?" he said. "He needs a man."

Immediately I was uneasy. The job sounded too attractive. It meant riding horseback through the rich farm lands to serve papers on people for various legal actions, stopping along the way to swap gossip or play a game of ball, living in the outdoors and getting paid for it. My notion of work was to be cooped up somewhere, in a store or office or tobacco warehouse.

Mac J. Davis was the County Sheriff. He had served in my father's regiment. He was offering me the job through Golay. It was mine for the taking.

"I haven't a horse," I said.

"We'll let you have one until you can provide it yourself."

Everything was arranged.

"Will I need a pistol?"

"Yes, but you'll have to get that yourself."

"How much does the job pay?"

"Seventy-five a month."

Seventy-five dollars a month! That was a lot of money. Where else could I earn that much?

"I'll take it."

My first assignment was to serve a paper on a farmer living near the Caldwell County line, about twenty miles away. I left at four A. M. on a plowhorse and got back at midnight. The horse was no good for a week and I learned to temper my zeal with common sense. After I got my own horse I left Hopkinsville each Monday morning and was away until Friday night, taking my papers with me.

The job was every bit as pleasant as I had anticipated. When possible I planned my days so that evening would bring me to the house of a farmer with a pretty daughter. If there was a dance or a church meeting in the neighborhood I would attend it, usually in the company of the daughter. In the morning I got up early, fed and curried my horse, and was off on another day's ride.

Perhaps that day would take me down near the Tennessee line, where the Barkers had their farms—Charlie, Tom, Doc, Trump, and others whose names I forget. This was prosperous land: there were darkies to open the gates, rubber-tired buggies, fine horses, lovely daughters, and it was said that the Barkers between them had a thousand hams put away. They were always glad to see me, because they were baseball fans. I pitched for their team, and they cheered for me until they were hoarse.

On Saturday, at home, I fished or played baseball. Sunday I went to church. In the afternoon I walked my bird dog. In the evening I attended Christian Endeavour and the church services. Next morning I got up at four, fed and curried my horse, and after a breakfast of oatmeal, bacon and eggs, and batter cakes with corn syrup or sorghum, started off on another week's work.

I rode every day of the year, and in winter the roads were lonely. Sometimes I passed no one all day but a country doctor or a farmer driving to town with a load of tobacco. Once during a ten day spell of snow, ice and sleet, I had to have my horse roughshod seven times.

It was during this storm that I started out one morning to ride cross-country from the Madisonville Road to the Buttermilk Road, just west of Empire. Sleet covered the ground, and the trees were loaded with it. Every now and then a limb cracked and broke under the strain. One fell as I was passing underneath. It hit me in the back and knocked me sideways. I fell to the left against a high bank that flanked the trail I was following.

When I regained consciousness I was lying on my side, my left foot still caught in the stirrup—and my horse standing quietly beside me. The big, white-bellied bay had proved the wisdom of kind treatment. I had bought him cheaply because he had killed one of his owners and won the reputation of being dangerous. I had treated him well. He had reciprocated.

The other thing that saved me was the fact that I was wearing a heavy jacket with a slicker over it. The padding broke the blow. I got up, remounted and rode to my destination. The man I was to serve was not at home so I headed for Squire Fuller's farm, near Buttermilk Road. When I got there I was almost frozen in the saddle. The Squire and one of his sons lifted me off the horse and helped me into the house. They took me to a spare room, built a roaring fire in the fireplace, brought in tubs of cold water, and stripped me. They sat me in the biggest tub and rubbed me until circulation was restored. I have never endured such pain. I had to bite my whole mouth to keep from hollering. Then they stood me in front of the fire and rubbed me with rough towels until my skin was raw. After that they gave me a hot toddy and put me in a feather bed. The next morning I felt fine and rode off on another day's work.

Being deputy sheriff in a county thronged with relatives and friends presented a problem. What kind of officer was I was going to be? Cold and hard-boiled? That was impossible. But I had to be firm. I decided to adopt a technique all my own.

Kentucky at the time was not far removed from the wild and woolly stage. You couldn't afford to be careless in approaching strangers or addressing friends. Tempers were quick and guns plentiful. Honor was more sacred than life. People who lived in the country were especially inclined to consider the law a private matter, to be administered among themselves.

Arresting a man was, therefore, a delicate problem, and if he had been drinking it was inadvisable. I once saw three men killed trying to arrest a man for a negligible charge. The man had come to town for supplies, had gone to a saloon, and was in just the right mood for trouble when the officers arrived. He was not a bad citizen—just a man with a high sense of freedom and a deep thirst. There were many more like him. Studying the situation, I decided that the right time and the right approach were the secrets of success.

Suppose a lad named Jack had gotten drunk and shot up a church meeting. It was a common offense—half a dozen young bucks would get hold of a jug of corn liquor and ride around the countryside looking for mischief. When they came to a church they would gallop around the building, shooting their pistols in the air. Sometimes there was a roughhouse; sometimes people were hurt.

The warrant for Jack would be given to me, to serve at my discretion. The first time I met him might be on a day when he was in town with his wife and children, or on a day when he was drinking. In either circumstance I would not bother him. But one day I would meet him when he was sober and alone. He might be passing by on the other side of the street. I would call to him to come and join me. I would not go to him. When he reached me I would say:

"Jack, I'm glad to see you. How're you feeling? How is that dear little wife of yours, and those grand kids?"

"Fine," he would say, expanding with pride, "just fine."

"Well, pardner, I'm glad to hear it. You going back out this afternoon? How about taking some candy to the kids for me? I haven't seen them in so long I'm afraid they'll forget me."

I would talk to him then about his crops, his horses, his land. Finally, lowering my voice to a confidential level, I would say:

"Jack, what in the world made you go and shoot up that church meeting the other night?"

I had made him aware of his responsibilities and riches—his family and farm—and the mention of bad conduct was a jolt to his conscience.

"I don't know. Just crazy drunk I reckon."

"Does your wife know about it, and the kids?"

"Not yet, but I reckon they will."

"Well, pardner, we'll have to see that they don't. They'd feel mighty bad about it, and we don't want them to be unhappy. Doggonit they're sweet, all of them.

"But, Jack, I've got this dad-blamed warrant for you. They gave it to me and I've got to do something about it.

"Tell you what we'll do. You take this paper and go around to a couple of your friends and get them to go bond for you. As soon as you get it signed bring it back to me. Don't give it to anyone else. Then you'll be free until this thing comes up, and it may not amount to much when it does—just some damage money probably."

Gratefully he would shake my hand and go off to look up two or three friends. Anyone who knew him would sign the bond—he was a responsible landowner and the charge was routine and inconsequential. But had I approached him while he was with his family he would have felt shamed and humiliated; had I gone to him while he was drinking he might have made trouble. In either case he would have disliked me. As it was, I had become his friend.

It was not always as easy as that. Occasionally real crooks entered our county and in the coal mining section there were strikes and other labor troubles. I had to learn to use my pistol—not fancily, or even precisely, but in the rough and tumble way to which a revolver is suited and for which it was invented. No criminal would ever let me raise a Colt to shoulder height and hold it at arm's length to aim, I knew. I learned to shoot coming up from the hip, and as long as I could keep a tin can rolling from twenty to thirty feet in this fashion I was satisfied. Anything more was just Fancy Dan stuff.

Five years passed pleasantly in this fashion. Then came 1898 and the war with Spain. I went to Lexington to enlist in the Rough Riders, along with a boy from Bowling Green named Hugh B. Wright, nicknamed Sleepy. When I returned to Hopkinsville the local unit of the National Guard was forming a company, and I was argued into joining it for the sake of civic pride. Reluctantly I gave up my chance to ride with Teddy Roosevelt and became a first sergeant of the Provost Guard.

My job was the one now performed by Military Police—keeping order among the soldiers. In Columbus, Georgia, a member of the Provost Guard was shot, and died in my arms, after telling me the name of his assassin. I caught the man in Atlanta, and while the court martial was going on my outfit moved on to Cuba, leaving me behind. Even so, I did more fighting in the United States than the rest of the company did on foreign shores. In Lexington, Kentucky, I fought the Battle of McGowan Street, then one of the country's most gilded and notorious red light districts. The soldiers appreciated the beautiful blue grass country around Lexington. They visited the great horse farms and the historic mansions. But they had been trained to fight and with no fighting at hand their energies frequently bubbled over—into Mc-Gowan Street. It wasn't much of a war on the whole, and soon we were all back in Hopkinsville, heroes to a man.

I went back to my old job, but the contentment it had held for me was gone. Something was urging me to move on, to seek greener fields.

One day in the spring of 1901, I stood on the platform of the railroad station in Hopkinsville watching passengers alight from one of the trains. My eyes fastened on a man getting off the Pullman. He wore a double-breasted blue suit with peg-leg trousers, an eight-ply high stiff collar, a red tie, a narrow-brimmed derby, and patent leather button shoes with cloth tops.

"Who is that?" I asked the station clerk, "The President of the road?"

"No," the clerk said, "he's one of the detectives on the line. He gets a pass to ride in the Pullman."

My eyes were glued to the man as he walked down the platform.

"That," I said, "is the job for me."

Next day I applied for a position as Special Agent for the Louisville and Nashville Railroad. Largely because of my record as deputy sheriff I got it, and spent a cold winter in the freight yards at East St. Louis. I didn't have a pass to ride the Pullman, or a double-breasted blue suit. I bundled myself in an eighty-five cent sweater and spent the nights ducking box-cars that ran after me in the dark. In the spring I was transferred to Birmingham, Alabama.

★☆★

CHAPTER TWO

Gentleman Bandit

In Birmingham I reported to B. M. Stark, superintendent of the division, a broad-shouldered, competent looking man with a clean-shaven, open face.

"Young man, I'm glad to see you," he said. "Are you afraid of work?"

"No, sir," I answered.

"Are you healthy?"

"Yes, sir."

"Can you shoot a pistol?"

"Yes, sir."

"You'll get $50 a month and it will be two years before you earn it. I'm not interested in particulars, I'm interested in results. If you need anything, come to me. So long as you're loyal and interested, I'm behind you."

My job was to protect valuable freight while it was in the yards at Birmingham and while it was being transferred, to keep pilfering and stealing to a minimum, to assist passengers and freight conductors in matters of safety for their passengers and freight, and to guard specific shipments or cars when so instructed. I had half a dozen watchmen working under me, scattered through the four or five miles of track that comprised the yards, and I cared for the division territory, riding both passenger and freight trains night and day. I had my pass now, and it was in constant use.

It was hard, steady work. I lived in hotels and rooming houses, stayed on the job twenty-four hours a day, and took most of my rest waiting for trains at way stations in the farm country. Birmingham in those years was a tough town. The steel industry was young and vigorous, and the coal mines worked convicts. When a convict was released his first act was to get a "blue steel" pistol—a nickel-plated gun would shine at night—and go for an officer of the law. I had five watchmen killed in the yards while I was there.

There was plenty of action all along the division. One of the nicknames I picked up was "Calera Bill," in honor of the many fracases I had in the town of Calera. One of them was most unpleasant, and caused me to change my way of carrying a pistol.

I was looking for a particular man in the Calera yards one night when I bumped right into him in the dark. He grabbed me and pinned my arms, so that my pistol hand, though partially free, could not reach the gun butt, which was behind it, in the holster strapped to my right side. He was a man of my size and just about my strength. We swayed back and forth silently, until with a thrust of energy I bent him down to the track and wrenched myself free. After that he gave me little trouble, but next day I strapped my holster to my left side, where in such a situation I would still be able to reach it. Later on I adopted a shoulder holster. In this I put a .41 Colt, while in the watch pocket of my trousers, enlarged for the purpose, I carried a "squeezer," a small hammerless Smith and Wesson revolver. This gave me access to a weapon in almost any predicament imaginable.

During these days in Birmingham I met and became well acquainted with one of the young lawyers of the city, Hugo L. Black. He handled many of our cases, and often I aided him in preparing evidence for the Grand Jury. Neither of us ever imagined at that time that his career would take him to Washington and the Supreme Court. To our way of thinking the capital was away up north, in a cold, disagreeable country with which we wanted nothing to do.

Meanwhile my old friend Sleepy Wright, with whom I had joined the Rough Riders, was also working for the L&N, as a Special Agent on the Nashville division. He had fought through the war with the Rough Riders and had become a great favorite with his commanding officer, Teddy Roosevelt, now become President.

One day in October 1905, Sleepy wired me that the President was making a Southern trip and invited me to go along as a member of the Secret Service Detail, which was to meet the train in Atlanta. My boss, Stark, was pleased. He decided that I was finally earning my salary.

We were to go from Atlanta to Montgomery and Tuskegee Institute, where the President was to meet Booker T. Washington, return to Montgomery, and from there go to Birmingham, where the President was to make an address at the Fair Grounds.

I boarded the special train at Atlanta and Sleepy took me back to the President's private car. Teddy rose to meet me, a strong man with a good, courageous eye. I shook his hand—he had a forceful grip, and the flesh was warm. He radiated energy and conviction. His smile under his clipped moustache made me feel at home, despite his formal morning dress and my $18 blue serge suit and $6 Stetson hat. The most valuable thing I had was a pearl-handled Colt which the plain-clothes men of the Birmingham Police Department had given to me.

In the next few days I saw a great deal of T.R. I listened to him talk and watched his personality work on crowds. I liked him. He was human and natural without effort. He talked with us about hunting and fishing and sports on a plane of complete equality—as a man who is interested in the outdoors talks to other men who share his enthusiasm. He was neither condescending nor did he lower himself. As men we were all, in his opinion, equal. It was only as President of the United States that he differed. In this role I watched him with interest, and I remember saying to Sleepy: "He's one of those dad-blamed practical idealists. He's willing to compromise anytime, so long as he wins his point." I remember saying this particularly because it came back to me with suddenness twenty-eight years later, when I met Teddy's cousin, Franklin Delano Roosevelt. I decided then that practical idealism must be a Roosevelt family trait.

My admiration for Teddy reached its peak after the visit to Montgomery. There was a farewell ceremony at Union Station, and as part of it a young girl—she could not have been more than eighteen—stepped forward to give the President an enormous bouquet of long-stemmed

American Beauty roses. In that moment I think she was the prettiest girl I have ever seen. She had great dark eyes, delicate aristocratic features, and a perfect complexion that glowed now with the excitement of the occasion. She trembled like a high-spirited horse. She was scared, but game. Marching up to Teddy she said:

"Mr. President, on behalf of the women of Montgomery I want to present you with these flowers. My father was an officer in the Confederate Army. My mother was a daughter—"

Teddy stopped her. Removing his high silk hat he swung it across his chest in salute, clicked his heels, bowed low, smiled—his teeth showing—and said:

"Young lady, such a pretty little giver needs no introduction to the President."

I muttered to Sleepy. "Hot damn! He's a man after my own heart. He talks just like a Southerner!"

Three hours later we reached Birmingham and were driven to the Fair Grounds. The path of the President's carriage into the grounds had been carefully roped off. I walked on one side of the carriage, Sleepy on the other. There were two Secret Service men from the regular White House Detail with us. One of them, Frank Tyree, was riding on the high seat in front of the driver.

A man leaped over the rope barrier and began to run alongside us, crowding close to the carriage. Tyree shouted at me to get rid of him.

"Get him outside the ropes and keep him out!" he ordered.

I hustled the man over the rope, but in a minute he was back again. I began to sweat. Again I chased him over the rope. Again he returned, running close to the carriage. My nerves got the best of me. I picked him up and threw him over the rope and into the crowd like a sack of corn meal. This time he didn't come back.

Later I was heartily ashamed of what I had done. I learned that the Secret Service combines firmness with tact. In the thirty years I spent at the White House I never spoke as loudly or acted as roughly as I did that day at the Fair Grounds in Birmingham.

When we returned that afternoon to the railroad station an immense crowd had gathered. Getting the President through it was a problem. Finally we surrounded him, Sleepy on one side, I on the other, and W. W. Brandon, then Adjutant General and later Governor of Alabama, as the spearhead. We ploughed through the crowd by bull strength, quickly and roughly. When we got him safely on the platform of the train Teddy rubbed his hands together gleefully and cried, "Bully! That was great! Just like a football game!" I've never seen a President since who could stand that kind of treatment.

I rode as far west as Memphis on the return trip, then went back to Birmingham. I had met and talked with a President, something I never expected to do. Moreover, I had discovered that he was just another human being, a good deal like myself in many respects.

In 1907 I was made Stock Claim Agent for the L&N, with headquarters at Flomaton, Alabama. This took me out of the field of excitement and danger, and for three years I led a dull and uneventful existence. Then, in 1910, I was offered the post of Chief Special Agent for the Southern Express Company, and my days of peace ended abruptly.

The territory covered by the Southern Express Company was approximately 30,000 square miles—everything east of the Mississippi and south of Washington. As a welcome to me the whole area erupted in a series of train robberies. I chased holdup men all over the South for more railroads than I can remember—the Mobile and Ohio, the B&O, the L&N, the Southern, the Atlantic Coast Line, the Alabama Great Southern, the Queen and Crescent, the Central of Georgia, the Nashville, Chattanooga and St. Louis, the Tennessee Central, the Gulf and Ship Island, and dozens of small lines whose names were then as familiar to me as the hammock in an upper berth.

Most of the robbers used the same technique. After stopping the train they cut out the engine and the express and mail cars, forcing the engineer to drive these several miles ahead of the coaches. At a suitable spot the express car was cut off and the engineer was told to drive ahead, with a man guarding him. The robbers then blew open the express car safe, took everything of value, and disappeared into the hills or swamps. Tracking them down was a long and arduous job, sometimes taking years, and there wasn't anything spectacular or glamorous about it. Like all crime detection it was largely a matter of perseverance and patient attention to detail.

Now and then, however, a case came along that had a little sparkle to it. One of these broke late in 1910, when a fast train of the Southern Railway was held up just south of Gainesville, Georgia, by three men who escaped with a large quantity of money, jewelry and foreign currency consigned to banks in Mobile and Pensacola. I was on a case in Winfield, near the Mississippi line, at the time, and while riding horseback to the railroad station was met by a messenger on a mule. They were flagging a fast train into Birmingham for me and I had only a few minutes to make it. I got aboard and found a telegram from E. M. Williams, the general manager at Birmingham, telling me to join the Atlanta general manager, J. B. Hockaday, at Gainesville. The executives were out in force.

At Gainesville nobody knew anything except that three men wearing black masks had held up the train. I questioned the train crew again, and after a full day's work got a few crumbs of information. One of the men might have been older than the other two. The points of his moustache, sticking out beyond the mask, were gray. Another one, when his head was turned, showed a crop of reddish hair. The older man seemed to be the leader. He spoke in a soft, polite voice, and was not very big. He had been very gentlemanly.

This wasn't much, but I had circulars printed containing the information, and offering $1,000 reward for each of the men. These were distributed all over the territory, and I and my men took to our horses and combed the hills, checking every hideout we knew. Day after day went by, and not a single clue turned up. We all returned to Gainesville for a council of strategy.

There wasn't much to discuss, and nobody had any suggestions. Sitting around a big room in the Hunt Hotel we were so disgusted that when the telephone rang nobody answered it. Finally, more to stop the noise than anything else, I picked up the receiver. Ex-sheriff Jim Davis of Dahlonega, up in Lumpkin County, was calling.

"I think I have some information for you," he said.

Three men have moved into an abandoned cabin in the Dahlonega hills. They said they were prospecting for gold, a plausible statement since the Dahlonega hills have yielded gold in small quantities for years and there was always a prospector or two in the vicinity. But these men had only a split shovel with no handlehold, a new tin bucket, and a rusty pan—hardly the equipment for serious mining. What did they look like? One was an old man with a gray moustache, a beak nose, and a slender build. The other two were younger. One of them, he thought, might be an Indian.

Over the phone I hired Davis at ten dollars a day to keep the men covered and told him to hire six assistants at the same price, two for each man in case the trio decided to separate.

"I'll meet you at the Dahlonega Courthouse," I said.

"Get here as soon as you can," Davis said, "I think they're getting jumpy."

It was then after seven P. M. I got a buggy and team of horses at a livery stable and started on the thirty mile ride, taking Bud Terrill, Route Agent for the Express Company, with me. The roads were bad, and it was after two o'clock when one of Davis' men stopped us just outside Dahlonega. He had bad news. The men had left the cabin and separated, the two younger ones going off together. They had gotten away, but Davis and two of his assistants were trailing the older man.

We went on into Dahlonega and found Davis waiting for us at the sheriff's office. He had his man. The old fellow had taken refuge in a mountaineer's cabin and gone to sleep. Under his pillow Davis found a three dollar mail order pistol, a considerable sum of money—part of it in foreign currency—and some jewels. This tallied with the shipment to the Mobile bank and I was sure we had the right man.

Still, when I saw him I was puzzled. He looked gentle and intelligent, spoke with dignity and great politeness, and asked for a comb for his hair and a chair to sit in. He earnestly desired to help me, he said, but he didn't know what I was talking about.

Later in the morning, after getting some sleep, I tackled him again.

When I mentioned that I was from Kentucky he showed some interest and admitted that he was from the same state. Then he looked at me as if to say, "How could you suspect a fellow Kentuckian of such a crime?" and I decided to let him rest for a while. With Terrill and a guide I drove into the hills to look for the two younger men.

We stopped at every cabin and made inquiries. After midnight our guide quit. Knocking at the doors of mountaineers' cabins in the dead of night was an unhealthy occupation, he said, and he wanted none of it. Terrill and I pushed on alone.

About three o'clock, riding along a ridge, I saw a light in the bottom land below. We turned our horses off the road and went to investigate. The light was coming from a cabin. Leaving Terrill with the horses I went up to the door and looked through a chain-hole. A group of men sat around a log fire. On a table behind them a coal-oil lamp was burning. In the double illumination I examined the men. Two of them did not look like natives.

With a long-bladed, deer-handled knife I reached through a crack in the door and lifted the inside latch. Then I stepped inside and covered the men with a pistol.

"Don't move, gentlemen," I said. "I'm an officer of the law. I'm looking for two men who held up a passenger train. I think these two in front of me are the ones I want."

One of the natives said, "I believe you're right, Mister, and we'll help you, but we'd like to see your badge."

I showed it to them and called to Terrill. We handcuffed the two men and searched them. Each had a cheap pistol and money and jewelry which tallied with the inventory I'd received from the express company. One of them had red hair and pock marks on his neck.

Next morning when Davis and one of his men arrived we hired a wagon, filled it with straw, put a jug of corn liquor under the seat, and started on the long trip to Gainesville. Davis drove; I sat in the straw with a prisoner on each side. I was handcuffed to both of them.

The old man had already been sent on from Dahlonega, and after his arrival at Gainesville an automobile was sent out to meet us. We were only a few miles from town when it reached us, but we were glad to ride the rest of the way on cushions. I got in the back of the car and sat with my prisoners flanking me. I was dirty, tired, unshaven, and hungry.

The automobile stopped just inside the city limits to get gasoline. In those days the pumps often were in the rear of a general store. While we were backed up to the pump three or four pretty girls appeared at the back door of the store and looked out. I could hear them talking.

"There they are sitting on the back seat."

"Oh, they're horrible!"

"Don't they just frighten you to death?"

"That one in the middle—I've never seen a worse face in my life!"

I was thoroughly miserable.

When we got to Gainesville, however, my spirits rose. Not only did we have the right men, but one of them, it seemed, was a prize. The polite old fellow was Bill Miner, alias George Edwards, Old Billy, Louis Colquhoun, William Morgan, California Billy, etc., a safe burglar, stage and train holdup man famous throughout the United States and Canada as one of the slickest robbers and prison breakers ever to bedevil the police. He had escaped from the New Westminster Penitentiary in British Columbia in 1907, but was thought to have been drowned going down the Mackenzie River in a small boat. How he got to Alabama I do not know.

His real name was George Anderson, and he was a native of Jackson County, Kentucky, where he was born in 1847. He went west when he was fifteen, and at nineteen was in San Joaquin Penitentiary for robbery. He stuck steadily to crime after that and was serving a life term in the Canadian prison when he escaped. I had to admire the old fellow for his persistence. He looked less like a criminal than almost any man I have ever seen, and he never deviated from his quiet, gentlemanly conduct.

When the judge asked him whether he had anything to say before being sentenced, he replied, "No. I took the money from the express company, and now you are taking my liberty from me."

As he was being led from the court room one of those righteous, busy ladies bustled up to him and said in a stentorian voice, with her head thrown back in moral rectitude, "Are you prepared to meet Jesus?" Fixing her with his kind, gentle eyes, the prisoner said, "Is He coming in now?"

For the Gainesville robbery he was given twenty years in the Milledgeville State Penitentiary. Within six months he had escaped. He was recaptured, but seven months later he escaped again. Again he was caught, but this time he was ill from exposure, and two months later he died. I was sorry to see him go. He had all the ingredients of a successful man except the right occupation.

Not all the robbers came from the hills. Some of them operated from within the company. The employees were subject to constant temptation, I knew, and I was never surprised—though it always saddened me, when one of them succumbed. Usually a $5,000 package of money disappeared. This seemed to be the favorite amount, and it was logical. An express company employee on a salary could not run up more than a few thousand dollars in debts. Five thousand would clear them up and give him something extra. In many of these cases I tried the friendly technique I developed in Christian County, and often it got results.

In the case of one young fellow, an express messenger, it had spectacular success. I had reason to believe that he was responsible for the disappearance of a package of money from his car, but there was no evidence and his record and his private life were above suspicion. I began to go with him on his daily runs. We became friends. On stopovers we shared a hotel room. Gradually I won his confidence. One night on a stopover, as we were getting ready for bed, he fell on his knees beside me, burst into tears, and told me he had a terrible burden on his conscience. He had stolen the money; it was hidden at his home. I comforted him, and we read together from the Bible.

Once I demonstrated this method to the satisfaction of my boss, W. S. McFarland, general manager of the express company. There had been a robbery and the police of Jackson, Tennessee were holding a stranger they had booked on suspicion. When I got to the hotel in Jackson I met McFarland and Tom Naylor, a Post Office Inspector. They had already been to the jail to interview the prisoner.

"He won't talk," McFarland said. "Come and have dinner with us and we'll all go down and see him later."

"I think I'll go and have a look now," I said. "I've got a lot of work to do and I don't want to lose any time if I can help it."

The jailer was just going out for lunch. He let me into the cell with the prisoner, Winfield, a big man with a moustache.

"Who the hell are you and what do you want?" Winfield said by way of greeting.

I told him my name and my job.

"Then who were those other fellows?" he asked.

"Didn't they tell you?"

"Hell, no, they just came in here acting mysterious and threatening me! Why didn't they say who they were?"

"Well, I've told you who I am. My job is to convict somebody for the holdup if I can. You're in jail. The fellows who were in on it with you are free. They won't help you. But you could help yourself—by talking."

He didn't answer.

"Have you had dinner?" I asked.

"No. I can't eat the fat, greasy slop they give me."

I looked through the cell window. Outside the jailer was passing by. I called to him.

"Stop by the hotel and ask them to send over two chicken dinners," I said, "and some cigars."

When the food came we both ate heartily. Then Winfield, lighting a cigar, said, "I've been thinking about what you said—me being in here and the other fellows out there. I'll talk."

The information he gave me was so exact that I was able to catch one of his accomplices within twelve hours, and the other in forty-eight hours.

Returning from the jail to the hotel I met McFarland.

"What kept you?" he asked.

"It took a long time for Winfield to write out his confession," I said, showing him the document.

That incident happened in 1913. In 1912 the Parcel Post had expanded its service to include heavier parcels at lower rates. The express companies were hard hit; their revenues dwindled. I would have to find another job or take a pay cut.

A job had been offered me by the Secret Service. On one of my trips to Washington—I went there frequently to ride south with valuable shipments—I had met William J. Flynn, Chief of the Service, and his assistant, William H. Moran. They had asked E. P. McAdams, their Birmingham agent, to approach me about joining the service. At the time I had declined. I was afraid of being sent north.

Now I went to McAdams and asked him if the job was still open. He said it was. I filled out an application, took an examination, and was accepted. After six months field work in Birmingham I was ordered to report to Washington.

★☆★

CHAPTER THREE

The White House—1914

IT WAS COLD and clear when I walked out of Union Station early on the morning of December 24, 1914. I could hear the newsboys shouting far across the plaza, and as I stood on the street car platform I could see the gleaming marble of the government buildings caught in the pale light of the rising sun. It didn't seem like a city. There was no noise, no smoke, no rush of laborers on their way to work.

I registered at the Stirling Hotel, 13th and E Streets, catty-corner from the National Theatre, and telephoned Assistant Chief Moran. He was at home—everyone seemed to be taking a holiday—and told me to report to the White House at one o'clock that afternoon. Self-consciously I bathed, scrubbing away the soot I had collected in years of railroading. Somehow the water didn't seem dirty enough when I finished, though I was obviously as clean as a man could get. My clothes were as clean as clothes could be, too, but they disappointed me. The idea of the White House had me enthralled. I wanted to shine like a knight in armor as I went to my new job. Walking past the Willard Hotel and the Treasury Department I was glad the streets were empty. I was as nervous as a hound dog baying at a full moon.

The White House seemed as deserted as the rest of the city. No one was on the grounds or at the gates. I turned in at the northwest entrance and walked to the Executive Offices. No one was at the door so I entered and found myself in the lobby, face to face with Joseph E. Murphy, Chief of the White House Detail of the Secret Service, a short, solidly built man in his late thirties, clean-shaven, quiet, and very formidable looking.

"You're Starling," he said. "Glad to have you with us. This is Dick Jervis, our advance man."

I shook hands with a handsome fellow of about my age. The eyes of both men were going over me like a sharp razor cutting a light beard. It made me uncomfortable, because I knew what they were looking for —a tell-tale flicker in the eyes, a weak muscle at the mouth, a sleekness along the jowl. How often had I looked for the same things myself, in other people!

"Sit down," Murphy said. "There's nothing doing today. The office force is having a holiday. The boss won't be over, but he may take a ride later."

We relaxed in the easy chairs provided for visitors, and they told me some of the details of my job. Guarding the President had been the task of the Secret Service since the assassination of McKinley by Leon Czolgosz.

"You are not working for the President," Murphy explained, "but for the Treasury Department, by order of Congress. So he can't order you to go away and leave him alone. That you must never do. His safety is your responsibility.

"The idea is to give him the maximum amount of protection with the minimum amount of inconvenience to his private life. When he goes to his living quarters on the second floor of the White House, we don't go with him. But from the time he comes downstairs until the time he goes back up again, he is under our guard.

"If he plays golf, we go along; if he attends the theatre, so do we; if he leaves town, we travel with him, and Dick goes ahead to make the arrangements."

Jervis began to tell me some of the intricacies of preparing for a Presidential journey. Every inch of railroad over which the special train was to travel had to be examined: weak spots were repaired, old ties were replaced, switches were spiked and guarded so that no one could get to them. The crew of the train was specially selected; the engine and coaches were checked and rechecked for mechanical faults; everyone who rode on the train had to be a certified member of the Presidential party, and the Secret Service men had to know him on sight.

Wherever the President travelled by automobile the road was inspected for bad spots, and if he rode through crowded streets extra precautions were taken. Then the Secret Service men watched the people and the buildings along the way, blanking out from their sight everything but the gesture or movement that meant danger—a handkerchief, something hurtling through the air.

If the party stayed at a hotel it occupied a complete floor, with the President in the center suite and Secret Service men in the rooms at each side. One elevator was appropriated for the use of the party, and no one could enter it without identifying himself. The other elevators were not allowed to stop at the reserved floor. All guests of the hotel were investigated, especially those on the floors immediately above and below that of the Presidential party.

I must have looked as confused as I felt, for Jervis stopped and smiled.

"There's a lot of routine to it," he said, "but you get used to it after a while. The main thing to remember is that no matter what happens, your only concern is the President. But when he's going through a crowd, turn your back on him. No danger will come from him. It will come from someone else—that's what you're supposed to look out for."

Murphy waved a reassuring hand.

"You'll get the hang of it," he said. "Anyhow, don't let it worry you. Come on, I'll show you through the offices."

The building was neither large nor complicated. The President's office faced us as we sat in the lobby. It was on the south side of the building, flanked by offices for his secretaries. The Cabinet room was on the southeast corner. Past the lobby on the north side were a reception room and another secretary's office. Beyond this was a door leading to the outside. The President used this entrance, coming from the White House by way of the basement alley or the rose garden.

We went back to the lobby and sat down. I was beginning to realize that more than twenty years experience as an officer of the law meant nothing in this job. Guarding a shipment of gold, which stayed where it was put and could not be hurt by bullets, was a lot different from looking after a man whose value was in his intelligence and judgment —things that could not be seen or touched—and who could be knocked out by a germ while I stood by, helpless and unknowing.

"What's this fellow like?" I asked. "Is he easy to get along with?"

My knowledge of Woodrow Wilson was limited. I knew that he was a Southerner, a Scotch-Irish Presbyterian, born in the manse at Staunton, Virginia, raised in North Carolina and Georgia, educated at the University of Virginia and Princeton, and a professor and college president during all of his career except for the past four years—two of which had been spent as Governor of New Jersey and two as President.

He ought, then, to be a somewhat austere person, completely devoted to his job and absolutely incorruptible. Somewhere I had read that as a boy he had met General Lee. Probably he knew Lee's famous statement that, "Duty is the sublimest word in the English language."

He ought to be a man who believed intelligence to be the greatest weapon that man of himself can wield, love being a gift of God. Being a Calvinist myself I understood this viewpoint, but I could see that it puzzled Murphy, who was a Roman Catholic. He had a softer, more mystical idea of religion, and he did not tell me that the President was a religious man. Yet I knew he must be, and I found myself nodding and smiling when Murphy said:

"He is punctual to the second, and he will not see anyone who is late for an appointment. If a man arrives five minutes after the time set for his interview, you don't even have to bother announcing him. He won't get in."

I would be that way myself if I were President, I thought. So would Cousin Matt Starling. I could appreciate it even more in a man like the President, whose labors were all mental. He would take it for granted that a trained mind meant a trained body, and a trained body would be on time.

"Part of your job is to learn as much about his personal habits as you can," Murphy went on. "This is in line of duty—it isn't snooping, and you don't have to do any of that. Besides, no matter what we see or hear never goes beyond our group. The 'Secret' part of the Service is very important.

"We'll tell you all we know, and you'll add to that yourself after you know the ropes.

"For instance, Mrs. Wilson died last August. The President misses her. He's lonely. Two of his daughters have married since he came here—Jessie to Francis Sayre, and Eleanor to the Secretary of the Treasury, Mr. McAdoo—and the other, Margaret, doesn't care much for the White House routine. She's away a good deal of the time. Right now he has only his cousin, Miss Helen Bones, for company. She was raised by his mother.

"Of course, it isn't our job to provide him with companionship and entertainment. But it's important for us to know that he is lonely and subject to fits of melancholy."

"Does he exercise?" I asked. "Does he ride horseback?"

I had been lonely all my mature life, unmarried and away from family and friends. The only way to fight it, I knew, was by action.

Murphy chuckled.

"When he came here last year he brought his bicycle with him, expecting to ride it around the streets of Washington," he said. "No, he doesn't ride horseback."

"He must know how," I interrupted, "he was raised in the South."

"Well, he doesn't ride, anyhow. Doctor Grayson, his physician—he's a nice little fellow—insists that he play golf. He doesn't like to do it, but he leaves here every morning for the links at 8:30. That means he walks out of the front door at 8:20, and if it happens to be your assignment you'd better be there waiting for him."

"Does he play well?"

"He's terrible. So is Grayson."

A melancholy prospect—following two poor golfers over a wind-swept course on a winter's morning.

"What happens when it snows?"

"He plays anyhow."

I should have known that he would. That was part of being a Scotch-Irish Presbyterian.

It was snowing now, lightly. The telephone rang. Murphy answered it, said "All right," then hung up.

"He's going for a ride," he said.

"In the snow?" I asked.

"Certainly," Murphy said. "It's not coming down very hard—may stop any minute."

We got into our overcoats and went outside. In a few minutes two big Pierce-Arrows, both open cars with right-hand drive, pulled up, the first stopping under the porte-cochère at the front door of the White House. Jervis and I went to the second car and waited. I was to ride on the left side of the rear seat. Murphy went to the first car. Jervis introduced me to Charlie Fredericks, the driver of our car.

When the President appeared I was disappointed. I expected him to sport a silk hat and an overcoat with a fur collar. Instead he wore an ordinary gray felt hat and an oxford gray overcoat that didn't seem to fit well. I could see nothing of his features except the sharp nose and jutting chin that showed in all his photographs. The young lady with him, slim and short, I took to be Miss Bones. They got into the car, the President sitting on the right. Murphy sat in front with the chauffeur, whose name, Jervis informed me, was Francis Robinson.

We followed at a proper distance. The route was a usual one, Jervis said, thoroughly checked from time to time by the Service. We went up Connecticut Avenue, crossed by way of Bradley Lane at the Chevy Chase Club to Wisconsin Avenue, thence through Bethesda to the Rockville Pike and to Kensington, Maryland. I will always remember that little town because on its outskirts I took a chill. I was suffering from malarial fever and chills, picked up in Arkansas, and I became reinfected in the cold, damp atmosphere of Washington's winter. I couldn't shake them off until April. But I did not miss a day of work during that time.

It stopped snowing while we were riding. When we got back to the White House it was dark. I stayed on duty until 11:30 but nothing else happened. As Christmas came I crawled into bed at the Stirling and shivered myself to sleep.

Christmas that year was on Friday, and there was not much doing at the White House until Monday. It was then that I met the President. Before this happened I was introduced to the members of the staff at both buildings—the Executive Offices and the residence.

First there was the President's secretary, Joseph P. Tumulty. He was very friendly, and struck me immediately as being bright and efficient and personable. For an assistant he had Warren Johnson, also an amiable and able man. Next came Rudolph Forster, a permanent member of the staff—i. e., he did not change with each administration. His title was Executive Secretary, and over his desk went all White House documents, state papers, proclamations, engagements, pardons, appointments, questions of government procedure and etiquette, matters of style, etc. His assistant was Tom Brahaney.

The President's private secretary and stenographer was Charlie Swem, who at that time was reputed to be the fastest typist and shorthand writer in the United States. He had his hands full with Mr. Wilson, they told me.

"The boss thinks fast and knows a lot of words," one of them said.

That started a discussion of the President's working habits.

"He can do more in less time than any man I've ever seen," one of the clerks said. "He sits in his office a few short hours, but when he's gone there's a day's work on your desk."

"He operates on a pile of papers like a starving man on a pile of flapjacks," another one said.

Mr. Forster explained.

"The President has a highly trained mind," he said. "He is almost all intellect. In addition he has been accustomed for thirty years to handling large amounts of paper work—examinations, for example. To be a successful teacher he had to learn to overcome detail. Otherwise he would have been a slave to it.

"Also, he isn't frightened by stacks of letters containing appeals, demands, supplications, and threats. As a college president he had that every day. He trained his mind to handle it swiftly. It is almost like magic, the way he weeds the important things from the unimportant.

"Then, too, he always knows where he stands in everything, so there is no hesitation about his decisions. He doesn't have to consult anyone. He's not a machine man and he has no advisers. He loathes politicians and he hates stupidity. He gets his work done and is off for an automobile ride while some other man would be chewing his nails over an inconsequential appointment."

As he talked the Executive Secretary's voice grew warm with admiration, and I could see that he adored his chief.

"He sounds like quite a fellow," I said.

"A genius," said Mr. Forster. "This job is just a vacation for him."

While we were talking, Murphy came in with the President, having escorted him from the White House. In a few minutes I was taken into the Executive Office and properly presented.

I saw before me a man slightly above medium height, well but sparely built, with a strong face, good gray eyes, and a lantern jaw. He had big ears that stuck out and a straight, sensitive nose that reminded me of my Cousin Lucy McGowan, whose little proboscis would flush, move, wiggle and point as her moods and feelings changed. The Wilson nose was like that; it would speak his mind before his eyes caught the message.

His mouth was straight, with full, well-shaped lips—surprising in a Scotch-Irishman, I thought—and his hair was a mixed gray, parted on the side. He wore a business suit of the same questionable tailoring I had noticed in his overcoat.

I forgot every one of these things when he spoke. His voice was so rich, so well-modulated, so vibrant with repressed energy that I was enchanted. His simple "How do you do?" said so much—it told of culture, of courage, of taste, of deep, sensitive feelings and of a natural warmth of nature. I was surprised. I had expected distant politeness. Instead I was made to feel that I amounted to something, that it was a good thing I had come, and that he was glad of it. In a daze I followed Murphy back into the lobby.

There were others of the staff to be met: Maurice C. Latta, Nomination Clerk, who carried all the President's nominations to Congress, and who could tell him offhand who was postmaster of Little Rock, Arkansas, or Naugatuck, Connecticut; Clarence Ingling, File Clerk; Ira R. L. Smith, Mail Clerk; E. W. Smithers, Chief Telegrapher; his assistants Jules Rodier and Fred Hohbein. There was also Charlie Wagner, assistant to the Executive Secretary in matters of correspondence.

Clarence L. Dalrymple was Captain of the White House Police, Pat McKenna was White House doorkeeper, Ike Hoover was Head Usher, Ed Norris was Chief Engineer—when it snowed I painted the golf balls red and set them to dry around his furnaces—Bill Reeves was Chief Florist, A. M. Thomas was Chief Electrician, and Colonel (of the Colored National Guard of the District of Columbia) Arthur Brooks was the President's valet and White House Custodian. There was also John Mays, a former Pullman porter brought to the White House by President Taft, who acted as Executive Barber and major domo of the hat check department.

I mention these men particularly because except where death has removed them,* they are still on the job. They were remarkable in their loyalty to the office of President of the United States, a feeling that I was to share with them. For thirty years I took off my hat whenever I met the President—and I had occasion to do so thousands of times—in honor of the office which he held. Whether the man himself deserved it I did not question; it was what he represented that was important.

Brooks, the President's valet, was a valuable and reliable source of information. I had to visit him often to find out what the President was planning to do. It was he who told me about Doctor Grayson's efforts to build up Mr. Wilson's health through diet. The President hadn't been eating correctly for years, it seemed.

"Those professors never get the right things to eat," Brooks explained. "They just don't care. When our boss came here he was just a hollow shell—all nervous energy, with nothing to back it up. Doctor Grayson

* Forster, Smithers, Hohbein, Norris, McKenna, Hoover, Dalrymple and Brooks are dead.

told me so. He said I'd have to work with him to help build the boss up."

This collaboration went on without the President's knowledge. Doctor Grayson told Brooks what to put on the breakfast tray, and Brooks reported to him on how much of each item was eaten, and with what relish or distaste. Thus they found out that oatmeal, chicken, steak, and Virginia country ham would always be eaten, whereas other things would be toyed with or ignored.

"It all depends on how he feels," Brooks told me. "If he's happy, he's hungry. Most of the time a meal is just a chore for him. He ought to eat as much as a pick and shovel man. This is a hard job he's got."

"They tell me at the Executive Offices that he handles it easily," I said.

"That's because he does his work before he gets to the office," Brooks said. "That's what Doctor Grayson is worried about. The man doesn't know how to do anything but think, so he thinks while he's exercising, while he's dressing or bathing. If he could relax while he's eating and exercising he'd be rejuvenated in no time."

Brooks uttered words like rejuvenated as if he had been speaking them since birth. He was a remarkable negro, intelligent, loyal, humble, and with beautiful manners. Years later Calvin Coolidge said of him, "Brooks isn't a colored gentleman. He's just a gentleman."

Another thing which worried Brooks was the President's wardrobe. I agreed with him heartily about this and said I would do what I could to help, though at the time I didn't see how I could be of any assistance. Most of his suits were equipped with box coats, so that they fitted him loosely in the back. At other places they were too tight, and the trousers were poorly cut. Left to himself he would choose a tie that disagreed with his suit.

"He doesn't notice it," Brooks said. "He's thinking of something else."

There was another side to it, however. When John Mays cut his hair, the President wouldn't let him clip the hairs in his ears. He didn't say why, but it was obvious that he did not intend to indulge in any notions that he considered plutocratic. He prided himself on being a man of the people. He was their spokesman, and he did not want to betray them in any way. During the Taft administration the Chevy Chase Golf Club, just over the District line in Maryland, had set aside on its grounds a small cottage to be known as the President's Cottage, providing a private dressing room and place of relaxation for any Chief Executive who cared to play at the club. Mr. Wilson would not use it. He considered the club too fashionable, and went instead to a small course called the Kirkside, at Chevy Chase Circle, or to the Washington Country Club, across the Potomac in Virginia. He also went to a Jewish Club, the Town and Country.

It was while we were on our way to the Washington Club one morning that I first became a personality in the eyes of the President—something more than a vague figure riding in the car behind him. It was a few weeks after my arrival, and I was huddled in the back seat of the Secret Service car, shivering in the cold, eerie glow of the January dawn. Suddenly the narrow, red clay road was blocked just ahead of us by a wagon. The horses had balked and turned it sideways, leaving the rear end directly in the way. The driver was excited and began shouting at his team, lashing them with a whip. They backed and reared but the wagon remained in the same position.

I waited for Murphy and Jervis to do something, but they sat quietly, waiting for the teamster to solve the problem. This he was not going to do, I could see—at least not very soon—so I left my place and went to the rear of the wagon. It was not very full, and not of heavy construction. I put my shoulders under the end, raised it up, and lifted it to one side. Now there was room for the cars to pass.

It is a trick every country boy knows, but as the President passed I could see him staring at me. So was Doctor Grayson. When we got to the golf course Murphy drew me aside.

"You made a great hit with the boss," he said.

Then he told me that, as I lifted the wagon, the President exclaimed, "Good heavens, Grayson! Look what that man is doing! Who is he?"

"I think that's the new Secret Service man, Starling," Doctor Grayson said.

Murphy confirmed this.

"He's a modern Hercules!" the President said.

Brooks, in his campaign for a smarter Presidential wardrobe, finally had some success. He wheedled his boss into being measured for a cutaway and gray trousers. They were executed by a first rate tailor, and when they were finished Brooks laid them out for Sunday morning. Rather dubiously the President put them on, but as soon as he saw himself in a mirror he was pleased.

"He wants to wear them all the time now," Brooks said happily, "and he's going to be measured for some evening clothes."

Complete reformation did not take place until spring, however, and then the credit did not go to Brooks. When Mrs. Galt—who was to become the second Mrs. Wilson—showed appreciation of his new dinner jacket, he was sold on the notion that clothes make the man. From then on he was a willing fashion plate.

The winter was dull and lonely for him. His companion most of the time was Miss Bones. Occasionally Miss Margaret was at home, and Miss Jessie and Miss Eleanor—Mrs. Sayre and Mrs. McAdoo—came for visits. Miss Jessie and Miss Margaret were blondes with blue eyes: Miss Jessie tall and raw-boned, Miss Margaret of the same general build but a little shorter. Miss Eleanor was a brunette with blue-gray eyes. Miss Margaret ran with a crowd of liberals, and was apt to show up with all sorts of long-haired, wild-eyed persons as her guests. She also sang, in a soprano voice that was not too good. Often it flooded the White House with its questionable beauty, creating a strange tension among the members of the staff.

The only other woman in the household was Miss Edith Benham, social secretary for the White House, who still fulfills that function, being now Mrs. James Helm, widow of the Admiral. All in all it was not much of a home, and a home was what the President needed. He was not a "man's man" in the sense that he enjoyed the company of other men, or liked to go to sporting events, or was athletic. The only man whose company he seemed to relish was Colonel E. M. House, who occasionally came down from New York to visit him.

Rudolph Forster, the Executive Secretary, with whom I had become friendly, gave me his theory of this situation.

"It's only a notion," he said, "but I've been reading this man's state papers for two years, and it strikes me that he is so highly developed as an individual—in his mind and tastes and habits—that it would be a rare man who could interest him and make him happy in a day-by-day companionship."

"What about Colonel House?" I asked.

"Personally I think Colonel House comes down here just to say 'yes' to him. I think he takes a lot of information from the old boy, but precious little advice.

"No, my theory is that this fellow needs female companionship—a woman who admires him and whom he admires.

"You see, in a charming woman there is nothing to irritate him. He doesn't expect her to measure up to him in intelligence, learning or wit. He doesn't want her to—she is supposed to admire these things in him, and give them a good audience, along with sympathy, understanding, and agreeableness.

"He wouldn't tolerate such an attitude in a man, because he hates fawning and kowtowing, though I think House gives him some of it in a sly way."

Forster was a shrewd observer, and I valued his observations. Ordinarily shy and retiring, he rarely expressed his opinions to other members of the staff, but often at one of our stag suppers at Jimmy Taylor's he would relax and talk about his job and his boss.

The Rev. James H. Taylor was pastor of the Central Presbyterian Church, 3045 15th St., N.W., which the President attended. I knew Taylor by reputation—he had preached to some of my relatives when he was at Anchorage, Kentucky—and when it turned out that he was about my age and a bachelor we pooled our loneliness and turned it into a rich friendship that perseveres to this day.

The stag suppers, at which Forster became a regular guest, were held at Jimmy's house and were usually precipitated by the arrival from Hopkinsville of a box containing smoked sausage, country ham, beaten biscuits, and jars of preserves, packed and sent to me by my mother, who never had me out of her mind, it seemed, and to whom I wrote each day.

It was more a pleasure than a duty to do this—it was the bright spot in my day—but I find now that I am indebted to that faithfulness for the details I am able to set down about those early days. I told her everything, and she kept each letter. In one of these I find recorded that I was being paid only four dollars a day and that I breakfasted on a cup of coffee and a soft-boiled egg. "I need to reduce," I explained. I must have been starving.

From the Stirling I moved to a small residential hotel a block and a half from the White House (it is now the Allies Inn), but twenty-five dollars a month rent was too much for my income, so I moved into a hall bedroom at Miss Nellie Green's at O Street and 16th, N.W., for six dollars a month. It was a long walk to work, but I could eat more, and that was the important thing. So long as my stomach was full my legs were strong.

By the end of winter I was settled in my job and liked it. I had found a few friends—Forster and Jimmy Taylor in particular—and my daily chills were growing less violent. The men with whom I worked—the regular Detail consisted of Murphy, Jervis, Jack Slye, Arnold Landvoigt and myself—were helpful and easy to get along with. Because most of them were married and lived in suburban districts with their families, they did not become my companions in off hours, but on the job they were team-mates with one idea in mind—don't fumble the ball. At first I was so tense that if anything had happened I would have been sure not only to fumble the ball but kick it all over the field. Gradually I relaxed, and pretty soon the task of guarding the President became the routine of my life. Actually it became my life, and stayed my life for thirty years. It was never just a job. It couldn't be. Whenever I got such an idea into my head history made certain that I did not keep it there long.

★★★

CHAPTER FOUR

Wilson—The Courtship

WHEN SPRING came, Rudolph Forster's theory received startling confirmation. Our boss was in love. He was courting a handsome widow, Mrs. Edith Bolling Galt, who lived "a piece up the way," as Kentucky folks say, at 1308 Twentieth Street. Since the President couldn't very well go out courting, it was all taking place at the White House, where Mrs. Galt was brought by her friends, Miss Bones and Miss Alice Gordon, Doctor Grayson's fiancee.

"She's a looker," Pat McKenna, the doorkeeper, told me.

"He's a goner," said Brooks, who was our barometer for Presidential moods.

I did not meet the lady until some time later, but I joined with the rest of the staff in wishing the boss good luck. If she was what he wanted, we hoped he would get her. Meanwhile, romance had come into my own life.

Each Sunday I accompanied the President to Jimmy Taylor's church, and sat where I could keep an eye on him and also on the congregation. After trying a number of pews I settled on one which gave me the best point of vantage for observation and action. In my pew sat a cute, saucy-looking lass who shared her hymnal with me and always smelled as fresh as a field of hay. Her hair was up off her ears and she had the look of being scrubbed both within and without. She was perhaps half my age, and I found myself wishing I had such a girl for a daughter. A man could miss a lot of nice things by not marrying, I decided.

As if in answer to my matrimonial cogitations I received a letter from

44

a woman who said she was madly in love with me. It was unsigned. We had met, she said, and a spark had been struck. She was aflame. How about me?

At first I suspected a joke, but when the second letter, and then the third, arrived, I knew that to one person at least the thing was serious. The woman, whoever she was, had a bad case. She said she now was sure I returned her love. She felt it whenever we met.

Met? But where? The only girls I saw regularly were those at the White House. My blood turned cold and I went sick at the thought. It couldn't be—but if, by some insane piece of bad luck, Miss Benham or Miss Bones had a crush on me, I was done for. I would have to leave the Detail.

Chills no longer bothered me. I had sweats. I made careful inquiries. I looked through the stacks of White House mail for duplicates of the stationery and handwriting of my mysterious lady. I found no clues.

More letters came. She was sure now of my love. I was so tender in my treatment of her. Why did I not speak, that she might leap to my arms and end the long agony? Singing "Lead Kindly Light," with my little lass of the hymnal, on a bright Sunday morning in May, I wished I had long ago married, and not lived to be chased by a wretched old crone—she must be old, I had decided—who had neither sense nor propriety.

Jimmy Taylor delivered a fine sermon that morning, and afterward cards were distributed for the mission societies. Each was asked to pledge an amount and sign the card. The girl in the pew had no pencil, so I offered her mine. Watching her sign her name my heart suddenly stuck to my ribs and refused to move. I was suspended from life. I knew that handwriting. She was the lady of the letters!

That night I took the matter up with Jimmy Taylor.

"Let me take care of it," he said, "and next week sit in another pew. But don't pick one with any women under sixty in it. Quite a spring we're having, isn't it?"

I followed his instructions, and thereafter sat directly behind the President. The young lady either changed her pew or left the congregation, for I did not see her again. Jimmy Taylor would give me no details. "I spoke to her mother," was all he would say.

On May 7 the *Lusitania* was torpedoed and sunk. It was the incident many people had been dreading. They were sure it would get us into the war.

"What will he do?" I asked Rudolph Forster the next day. For answer he took me into his office and showed me the text of a speech the President had written for delivery at Philadelphia on the tenth, two days later. It contained a phrase which became famous, "too proud to fight."

"He hasn't revised it," Forster said, "and I don't think he will. He believes war is a low-class way to settle an argument. He's a civilized man. There may be smarter men, and there may be nicer men; but I don't think there's a more civilized man living. He'll use words, and nobody can beat him at that."

"I don't think it's a matter of being civilized," I said. "He's just being Christian. Christ didn't believe in war."

"Wasn't He civilized?" Forster asked.

Watching the President deliver the speech, unchanged, a few days later, I was struck by his mannerisms on the platform. When he began he was nervous. He rocked back and forth on his heels. He didn't seem to know what to do with his hands: they were at his lapels, at his pockets, folded over his stomach. But as the audience reacted to his oratory, and the applause began to come at the right places, he relaxed. He stood firm and still, with his hands behind him. The left hand held the right, and the third finger of the right hand tapped out the rhythm of the speech on the thumb, striking, just as his voice struck, on the key word of each sentence.

Although the President seemed determined to keep the country out of war, none of us considered him a pacifist. A pacifist was a man who wouldn't fight no matter what you did to him. Bryan was of that type, and soon rumors were heard that he was about to resign. It was obvious to those of us who watched him come and go at the White House that he was deeply troubled by the trend of world events, and the danger of

America being drawn into the war. It was whispered that he did not like the way the President had phrased the first *Lusitania* note to Germany and feared that the language of the second would be too strong. He was hurt, too, because the President and Cabinet had been against using his arbitration treaty, which had never been ratified.

Bryan struck me as a man of wonderful personality—his physical vigor at that time was unimpaired—whose power of speech surpassed his power of thought. He also struck me as rather too commercial-minded, for like other people I was offended by his speeches on the Chautauqua circuit. He received fat fees, but he lowered the dignity of the Secretaryship of State. I talked with him a good deal, and always pleasantly. Once I went with him when he made a speech in Baltimore. The crowd was enormous. The enthusiasm was tremendous. I wondered as I heard the cheers how a man who could gain such a hold on the people could have missed the Presidency. But I was a little distrustful of his eloquence; I could not help thinking of the old maxim, "You are slave of your spoken word but master of your unspoken word."

Forster, my political mentor, explained the situation to me. "Bryan is a political debt," he said. "In the 1912 convention he threw his weight to Wilson and got him nominated, so he was rewarded. Ordinarily he would just be a poor Secretary of State, but in times like this he can do the country great harm. The President is acting like a gentleman in the *Lusitania* situation. Bryan wants him to be a doormat for the Kaiser."

He shook his head. "The boss is a political freak," he said. " 'Sugar Jim' Smith picked him for Governor of New Jersey and nobody yet knows why. He's never taken an order from the organization to this day. He figured they chose him for his ability, and he's acted that way ever since."

"Maybe they did," I said. I was pretty naive about politics in those days.

"Maybe Somebody Else did," Forster said, staring at me with his mild brown eyes. "Those things happen."

I nodded. With this shy, modest man, who had many friends but few intimates, I was beginning to share a feeling for the events swirling about us which was, I now realize, fatalistic. We thought of it as religious—I linked it to predestination. At any rate, we had a system which put small things into the hands of man and left large things to the plan of God. It was an attitude which over the years proved to be my salvation. So long as I was doing my best to safeguard the President I did not worry further about his well-being. That was in the hands of destiny. Thus my nerves remained steady and my health was unimpaired through nearly a third of a century on a job that is notorious for ruining digestion and breeding insomnia. I never had recourse to bicarbonate of soda, and the only meals I missed were those I could not afford to buy.

I remember a few meals that Murphy and Jervis missed, though, and gladly. In that same May of 1915 the President went to New York to review the Atlantic Fleet. He and his party made the trip on the *Mayflower,* with Murphy and Jervis along. I took the automobile to New York and met the party at the dock. Except for the President they looked pretty haggard. Murphy and Jervis were pale green, tinted with yellow. There had been a storm, it seemed, and most everyone had been seasick. Even Brooks had succumbed.

"Have you had breakfast?" I said to Murphy.

He groaned. "I will never eat again," he said.

Later that day I showed him the New York newspapers, which carried flattering stories about the Secret Service men, who had descended from the *Mayflower* "hollow-eyed" from an all-night watch over their precious charge.

"You're heroes!" I said. "You saved the President's life!"

"My Lord!" Murphy said, "the boss was the only one who stayed on his feet. He didn't have any more protection than a silk hat in a high wind!"

The weather was calm and bright for the review. As the ships steamed by Jervis looked at me uneasily.

"There aren't very many, for a war," he said.

I agreed with him. Preparedness was a question that was in everybody's mind. Should we build up our army and navy, even though we did not intend to get into the war?

"Why doesn't he do something about it?" Jervis said, indicating the President.

Watching the straight, slim figure, standing with hands clasped behind, I felt that I understood his feelings. He was still a gentleman.

"I reckon he figures it would be too much like spitting on his hands," I said.

In a few weeks Bryan's resignation was accepted and Robert Lansing was appointed in his place. By now it was June, and plans were being made for the summer. The President rented the home of the American novelist, Winston Churchill, at Cornish, New Hampshire. It was called Harlakenden House, a fine country home with an excellent view of the Connecticut River valley and the surrounding mountains. There the President planned to spend as much time as he could spare away from the White House. I first met Mrs. Galt at Harlakenden.

She was, indeed, a fine figure of a woman, somewhat plump by modern American standards, but ideal from the viewpoint of a mature man. Her face was not only lovely but alive. She laughed easily, and after she had grown accustomed to my presence in the gardens back of the house, she would come out there with the other girls—Miss Bones and Miss Benham—and join in the official sport of teasing me. As I saw her eyes dancing and her lips trembling with the effort to keep laughter back I thought, "Lordy me, lady! I'll bet you're driving the boss wild!"

He wasn't able to get away from Washington as often as he would have liked but whenever it was at all possible he was at Harlakenden House, and the romance prospered. At least it seemed to prosper. What was going on in the lady's mind nobody knew but herself. What was going on in his mind was obvious. He was in pursuit. She was retreating, but how rapidly, and with what purpose in view, no one knew.

Automobile rides were in order whenever the weather permitted, and I began to get acquainted with the New England countryside, so different from the rolling hills of Christian County. The President was accompanied by Mrs. Galt and Miss Bones. Murphy sat in the front seat with the driver, and the rest of us followed in the Secret Service car.

One day the President ordered a stop in front of a typical farmhouse, which turned out to be a tea room. Instantly we went into action. Such situations are loaded with peril. We knew nothing about the house or the people in it, and had no chance to make an investigation before the President was out of the car and up the path. Anything could have happened, and the fact that it didn't proves nothing. It might have. Such things as this—unscheduled stops and visits to unguarded places—are what make fatalism the only friend of the Secret Service man.

As quickly as possible I got to the rear of the house, inspected the approaches, and took up my vigil. Only one man was in sight. He was in the garden, picking strawberries. I went to talk to him, and discovered he was the owner of the place.

"Nice berries you have," I said. The mountain air and the ride had stimulated my appetite. The berries were large and red, and I caught the breath of them in my nostrils.

"Thought I'd pick them for supper," he said.

I began to bargain. Finally I got the bowl, with a dab of sugar and two spoons, for forty cents.

"The wife won't like it," the man said as I gave him the money.

I called Jack Slye from the side of the house and gave him one of the spoons. We had just finished the last berry when the man reappeared. He was hopping mad.

"Damn it!" he said. "You fellows got me in a fine fix. The President of the United States is inside with two ladies and he's ordered tea and cake and berries"—he pointed to the empty bowl—"and you've eaten the last piece of fruit on the place! I've got to go borrow some from the neighbors and keep the President waiting, and the wife is raising hell!"

He stormed off through the garden. Jack went back to his post and I guiltily put the bowl on the back porch.

I made up for my delinquency a few days later when, returning home on a muddy road after a shower of rain, we came up behind a farmer driving a two-horse team hitched to an empty wagon. Robby, the President's chauffeur, sounded his horn several times, but the old fellow didn't pull over. I ran ahead and asked him to make way.

"It's the President of the United States," I said.

"Don't care who'tis," said the old fellow. "I got's much right to this road's anybody and I intend to stay where I'm a-settin'. Don't care whether the whole dad-gummed population of Washington wants to get by."

He was a Republican, obviously.

"Pardner," I said, "where I come from it's mighty bad manners not to let a body by when he's a mind to go by."

He got the point.

"I'm a-settin'," he said.

In a small way the Civil War was being fought again, only this time the Starling banner was on the side of the Confederacy.

"You're a-movin'," I said.

I took hold of the bridle of the left hand horse, gave him a friendly kick in the ribs, and led the team off the road.

"We have horses in Kentucky, too," I said.

As the President's car passed I bowed, and he and the girls laughed. The old man didn't say anything, but I felt his eyes burning holes in my back. Without turning around I got into the Secret Service car and we drove off.

When Mrs. Galt returned to Washington in September my role in the romance became more personal. In order to be alone—or as much alone as was possible—with her, the President changed the routine of his afternoon automobile ride to include a walk in Rock Creek Park. It was my job to follow them on this daily stroll, and to keep my eyes on the President every moment. I wanted to look away; I wanted to let a tree get between me and the two of them. But I couldn't. Something might happen.

He was an ardent lover, and a gay one. He talked, gesticulated, laughed, boldly held her hand. It was hard to believe he was fifty-eight years old. He had a natural lightness of foot, and walking along the woodland paths he leaped over the smallest obstacles, or skipped around them.

Every now and then they would glance back at me, as if my name had been mentioned—he with the embarrassed half smile of a man who wishes you would go away and leave him alone; she with the frank laughter of a woman who is enjoying the predicament of both men. She was having a wonderful time.

People who are familiar with Washington may be interested in the geography of those walks. The car would go out Beach Drive, past the old Pierce Mill, and along Military Road to Ross Drive. Here the President and Mrs. Galt would get out and take the footpath which goes through the park for about half a mile to the west. The car met them again at the point where Ross Drive runs into Ridge Road, just after the latter descends Snake Hill and intersects Beach Drive.

By this time the newspapermen were nosing around for the story. They were polite, but they were persistent, and they were everywhere. Washington has a lot of reporters, and they have a lot of friends. As a protection—meaning no offense to the lady—we referred to Mrs. Galt among ourselves as "Grandma," and we all hoped that the engagement would soon be announced so that the strain might end. But just at this point something happened that made us certain the whole thing had blown up.

For three days the President remained indoors. He was ill, we were told. Brooks reported that it wasn't anything the doctors could help.

"He's just down and out," he told me. "She must have refused him."

I didn't believe it. I was sure she loved him. I decided it was a lover's quarrel. Then I remembered something.

"Wasn't Colonel House here a few days ago?" I asked.

Brooks admitted that he was.

"There's the trouble," I said. "I don't like that pussy-footer. I'll bet he's at the bottom of this."

Brooks smiled. "The President thinks a lot of him," he said.

My dislike of House was founded on nothing more substantial than my personal reaction to his appearance. Deliver me from a man who smiles, rubs his hands together, and calls me "Brother." House struck me as that sort of person, and later I learned that I was right in suspecting him in this particular matter. He was afraid that another woman— a Mrs. Peck, whom the President had known years before—would make trouble if an engagement were announced. He was also afraid of the public reaction to a marriage so soon after the death of the first Mrs. Wilson.

The suspense ended one afternoon with a visit by Mrs. Galt to the White House. The President's recovery was almost instantaneous. The romance was on again. Years later, in Mrs. Wilson's "Memoir," * the details were told. The President sent Doctor Grayson to tell Mrs. Galt of Colonel House's fears about Mrs. Peck. Rather than risk a scandal for her he said he was willing to give her up, though he himself did not care what was said or done. While waiting for her reply he fell into a melancholia that had all the appearance of an old-fashioned "decline." She sent him a letter saying she loved him, that this was all that mattered, and that she would marry him, if he wished her to, under any circumstances. But he was too frightened to open the envelope—he was sure it contained a farewell—and she had to make a personal visit to reassure him.

The engagement was announced on October 7. Next day we left on a trip to New York and Philadelphia, where the President attended a World Series game. It was his first public appearance with Mrs. Galt. Colonel House's estimate of the public's reaction was completely wrong. The people showed increased affection for the President, and when they saw that Mrs. Galt was pretty they loved her. I find the story of this little excursion well preserved in a letter to my mother.

Washington, D.C., October 10, 1915.

Dear Mother:

Well, we are back from another arduous trip full of hard work, loss of sleep, nervous tension, and anxiety. Today we will again resume our usual mode of living by going to church and doing our Christian duty,

* "My Memoir" by Edith Bolling Wilson. Bobbs-Merrill, 1939.

and to me this is more pleasant than being in a crowd of crazy people.

Enclosed find a $5.00 baseball ticket to the second game of the World Series. You can give it to Guy. I was right behind the boss with my arms thrown out on each side, and had to pass up the ticket collector. It was a great game, but too much of a crowd for me. I suppose there were about 21,000 people present and great crowds greeted us all along the street to the ball park.

We arrived at New York about 3 P.M. Friday afternoon, and drove straight to the St. Regis hotel, where we left Mrs. Galt, Mrs. Bolling (Mrs. Galt's mother) and Miss Bones. We then took the boss to Col. House's residence, where we stayed for a few minutes, then went back to the hotel, secured the ladies, and took a long automobile ride along the river speedway, passing Grant's Tomb and Columbia University. We also rode thru most of Central Park. We returned to the St. Regis hotel about 5:45 P.M., left the ladies, and went to Col. House's residence, where we stayed about thirty minutes, when we again returned to the hotel, secured the ladies, and brought them back to Col. House's residence for dinner. At 8:15 P.M. we automobiled to the Empire Theatre and saw "Grumpy." I left them at the theatre and went to my room to get some sleep, as I had to get up at 3 A.M. and go to Col. House's residence and keep the boss from harm. I did not mind the early rising and enjoyed a good book in Col. House's residence. That morning we took another long automobile ride on the speedway and the parks and then went to Penn. Station. At 11 o'clock we boarded a private car for Philadelphia to see the second game of the World Series. We landed in Phila. about 1 P.M. and were met at the station by a vast throng, which the policemen could hardly handle. At 1:25 P.M. we rode out to the baseball game, 26 squares from the depot. I rode on the running board of the automobile all of the way and literally pushed the President and his crowd through the entrance of the ball park. The police seemed to be powerless to keep them back. In the ninth inning I had to go along the aisle and request the people to keep their seats until the President and his party passed thru. We hurried back to the depot, people yelling all the way, and it was certainly with a sigh of relief that I felt the train move forward in the direction of Washington, D.C. We were so busy with the President that we did not have time to eat our noon meal so we had to go to the game on empty stomachs. When I got settled down, after we started, I went back to the kitchen and had the cook give me a squab sandwich and I then went into a drawing room and enjoyed my first meal since seven o'clock that morning.

I got to sleep about 9 o'clock that night and slept about ten hours. I got up Sunday morning, strolled down to the city, had my breakfast and arrived at the Executive Office. All of a sudden the phone bell rang and summoned the two men on duty to come to the White House at once. Our Operative in charge not being at the office I had to grab my coat and cap and rush up to the White House, and you can imagine my surprise when I was informed that he was going to Baltimore. Well, we arrived at Baltimore at 10 A. M. We went to church, had communion, then went back to his brother Joe's apartment to dinner, and left at 3 P. M. for home where we arrived at 5 P. M. At about 6:15 P. M. while I was waiting with the Operative in charge for the other Operative to show up, the phone called us on the jump and I ran my tongue out to get up with the President, who was walking towards the gate. When I caught up with him he informed me that he was going to eat dinner with Mrs. Galt and walk back later on. Well, I kept my eye on the house until 11:50 P. M. when he appeared, and we walked home. You can see how long I was on duty and imagine how tired I felt when I hit the bed that morning about 1 A. M. I got up at 6 A. M. and was on duty until four-thirty this evening. He is speaking to the D.A.R.'s this evening at their hall. I had to come back tonight to see if he intended going to the theatre, and on finding that he was not I took the chance to write you this letter.

Now that he was free to visit the little house on Twentieth Street the President did so frequently. He had been communicating with Mrs. Galt by letter each day, but now a private telephone line was installed between the White House and her residence, and when they were not together at one place or the other, they were telephoning.

Almost every night we took him to see her, then waited outside the house until he reappeared. That was never before midnight, and on

Sundays the vigil was frequently from 1 P. M.—after church—to 1 A. M. We didn't mind. We were all romantic, and we were glad the boss had made good.

Often he wanted to walk back to the White House, and I welcomed this decision, for it was my job to walk with him, and the chance to get some exercise after four or five hours of inactivity was one I appreciated.

I remember those October and November nights—the air was clear, and just cold enough to make me conscious of my skin and the tip of my nose. The sky was spattered with stars, and sometimes there was a moon. We walked briskly, and the President danced off the curbs and up them when we crossed streets. If we had to wait for traffic— delivery trucks were about all we found abroad at that hour—he jigged a few steps, whistling an accompaniment for himself. There was a tune he had heard in vaudeville which he liked, and almost unconsciously, it seemed, he would whistle it as he waited for something— for the caddy to hand him a club on the golf links, or a milk truck to pass us on the corner of N Street. He whistled softly, through his teeth, tapping out the rhythm with restless feet: "Oh, you beautiful doll! You great big beautiful doll! Let me put my arms around you, I can hardly live without you. . . ."

Thus he walked from Twentieth Street to DuPont Circle, down Connecticut Avenue to Farragut Square, through it to Lafayette Square and thence to the White House. There I left him and walked the fifteen blocks back to my room, knowing I had to be at the porte-cochère at 8:15 to take him golfing. They ought to rewrite that old adage; it is a man in love who has the strength of ten.

The newspapermen were openly on our trail now, and we gave them all the help we could, at the same time doing our best to protect the privacy of the President. The photographers were particularly pestiferous. We told them that no pictures were to be taken of the President as he was entering or leaving Mrs. Galt's house. You have only to know the character of news photographers to realize that this was like waving a red flag in front of a bull. It was particularly a challenge to Eddie Jackson, a cameraman who spurned all but the most difficult assignments, and who for more than a quarter of a century has been a top man in his field. We have been good friends for many years, but our first meeting, on an afternoon of that autumn in 1915, was far from peaceable.

Eddie was hiding behind some shubbery near the Twentieth St. house, his camera trained on the entrance. Sneaking up behind him I put my hands under his armpits and lifted him off the ground. Then I whispered into his ear, in my deepest and most sinister voice:

"Young man, there are times when it is necessary for me to do things which are contrary to my Christian principles. We've been very patient with you boys, and now you're going to force me to spoil the barrel of my brand-new pistol by bending it over your head. And maybe you're going to make me get out my knife and cut another notch in the handle of my favorite Colt, and I don't want to do that, because the design I was carving is all finished."

I set him down then and turned him around so he could see me. He was scared.

"Now will you go away and not bother us any more?" I asked.

He went. Later, when we knew each other better, we laughed about the incident. Eddie had heard that the new man on the Detail was from Kentucky, and Murphy and Jervis had fed him some tall tales about my exploits. He was ready to believe that my pistol butt was full of notches, and that my trigger finger was itchy.

So the days went. On October 29th I wrote to my mother:

Dear Mother:

Well, I am here on duty while the boss is eating dinner with his fiancée. He certainly has me on the go these days. We never know when he is going to start something. He is hooked hard and fast and acts like a boy in his first love experience.

The other night we were at the Cordova Apt. house, where Mrs. Galt's mother and sister live. Three of us were on duty downstairs— Murphy, Jervis, and I. It was about 6:35 P. M., and none of us had been to supper. Finally Murphy sent Jervis to telephone the White House and find out where the President was going to eat dinner. Jervis reported that he was going to have dinner with Mrs. Galt's mother at the Cordova. Acting on this information Murphy and Jervis hiked off to dinner, leaving me alone. Imagine my surprise when the President and Mrs. Galt came tripping down the steps and made for the door. I of course stepped quickly to the door and opened it—the doorman being out—and off we walked, landing at Mrs. Galt's house, where they had dinner and where I stayed until 11:30 P. M. Murphy and Jervis surmised what had happened when they returned and found me gone, and followed me to Mrs. Galt's, so that I finally got a chance to eat my own dinner.

Walking to her house the President acted like a happy young boy lover. He laughed most of the time and kept me grinning at his antics. However, I was glad when I put him in her house, for three of us are supposed to stay with him at all times now, for these are considered dangerous days when anything is apt to happen at any moment.

An amusing incident happened to me the other day when we automobiled to Emmitsburg, Md. I had just followed the President, Mrs. Galt and Miss Margaret Wilson to the front door of Mrs. Sterling Galt's home and had returned to the pavement in front of the house, when a crowd began to gather. A one legged man walked up to me and said, "Gray is my name. Are you the man they call the President?" I hastily denied the honor.

The next Monday morning we were in the President's office receiving several small delegations, when a woman walked up to me with her hand out and a smile on her face, and said, "Why, how do you do Mr. Tumulty? I am very anxious to have a private talk with you." I again declined the honor.

Yesterday evening we took the President and Mrs. Galt out to play golf. On returning the President stayed at Mrs. Galt's, and two of us hurried back to the White House to get rid of the golf clubs. We drove up to the White House steps. I was on the back seat wearing a raincoat and English cap which I had pulled down in order to keep it from blowing off. The negro footman rushed out and opened the car door. He bowed and said, "Howdy do, Mr. President." "Howdy do yourself you old rascal," I said. His face popped with amazement as he looked at me. Then he laughed and said, "Mr. Starling, you're a mess."

I am afraid we will be pretty busy all the rest of this year. We are expecting daily to hear an announcement of the wedding date, but nothing has been given out yet.

The date of the wedding and some of the details were revealed to me inadvertently one week-end in New York, while the President was visiting Colonel House. On these occasions—and they were frequent during that period—I was assigned to a settee opposite the elevator and just outside the entrance to Colonel House's apartment. I had to meet all visitors and make sure they had appointments before letting them in. On this particular day the last caller left the door ajar. Going to close it I heard the President say to Colonel House, "Edith and I will be married at her home sometime in December. We will go to Hot Springs, Virginia, where we shall spend at least two weeks at the Homestead Hotel." I closed the door, glad that I knew at last when the wedding was to take place, but a little unhappy to be burdened with the secret of it. I did not even pass on my discovery to the other members of the Detail.

These week-ends in New York were hectic. I described one of them in a letter to my mother dated November 7.

Dear Mother:

We have had a strenuous week and I was glad to get back to Washington Friday night.

On Tuesday, November 2, we left Washington at 8 A. M in a private car for Princeton, New Jersey, where the President voted. We arrived at Princeton at 12:25 and departed at 1:55 P. M., reaching Washington about 6:35 P. M. Fortunately I was not on duty that night, so I did not have to look after the boss while he courted his sweetheart until midnight. I did not come on duty until Saturday evening at 1 P. M and I caught it that night. Thursday morning at 10 A. M. we left for New York where we attended a banquet that night at the Biltmore Hotel, given by the Manhattan Club. Next morning I went to Col. House's residence about 9 A. M. I heard the doorknob to the boss' room turn, so I jumped up and was waiting when he and Col. House walked out. I touched the button for the elevator and then returned their salutation. Col. House put his hand on my shoulder and said to the President, "Talk about 'Watchful Waiting.' This is it." To which the President replied, "Yes, Starling has been my faithful friend." It was hard to hold me the rest of the day.

A very interesting incident occurred in connection with Mrs. Galt. It seems that we were invited out to a Mr. Dodge's place to lunch and that on account of the large crowds waiting outside to see the President and Mrs. Galt together, and also to avoid the moving picture and newspapermen, it was decided to take Mrs. Galt out through a secret exit leading to Fifth Avenue (the crowd was in front of the hotel on 55th St.), put her into a waiting automobile, pull down the blinds, rush the car around to the front entrance on 55th St., and there allow the President to walk out and get into the car. Jervis and I were selected for the job and promptly at 12:15 we took Mrs. Galt in an elevator from the tenth to the third floor, got off there, and were guided to a secret door that led into a narrow hall or alley where we had to stoop to get through the door. Then we walked down some narrow, dark steps, two floors down to another door leading to Fifth Avenue. There we put her in the car and drove around to the front entrance, where the President walked out and got in. We drove away and no one was the wiser until suddenly a newspaperman shouted, "She's in the car!" Of course our car was right behind theirs and no car was allowed to pass our car, so we foiled their hopes of getting pictures. On leaving Mr. Dodge's for the train Mrs. Galt was taken out through the back entrance and driven straight to the depot, again avoiding the moving picture men. I got to bed that night at 12:45 and was up again at six.

I have about finished the nut bread and rummage pickle, both of which I enjoyed very much. I have been with the boss most all day. We went to church this morning, where we had a splendid service and I sang with more vigor than usual. Only the President and Miss Bones attended, and we carried Miss Bones back to the White House before taking the President to his lady love's where I stayed until 4 P. M. I am out for dinner now and will go back to watch until he leaves, which will be about midnight. I will be glad when he gets married, for he certainly has us on the go.

The wedding took place on December 18, at eight o'clock in the evening. It was a small affair, with members of the two families and a few close friends attending. Two clergymen officiated, Jimmy Taylor, and Dr. Herbert Scott Smith, of St. Margaret's Episcopal Church, which Mrs. Galt attended. We had little to do at the ceremony. Our job was to see that the bride and groom got out of town without meeting the newspapermen and photographers. It was a perfect occasion for cranks and emotionally unstable persons, and we couldn't risk it, much as we would have liked to accommodate our friends of the press.

To make certain that our plan was successful it was necessary that only the key men know about it—Murphy, Jervis, and myself. Everyone else was encouraged to believe that the party would leave from Union Station. On the day of the wedding we loaded the two automobiles—ours and the President's—into the baggage coach of our special train. The two chauffeurs were told to report to Jervis at the stationmaster's office with their bags packed for a two weeks' stay. They were given no hint as to what climate they would be in.

The train crew didn't know the destination either. Suddenly they were ordered to depart, without the President. The engineer was told to pull into a siding at the edge of the freight yards in Alexandria. This was a spot I had chosen, and I was stationed there. It was remote from the activity of the yards, and easily accessible by automobile.

Murphy was with the President and Mrs. Wilson. After leaving the Twentieth Street house he directed the chauffeur street by street, timing his approach to Alexandria so that the car entered the yards at the same moment as the train. I winked my flashlight three times, the car slowed, I leaped aboard and guided the chauffeur to the side of the President's car. In a minute they were aboard, Murphy and I swung up behind them, and the train pulled out. But even Murphy and Jervis didn't know where we were going. The engineer was only then getting his orders from officials of the Chesapeake and Ohio, who were aboard to see that all went well. Murphy and Jervis gasped when I showed them the clothes I was carrying in my bags. They had packed for all the possibilities, including Florida. When I confessed that I had known where we were going for nearly two months they didn't know whether to commend me or cuss me out.

We ran into the siding at Hot Springs about seven o'clock the next morning. Soon after we stopped I went back to the private car. I entered quietly and walked down the narrow corridor flanking the bedrooms. Suddenly my ear caught the notes of a familiar melody. Emerging into the sitting room I saw a figure in top hat, tailcoat, and gray morning trousers, standing with his back to me, hands in his pockets, happily dancing a jig. As I watched him he clicked his heels in the air, and from whistling the tune he changed to singing the words, "Oh, you beautiful doll! You great big beautiful doll. . . ."

★☆★

Wilson—Re-election

The Homestead
Hot Springs, Va.
Jan. 3, 1916

Dear Mother:

We received hurried orders this morning to prepare to leave here tonight for Washington. We will arrive there tomorrow (Tuesday) morning. I knew what was coming, for I have been deciphering code messages from Secretary of State Lansing to the President, and sending the replies. Lansing kept after him to hurry back.

I am very uneasy about our continued submarine troubles, and I am afraid we will be forced into war whether we want it or not. I believe we have lost the respect of other nations, who seem to think we are afraid to fight. It is not fear—the President has been a scrapper all his life, but he fights with his brain and he always has a cause in which to believe. He doesn't want to get into this thing, which is just a brawl between a lot of bullies, and I agree with him. I would almost go so far as to say that I am for peace at any price. And you know that I am not afraid to fight.

What I am afraid of is that some of the people and some of our hot-headed representatives and politicians, will get up a big stir and try to get us into more trouble than we can take care of, especially while we are in such a state of unpreparedness. In fact at present we could hardly afford to fight Mexico.

The President and his bride had a good time, even though their visit was cut short. For ten days I did not see him at all; he stayed in the bridal suite. On the tenth day he stuck his head out of the door and said, "Starling, if Malvina comes will you let her in?" "Yes sir," I said. "Who is Malvina?" "She is Susie's sister," he said, closing the door. Susie was Mrs. Wilson's maid.

The next day they played golf and took a ride through the surrounding countryside, and for the remaining three days of the visit this schedule was repeated. During one of the rides the President spotted a promontory which promised an excellent view. He decided to walk up to it, taking Mrs. Wilson along. It was a stiff climb, but he was ready for anything during those high days.

When they returned to the automobile the President's shoes were very muddy.

"If you'll put your foot on the running board I'll clean it off," Robby, his chauffeur, said.

The President accepted the offer. Mrs. Wilson looked down at her feet.

"My shoes are not muddy," she said. "I was more careful. But I have a lace untied."

She looked at me expectantly. Immediately I dropped to one knee. "May I tie it for you?" I said.

She rested her foot on my trouser leg, raising the skirt of her handsomely tailored suit at the same time, to reveal a shapely ankle.

"Thank you," she said.

I tensed my shoulders to keep my hands from shaking. Remember this was twenty-five years ago. When I set her foot back on the ground she said, "You make a very neat bow." Then she looked beyond me and smiled.

The President was standing by the car, staring straight ahead, his nose pointing and his jaws working—tell-tale signs of his anger. Quietly I went to the Secret Service car. He didn't speak to me for two weeks.

Back in Washington the social season began, and Mrs. Wilson made her debut as White House hostess. She had the grace and manner of a woman born to the position, and her gowns were exquisite. The President was proud of her, but her presence at official functions had a practical use; it took a great deal of the strain of meeting people off him, and turned what had been a tedious chore into a pleasure he began to anticipate.

I also made my White House debut that winter. We had to be at these social affairs, and we had to provide ourselves with full dress suits, dinner jackets, etc. We were posted at various points, and my position was along the receiving line, a few feet from the President, where I could look for bulging pockets, handkerchiefs that might have something concealed in them, and eyes with a fanatical gleam. I tried also to memorize faces and names, so that I would know them when they appeared again. Thus I got to know most of official, diplomatic, and social Washington.

Some of them got to know me, too, or at least they thought they did. One night there was a D.A.R. reception in the Blue Room. Members of the White House domestic staff waxed the floor, but forgot to tone it down. It was extremely slippery, and we were all watching our step. As I stood in my accustomed place a sweet-looking old lady stepped toward me from the line, put her hand in mine, and said fervently:

"Thank God you are our President! You have kept us out of war!"

As she uttered these words her feet went out from under her and she straddled my legs. I held firmly to her hand and raised her quickly from the floor, but not before her long dress had slipped up over her knees and all who were assembled had seen that she was fully sheathed in long red flannel drawers.

"Red Raven Splits," I thought.

I apologized for the condition of the floor, thanked her for her mistake in identity, and escorted her to the President, who smiled broadly—having seen the incident—while she repeated to him what she had told me.

Because of the number of times I was mistaken for the President, whom I in no way resembled, my superiors decided that if things got really troublesome I would double for him. Moran thought it was a fine idea. His wife was not so sure. Mrs. Moran and I were good friends;

we went to the moving pictures together, and she shared her hot ginger-bread with me. The President was only a man, so far as she was concerned, and might conceivably be replaced, but one of her boys, who took her to the movies and ate her gingerbread, was irreplaceable. I must confess that there was a daughter, Aileen, and it is an indication of my callousness and greed that I courted the mother instead, for it was she who made the gingerbread, God love her, as the Irish say.

Mrs. Wilson moved into the stream of White House life without disturbing its even flow. She went golfing each morning with the President, and he got a great deal more fun out of the game with her for partner. Because of Dr. Grayson's watchful care, he had become far more vigorous physically. At first he had been little more than the shell of a man, with no vitality or reserve vigor; now he had genuine resilience. The President and Mrs. Wilson were inexpert golfers, he averaging about 115 and she about 200. She used a niblick most of the time, and depended on me to keep her out of trouble. I cheated for her, retrieving the balls she knocked into the woods and dropping them on the edge of the fairway.

"You could beat all of us if you were playing," she whispered to me one day.

"I would rather caddy for you than be the best player in the world," I replied.

She blushed prettily, and my day was made. There is not a bit of use in denying it—I was her slave.

Neither of them really cared about the game. Walking along the fairway between shots the President regaled her with dialect stories and gave impromptu impersonations, one of his best being an interpretation of serious little Dr. Grayson addressing a ball. One day, tired of carrying her niblick, Mrs. Wilson laid it across her husband's shoulders and bent him forward so that it would not slip off. Immediately he changed his stride to imitate the lumbering gait of an ape. When he tired of the jest he bent forward, let the niblick roll over the top of his head, and caught it as it fell. They both laughed—they laughed at anything and everything in those days. They were completely happy, and the increasing burden of his job rested lightly on the President's shoulders.

They played until ten o'clock, then returned to the White House. The President was due at his office in the Executive building at eleven. A few minutes before that hour he would appear in the rose garden, walking slowly and talking animatedly to Mrs. Wilson, who clung to his arm. At the office building he would look at his watch, kiss her, then stand gazing after her as she walked back along the path. When she reached the other end she would turn and wave at him. He would look at his watch again. There was still a minute. Quickly he would walk to meet her. Again they would embrace, again part. Finally, at the stroke of eleven, with a final reluctant look at her retreating figure, he would enter the building. He was never late, but after the marriage he was never early.

He made a speaking trip that winter—New York, Pittsburgh, Cleveland, Milwaukee, Kansas City, Des Moines, and Chicago. At the Blackstone Hotel, Jervis, who was standing in front of the building, got a scare when he saw the body of a man hurtle to the street. He rushed upstairs and asked Dr. Grayson to check on the President's safety. "Sleeping like a child," the doctor reported. "I wish I could," Jervis said sadly. The mysterious body was a suicide, a business man who had leapt from a window several floors above the President's suite.

It had become evident during the winter that the Secretary of War, Lindley M. Garrison, had grown discontented with the Administration's policies. He was a strong man, of great mental energy and determined convictions. He never descended to the level of a "yes man." It was obvious that he had not only a deep respect for the President but a strong affection. But he had his own views and stuck to them. I remember an episode which first showed me that he could disagree sharply with Mr. Wilson. Once during the troubles with Mexico the President took a conciliatory step that Garrison condemned; and the newspaper boys said that the handwriting was on the wall—that some day he would part ways with the Administration. Now the breach came. The Congressional leaders failed to take the strong measures for military preparedness that Garrison thought were imperative. Many of them favored raising the new forces on a State basis, while Garrison wanted them put on a national basis. Wilson could be positive enough on some legislation, but in this matter he let the Congressional committees have their way. The result was that Garrison, after a number of protests, resigned. I could see that it was a tragedy to him.

As the new Secretary of War we got Newton D. Baker, who came to Washington with considerable reluctance; I heard that he protested to Wilson that he had no military knowledge whatever. When he first appeared, the newspapermen and I over-hastily sized him up—he was short, slight, and very quiet—a bit effeminate. We nicknamed him "Violet." But that name did not stick, for he turned out to be one of the best-equipped members of the Cabinet. None of us could talk to him without seeing that he had an unusually well-ordered mind and an independent way of looking at matters. He walked, talked, and acted quietly and deliberately, but with perfect self-confidence, as if he had this job well in hand; he never allowed himself to be handicapped by hurry; his poise and self-control were perfect. He came more frequently to the White House than Garrison had done, and I saw plenty of evidence that the President was consulting him with implicit confidence. When the newspapermen talked with him in my hearing, he had a canny way of picking out essentials. He soon gained and always held their complete respect.

The new Secretary quickly had a job, for on March 9 Pancho Villa, the Mexican bandit, raided Columbus, New Mexico. The statement I had made to my mother—that we were hardly in shape to fight Mexico, proved truer than I knew. We couldn't catch Villa, and our efforts to deal with Carranza, a double-crosser by nature, began to make us look silly. But our unpreparedness was now obvious to everyone, even the pacifists, and the danger that we might be drawn into the European war was mounting daily. Preparedness became popular, and the President endorsed it and marched in numerous Preparedness Day parades. Once he had given himself to the idea of preparedness he enjoyed the marching, for he loved music, moving feet, and the cheering of crowds. He wanted more than anything else to be the people's champion, their leader and their guide, and the best assurance he could have that this was true was the sound of their cheers as he passed.

In parades I marched on one flank of the President's line, and another member of the Detail took the opposite flank. Once in a parade on Fifth Avenue in New York a news photographer got a picture which included me but missed the Secret Service man at the other end of the line. The last man on the line was not known to the picture editor of the *New York Times,* however, and in the rotogravure section the following Sunday he was identified as "a Secret Service man." Actually he was a young Texas millionaire who was just then emerging into prominence, and I think that today any of the *Times'* editors would recognize Jesse Jones.

There were lots of parades that year. If no one else was marching the Suffragettes at least were abroad. Sometimes they were a joke; sometimes they were a nuisance; always they were determined and a little frightening to us men.

One parade that passed the White House I remember well. It was a company of cavalry volunteers, recruited in the District of Columbia. They were marching on foot, with full pack, to their camp in Virginia. Idly watching them pass, we spotted a little fellow, almost lost under his pack. He was Joseph P. Annin, a Washington newspaperman who until a few days before had been covering the White House for the *Herald.* We all knew him; he was, in fact one of our favorites, for although not much more than five feet in height, he had wit and spirit enough for a man twice his size. Sternly we called him to account.

"What's the idea of impersonating a soldier?"

"You reporters will do anything for a story."

"What's in the pack—cotton?"

"It's a fake pack. It's a balloon full of gas, to keep him up."

Joe viewed us with contempt.

"I'll put you all in the hoosegow," he said. "You're interfering with an officer of the United States Cavalry."

"Cavalry? But you have no horses!"

"They're at the camp. And we aren't marching by the White House to show off. It just happens to be along the line of march."

"But Joe"—I softened my voice and adopted an air of solicitude—"that's apt to be tragic. You can't ride a horse!"

I had seen him time after time on the bridle paths of Potomac Park. I knew he was proud of his horsemanship. Without saying a word he walked away from us and rejoined his company. When it had passed we went back to the Executive building.

In a few minutes there was a clatter in the driveway. Jervis called me to come outside and look. There was Joe, on an enormous old drayhorse, riding solemnly up and down West Executive Avenue, looking neither to left or right, solemn as an owl. We gave him nine long cheers, after which he bowed stiffly and rode off. He told me later that he hired the horse from a junk dealer he met a few blocks from the White House. After paying the man two dollars he unhitched the horse, mounted him, and rode to the Executive Offices.

Spring came early that year, and was dry and hot. I had not suffered from malaria that winter, but I was glad to feel the sun on my back again and get my bones thawed out. We went to Charlotte, North Carolina, in May, for a ceremony celebrating the anniversary of the Mecklenberg Declaration of Independence. One of the local political bigwigs made an interminable speech—it was the chance of a lifetime and he took it, coattails flying and arms waving (from that day it became part of the advance man's job to see that no such long-winded speeches were on the program). It kept getting hotter and hotter, and the members of the Marine Band, standing at attention in the sun and wearing winter uniforms, began to succumb. One by one they dropped, but the speaker went on and on. Personally I felt fine; the last bit of winter was being fried out of me.

Next day the Charlotte newspaper eulogized the "courage and endurance of the tall Secret Service man who stood behind the President during all the ceremony without showing fatigue." I hadn't been so comfortable in years.

That was the spring my old friend Charlie Barker came to town to see about the dark tobacco situation. Charlie had a voice trained in the broad fields of the Barker farms in south Christian County. He was used to carrying on a conversation with someone half a mile away, and he had lost the trick of cutting down the volume to suit a room.

"How's the old arm?" he roared, while the windows rattled. "I brought some flowers for the little woman!"

The "little woman" proved to be Mrs. Wilson. I took the flowers—dozens of them—and sent them over to the White House with a note to Mrs. Wilson about their donor. Then I took Charlie in and introduced him to the President. Charlie swung his arm and caught the President's hand in a grip that would have made a gorilla wince.

"I'm honored, sir, honored!" he said, and the papers on the desk shook as if a wind were blowing.

"How do you do?" the President said. His eyes twinkled, and I could tell by his nose that he was amused.

"I'm from Starling's country, down Kentucky way," Charlie boomed. "We're all for you down there. Follow you anywhere you want to go!" He lowered his voice to the approximate pitch of a steam calliope and said, "Maybe we ought to go over there and settle that business, eh?" He raised his eyebrow and jerked a thumb in the approximate direction of the Atlantic Ocean. "Glad to do it for you."

The President smiled.

"I hope we won't be brought to any such expedient," he said.

I wondered about that smile. He was amused at Charlie, of course, but the smile conveyed something. Was he looking for approval of a declaration of war? Were things that bad? His whole campaign for re-election was going to be based on the fact that he had kept us out of war. Was he going to take us into it now? He wouldn't unless he had to, I was sure of that.

The following September the President met some more of my Christian County friends, when he went to Kentucky to dedicate the shrine of Lincoln's birthplace at Hodgensville. Two of my dearest Hopkinsville friends were on the committee, Tom Underwood, editor of the *New Era,* Hopkinsville's newspaper, and Joe Moseley, the postmaster and local Democratic boss. Tom met the special train and I introduced him to the President, who granted him an interview.

Driving by automobile from the train to the shrine we saw a giant of a man striding across the fields toward the road. The President said to me—I was on the running board of his car—"Starling, who is that tall man with his coattails flying?" "I'm not sure," I said, "but it looks like Joe Moseley, the Democratic boss of my county. But I've never seen Joe in clothes like that." The man wore a pearl gray cutaway suit with tails to his knees and a pearl gray Stetson hat.

It was Joe. I could tell by his handle-bar moustaches. When he got to the car he said, "Bill, I want to have the honor of being introduced to the President by you."

The President laughed and put out his hand.

"By now I know what kind of friends to expect of Starling," he said, "and I'm glad to meet them." Turning to me he said, "This place produces remarkable men—Lincoln, Barker, and now Moseley."

The climate of Washington lived up to its evil reputation that summer.

Now and then we got away for week-end trips down the Potomac on the *Mayflower*. Otherwise the President and Mrs. Wilson found recreation in early morning games of golf and automobile rides in the evening, after the sun had set. Rock Creek Park was a favorite spot for cooling off, and they had a sentimental feeling about it, since it was the scene of much of their courtship.

But the President worked hard that summer; in fact he always worked hard. Late at night I would often hear him pounding his typewriter on some message or speech. He would sit in his study in the White House proper, and peck away at the big old machine, which Charlie Swem had oiled and put in good running order; and we knew that Mrs. Wilson was sitting beside him reading.

On Sundays they alternated between Jimmy Taylor's church and St. Margaret's Episcopal Church—at least they did until a minister at the Episcopal church one Sunday delivered a eulogy on a dog. The President had nothing against dogs, but he had plenty against a man who would write a sermon about them. He was plainly disgusted, and after that we almost always attended the Central Presbyterian Church. He was an Elder of this church, and faithfully attended the meetings of the board. Often, too, he went to the Wednesday night prayer meetings.

One Sunday morning during that summer we returned to the White House to find the usual groups of sightseers scattered about the grounds. There was no restriction, then, on their entrance, and they were free to wander about the walks. Some of them were gathered at the porte-cochère covering the entrance to the front door. Among them was a little crippled girl. She waved at the President and Mrs. Wilson as they walked up the steps. Mrs. Wilson, seeing the gesture, suddenly left her husband's side, descended the steps, and went to the child. She patted her head, spoke to her and to her mother, who was by her side, and shook hands with both.

The President, missing his wife, turned with a look of annoyance on his face. When he saw what was happening he smiled. Then he also went to the little girl and spoke to her and to her mother. Mounting the steps again he looked at Mrs. Wilson with frank adoration, and took her hand in his as they disappeared into the lobby.

The decision to remain in the city until September was influenced not only by the press of events, but by the President's decision to wage his fall campaign for re-election away from the White House. It was typical of him that he wanted to be identified with the White House as little as possible while a candidate. He did not feel that it was fair to his opponent, Charles Evans Hughes, to campaign from the White House.

All summer long Vance McCormick, chairman of the Democratic National Committee, was a frequent visitor. He became a familiar figure to all of us associated with Wilson. A cheery, robust man, of unfailing tact and discretion, he was universally liked; and both the President and Mrs. Wilson soon made him a favorite. Later on, of course, he became head of the War Trade Board, and he was to go to Paris for the Peace Conference. Wilson always liked to have him about. I think I may say that next after Colonel House, he undertook success-

fully more confidential missions, big and small, than any other man connected with the Administration.

On September 1 we moved to Shadow Lawn, New Jersey, an estate of eight or nine acres near Asbury Park, which was to be the President's home until after the election. It was a large, roomy house, and a speaker's platform was built in front of it for the ceremonies of Notification Day, the second of September. My fellow Kentuckian, Ollie M. James, who had been chairman of the Democratic Convention, delivered the notification speech. He, like Alben Barkley, came from what was called the "pennyroyal district" of my State, as I did, and both he and his wife were old friends. With his big frame, well filled out, he was physically perhaps the largest man in the Senate. He loved the good things of life; a steak dinner, accompanied by a suitable number of bourbons, with a ride out around Rock Creek Park afterwards. His speech at Shadow Lawn that day was a masterly piece of eloquence, and I can remember yet how proud I was of his imposing appearance and his beautiful language.

After that day the President used the platform frequently to address various meetings and delegations, crowds that varied from 500 to 2,000 persons. But it was not entirely a front porch campaign. Frequently we left Shadow Lawn, and once we swung through the Middle West, visiting Detroit, Chicago, Omaha, and other cities.

The offices of the temporary Presidential residence were in Asbury Park. There Tumulty and his private secretary, Warren Johnson, and Charlie Swem, the President's private secretary, stayed. I had a room in a small hotel, and, without meaning to, became something of a hero one morning when the structure caught fire. The corridor was full of smoke when I came out of my room, and the stairway was choked with a white, billowing mass. I was on the fourth floor, but I made it to the bottom and safely out the front door, carrying with me an old gentleman from my floor who was too weak to travel by himself. The reporters gave me a big hand; news was scarce that day.

At Shadow Lawn I was stationed in front of the house, passing on all visitors before they were admitted. There were a great many every day, a few of whom I remember—Henry Ford, Ignace Paderewski, and Dr. and Mrs. Simon Baruch, whose son, Bernard, was soon to come into prominence. I also remember a certain New Jersey political boss, who arrived one day without an appointment. He should not have been allowed to pass the gate of the estate, but he had convinced the man on duty there of his importance and now he demanded that I give his card to the President. Rather than take the responsibility for throwing him out myself I did as he asked, first taking the precaution of sending him back to the gate. The President came to the door from the luncheon table. For a full minute he studied the card, then he said, still staring at it, and in a very precise, flat voice, as if he were a child reading a sentence from a primer, giving each word the same dull, heavy emphasis:

"I–will–not–see–the–son–of–a–bitch!"

I laughed to myself as I descended the steps, thinking of the New Jersey politicians who had chosen him for Governor because they thought he would make a good "front" for the organization.

Still, such a man might be difficult for the organization to elect, considering his independence and his refusal to cooperate with the bosses. I didn't know much about politics, but I knew the boss had a tough fight on his hands. Hughes was a man of recognized ability and integrity, and the money, as always, was on the Republican side. Tumulty was worried and morose, and the President would have been worried too had he not been trained, as I was, in the Presbyterian doctrine of predestination. He was completely calm, having decided that he had done his best to fill the job and his future in it was in the hands of God and the people. He asked his advisers what effect his defeat would have upon Europe. He was told that it would be construed as a rejection by the country of his peace aims. Because of that he wanted to be re-elected. Otherwise he would have been glad to retire and enjoy the happiness he had found with his new wife.

He had gone to Washington with certain plans in mind and these had been carried out—things like the Federal Reserve Banking system and the reduction of the tariff. That was his specialty—social and economic reform. He had no intention of getting tangled up with international diplomacy or a war.

Rudolph Forster told me: "The boss knows this country like a book, but he's not so well up on the fellows across the water. The way I figure it is that the other fellows are so far behind what he thinks is modern and civilized that he hasn't paid them much mind.

"What he'd like to do, if they'd let him, is act as peacemaker and then fix them up with a system like ours, so they could get rid of their armies and live together without squabbling."

My own feelings about the election were so bound up with personal fortunes that they had little relation either to politics or the war. For the first time I realized how precarious my job was, and what a difficult and thankless task I fulfilled. A new President could not fire me, but if he disapproved of me I would quickly be removed from the Detail. I wasn't sure I wanted to stay anyhow. I had worked for two years without taking a day off, yet I was in debt, for my salary barely covered living expenses and I had been obliged to purchase evening clothes, a dinner jacket, and morning clothes for which I still owed the tailor. I liked the President, and I particularly liked Mrs. Wilson, but I was lonely and despondent and homesick.

The night of the election, November 7, I and some of the boys went into New York to see what we could find out about the results. Everything indicated a Republican victory—the East and Middle West were piling up big margins for Hughes. The South was Democratic, of course, and no returns had come from the West. We visited Republican headquarters at the Astor Hotel, where Frank Tyree was assigned to Hughes. The place was a bedlam—everyone was celebrating the victory.

Next day we sat around the office at Asbury Park, waiting for the final word. Tumulty was sunk in gloom. Everyone but Doc Smithers, Chief White House telegrapher, was convinced that Hughes had won.

"It's not over yet," Doc kept saying. "The West could swing it."

I can see him yet, sitting at his key, a powerful, well-built man, his large brown eyes shining hopefully from his kind face. Doc had worked for the Southern Railway; for many years he had been stationed at Gordonsville, Virginia. He wanted the boss to win.

Things at Shadow Lawn were quiet. The girls were busy trying to get more news—Miss Bones, Miss Benham, and Miss Margaret—but I saw no evidence that either the President or Mrs. Wilson was unduly disturbed. Miss Margaret was particularly anxious, and made several trips to New York. Meeting the young ladies on the grounds of the estate I found them all highly indignant; a country which would not re-elect their hero could only be ungrateful.

The next afternoon we drove to Spring Lake for golf. The President seemed as calm as ever, and played just as poorly. There wasn't any laughing or joking, but he and Mrs. Wilson talked good-naturedly and smiled at the usual things. Somewhere along the way Dr. Grayson rushed up with the news that California seemed pretty safe, which would clinch it for the Democrats. The President made no unusual comment and went on playing. Surely he had put the matter away from himself and in the hands of God. Either that or he had a good poker face.

That night we drove to Sandy Hook and boarded the *Mayflower*. It was a calm night, warm for November. The suspense about the election made everything so tense that I wished the wind would blow, so that the air would be cleared. We were all so repressed, so worried, so silent.

Since my days as a deputy sheriff I had been in the habit of getting up at five o'clock every morning. On the *Mayflower* it was my custom to go to the cook's galley and get myself a cup of coffee. The next morning about half-past five I met Brooks there. He was smiling broadly; he waved a wireless message in my face.

"Safe at last," he said. "The boss has won for certain!"

"Does he know?" I asked.

Brooks shook his head.

"You know what would happen if I woke him up to tell him," he said. "I'd be fired! Nothing is so important that it can't wait until breakfast, he thinks."

Sipping my coffee, blowing away the steam, I felt my doubts, my loneliness, and my homesickness ebbing away. The boss was in for rough times. However unimportant, I was a member of the team.

Suddenly I realized that I was a Wilson man, that I believed in the things for which he stood, that like Charlie Barker I would follow him wherever he led.

I am still a Wilson man. I always will be. Standing in the galley of the *Mayflower* in the darkness before dawn of that November 10th twenty-eight years ago I realized that the man on that boat who as yet did not know he had been re-elected President stood for something bigger than me, bigger than himself, bigger than America. He stood for the hope of the world.

"It was a funny election," I said to Brooks. "The Republicans celebrated and the Democrats won."

★☆★

CHAPTER SIX

The War

THE CABINET met at the usual time, 2 P. M., on Friday, February 2, 1917. I was stationed outside the door. As the members walked past me into the big room, worry, tension, concern showed in their faces. Things had changed dramatically since last they had assembled on Tuesday. On Wednesday, January 31, Germany had announced her campaign of unrestricted submarine warfare. I had not seen the President since then. Colonel House had arrived the day before, and the only report I got was from Brooks, who said, "They're just sitting around looking sad."

The Cabinet members arrived separately, spoke to me quietly, almost gloomily, I thought, and went in: tall, cadaverous William Gibbs McAdoo of the Treasury, who had married Miss Eleanor Wilson; small, dark, bright Newton D. Baker, whose department would have the job of running the war for us if we got into it; solid, strong, silent David Franklin Houston, Secretary of Agriculture; handsome Robert Lansing, who had replaced Bryan in the State Department; friendly, teetotalling Josephus Daniels, of the Navy; Redfield of Commerce, Lane of Interior, Wilson of Labor, Attorney-General Gregory, and Postmaster Burleson. Houston and Daniels smiled at me. Daniels patted my arm as he said, "Hello, my son. Watching over your sheep?"

The President, when he arrived, looked more careworn than I had ever seen him. His plans were upset, I knew. He did not want to get into the war. He wanted to make the peace. He had suggested it only six weeks before, and again on January 22, when in his speech before the Senate "on behalf of humanity" he had asked for "peace without victory" and put forward the idea of a "definite concert of powers" to see that peace was kept. The echoes of that speech, with its possibility of ending war by agreeing to fight for its opposite, were still reverberating when the Kaiser made his fatal pronouncement. It looked now as if the President would have to put away the olive branch and take up the sword.

For the first time I wondered what was going on in the room I was guarding. Cabinet meetings, I had always thought, must be dull business. But this one had the flavor of history. One way or the other, something momentous would be decided.

Their faces, as they emerged, had a common expression—grimness. The President's jaw was set and thrust forward. "We're in it," I thought. Next day we went to the Capitol and the President announced the severing of our diplomatic relations with Germany. Only one step remained to be taken.

How quickly the atmosphere changed at the White House! On January 24th I had written to my mother:

Last night we had our Congressional Reception, and quite a mob was on hand.

I was very fortunate in being introduced to a very charming lady, Miss Elizabeth Perkins, who last year attended Ward Belmont College and knew Edith Bailware. She was introduced to me by Miss Alice Wilson, niece of the President and daughter of Joe Wilson, the President's brother, who formerly lived in Nashville but now resides in Baltimore. I spent some time with the young ladies and both gave me roses from their bouquets when I said goodnight.

This afternoon at 2:30 we go to the Capitol where the President is spending about three afternoons a week in order to make both houses get down to business. It is causing quite a lot of comment by various Senators.

The stuffed dates were delicious.

On February 10 I wrote:

I am rather enjoying my stay at the White House, where I am on duty now at night. I love the seclusion. The only bother I have is with the policemen stationed inside. They are great talkers, and get tiresome at times, though they mean well.

Last night after the President and Mrs. Wilson had finished dinner—no one else was at the table—I walked into the State dining room and stood before the massive fire place. A great log fire had burned down to a bed of coals. The room was full of shadows. I stood and thought of home, of you, and how I miss the life I might have had in the place I love. How often do I wonder what I am doing here, so lonely and so far from all I cherish.

It is my job to go over the whole house at times, say once or twice a week. I wish you could see the rooms—they are lovely, but haunted, I think. There has not been much happiness here. The Presidency is not that kind of a job.

This morning the President and Mrs. Wilson played golf. It was pretty cold, but dry and windy, and I enjoyed walking over the links immensely. Mrs. Wilson is a dear, lovable woman, and I like her better each day.

We are very careful now and watch everything that goes on, and it is therefore hard on me both physically and mentally, but especially physically. I pray every night for the President's safety, and for courage and wisdom for myself in performing my duty. However, I am used to things of this kind, and I greatly enjoy anything that savors of risk. So let 'em come. I am ready to go to the limit.

By this time I had gotten well acquainted with all the members of the Cabinet. One of the men I liked best was the breezy, kindly, thoroughly sincere Josephus Daniels, who was a much better Secretary of the Navy than most people supposed. A great many amusing stories were told about him. One came to me from Franklin D. Roosevelt, the young Assistant Secretary of the Navy. According to this tale, soon after Daniels became Secretary the Atlantic fleet anchored off the mouth of the York River, and the President and Daniels went down to review it. In fact, I recall that occasion myself, for I was with Mr. Wilson on the *Mayflower*. The fleet, drawn up in precise formation, was a beautiful sight. The *Mayflower* moved along the whole line so that the President could take the salute. Then the admiral came to pay his respects to the President and Secretary, and when he left, Daniels accompanied him to the flagship to spend the night. After dinner that evening, he and Roosevelt were seated in the admiral's quarters when the officer of the day came around, knocked, and was told to enter. He stepped inside, came to attention, and saluted. Then, looking at the admiral, he said: "I wish to report, sir, that all is secure." The admiral looked at the Secretary. Daniels, quite nonplused, looked back with a blank expression. The admiral nodded to him. It then dawned on the new Secretary that he was expected to receive the officer's report. He rose to the occasion by exclaiming with hearty cordiality: "Well, I declare! That's fine! I'm mighty glad to hear it!"

William B. Wilson, the Secretary of Labor, was another lovable man, with character in every line of his fine old Scottish face. He had the respect of every workingman in the United States. Samuel Gompers, as I had reason to know, liked him and often came to him for advice. Thoroughness was one of his virtues, and he was familiar with every item of business in his department. If he could not be called brilliant, he was one of the most intelligent Cabinet officers a President ever had. Not many people knew, as we about the White House did, that he carried the burden of an invalid wife. His devotion to her kept him from playing any part in society. When not in his office he was at home, and so was his daughter, who acted as secretary to her father, and nurse to her mother.

Very different from the genial Daniels and the frank, open Secretary Wilson was Postmaster-General Burleson, who looked and acted like an extremely sly gentleman. He was so astute and secretive that his left hand never knew what his right was doing. He used to come over from the Postoffice Department through the east entrance of the White House, along the lower corridor past the laundry, following in part the same passageway that the President used in going between the White House and executive offices. Rain or shine, he carried an umbrella and briefcase, and if the weather was bad he wore overshoes, tiptoeing as he walked. We finally began to call that passageway "Pussyfoot Alley."

On February 3, at noon, President Wilson had announced to both Houses of Congress the rupture of diplomatic relations with Germany, and that same day the German ambassador was handed his passports. I had seen a good deal of Von Bernstorff in his comings and goings. It was easier to respect him than to admire him. He was a smart, efficient German diplomat who looked the part and acted the part. His subordinates Boy-Ed and Von Papen had been up to their necks in intrigue, and of course he knew all about their activities. But he wished to keep peace with the United States; he would have prevented the renewal of unrestricted submarine warfare if he had been able, and to the end he worked hard to keep his government from following the suicidal path that it took. He never spared himself. He was always admirably correct in his public appearances. While we did not love him, we felt that his going was a personal tragedy.

For the British ambassador, Cecil Spring-Rice, I grew to have a warm personal regard. He and his wife, in fact, became very dear friends of mine. He was a lovable personality, with some really wonderful traits. He was witty and learned; he was one of the most experienced diplomats of his time; but he believed in gaining his ends, above all, through kindness, thoughtfulness, and patience. Once I accompanied him on a short cruise out of Baltimore on J. P. Morgan's yacht the *Corsair,* and I have a vivid recollection of his interesting conversation—for he unbent and talked to me as to an intimate.

Our particular attention was centered on the coming Inauguration. March 4 was due to fall on Sunday, so the public portion of the program was put off until Monday. We would have been happy had it been cancelled altogether. Threat letters were reaching a new high, and despite the fact that every building along the route had been inspected, and every tenant investigated, we were nervous and apprehensive.

At the Capitol, we felt more sure of ourselves, for it was often under our surveillance. Whenever the President was to appear there it was the duty of the Detail to get in touch with the Speaker of the House, who then sent for the Sergeant at Arms of the House and the architect of the Capitol, David Lynn, together with Lynn's assistant, Gus Cook. If the President was to appear on the Senate side we notified the Majority Leader and the Clerk of the Senate, Ed Halsey. After that the Capitol was in our hands, and assisted by Metropolitan Police, Capitol Police, and soldiers and marines, we guarded it until the President completed his visit and was safely away. We inspected the building from head to foot, overlooking no closet or cubbyhole big enough to hide a midget.

While arrangements for the Inauguration went forward a few members of the Senate stirred up trouble for the President by blocking the bill to arm our merchant vessels. It was on this occasion that one of my favorite Wilsonian phrases came into being, as a description of the Senators who opposed the bill. The welfare of the nation, the President said, was being jeopardized by "a little group of willful men." I have never seen a time when there was not "a little group of willful men" in the Senate. Also that February the Zimmerman Note was made public —Germany was offering Mexico the restoration of Texas if she would make war on us. We joked at the idea of Mexico trying to occupy Texas, but the incident had a serious side. Mexico as an active ally of Germany would be no laughing matter.

It was my first Inauguration, but I was so consumed by my job that I remember few of the details. The mile from the White House to the Capitol was the longest I ever rode.

The trip on Sunday was uneventful. There were no crowds, and no guests other than Mrs. Wilson, Vance McCormick, and Colonel House. We went to the President's room, which is on the Senate side, and there, after putting his signature on bills that had been passed, the President was informed that the work of the Congress was finished. He then took the oath of office from Chief Justice Edward D. White. As he put his hand on the Bible—the same he had used four years before, and when being sworn in as Governor of New Jersey—I felt a tingling along my spine. The man and the Book were one, I suddenly thought, and come what may, he would do its bidding. He meant every word of the oath he was repeating. He would keep the faith.

I stole a look at Mrs. Wilson. With shining eyes she watched her husband, proud of him, her head held high, a little smile on her lips.

The ceremonies next day went off without incident, although I cannot recall a word of the President's speech. I have a memory of upturned faces, the sound of that winning, musical voice, and bright sunshine that had come after a morning of rain and heavy clouds. With the Presidential party safely back in the White House I relaxed. One ordeal at least could be forgotten for another four years.

But there were others. German submarines were sinking our ships. We were fast heading for war. The President ordered our merchant vessels armed, in defiance of the Senate. He ordered Congress to reconvene on April 2 for a special message. He was going to ask for war. I could tell by the way he acted: his jaw was set, he was moody; he looked past us with a melancholy, preoccupied air. When he spoke his voice was soft, as if the whole world were a sickroom through which he was tiptoeing. I was sorry for him because of the decision he had to make. On March 29 I wrote to my mother.

We stayed in the whole afternoon and evening. The President held several conferences. I had a talk with Secretary Daniels, who was in the Green Room waiting for the President. He said, "Starling, these are tense times. The strain is awful. I don't know what I'd do if it weren't for that man upstairs." "Yes, sir," I said, "but we must remember that he is human too. I think this is a time when we should go even higher than upstairs. It would help us all to talk this thing over with God, and it would lighten the load on the President if we leaned a little bit on Somebody Else." His face lighted up, he squared his shoulders, and looking me straight in the eye said, "Young man, that's good advice. I appreciate it. It helps me more than you will ever know."

It was presumptuous of me, of course, but I am a Presbyterian, and we are apt to be presumptuous in such matters. One of my young newspaper friends who amused himself writing jingles once gave me this one:

The Presbyterian is tough
Because his way of life is rough.
He knows that sin and death are fated,
And all his acts predestinated.

My diary records the events of the next few feverish days, in matter-of-fact language.

Friday, March 30

Arrived White House 8 A. M. Discontinued 1 P. M. From 3:30 to 4:30 engaged wtih Operator Ahern investigating certain information. At 5:20 relieved Operator Slye. At 5:25 accompanied President and Mrs. Wilson walking down F Street to 5th Street, and then back to the White House. Dinner at 6:30. Returned 7:30. Discontinued 8 P. M. Picture show.

Saturday, March 31

Arrived White House 1 P. M. At 5:35 accompanied President and Mrs. Wilson automobiling. Returned 6:35. Dinner 6:40–7:35. At 8:15 accompanied President and Dr. Grayson, walking to Belasco Theatre, where we attended the play, "So Long Letty." I could not hand the performance much. Neither could the President. Returned to White House 11 P. M. Discontinued at 11:45, when President retired.

Sunday, April 1

Up at 6. At White House at 7:30. At 10:50 accompanied President and Mrs. Wilson to Central Presbyterian Church, where we had communion. Returned to White House 12:20. Engaged through out afternoon interviewing certain persons. Discontinued 9:30.

Monday, April 2

Arrived White House 1 P. M. At 4:40 accompanied President, walking to offices of Secretary Lansing and Secretary Daniels. Returned to White House at 6. Relieved for dinner at 6:15. Returned at 7. At 8:20 accompanied President to Capitol where he appeared before joint session of Congress and asked that a state of war be declared to exist between this country and Germany, also that liberal and sufficient appropriations be made. Returned to White House at 9:30 and was relieved as we were all on our tiptoes for anything. I walked with the President, my right shoulder to his left shoulder. It seemed to me he kinder leaned against my good right arm. He was very tired when he got into the automobile to return to the White House. Discontinued 11 P.M. when the President retired.

How well I remember that night—the soft spring rain falling on us as we moved down Pennsylvania Avenue, while ahead the Capitol was aglow, illuminated for the first time by the indirect lighting system which since then has made the Hill and its white dome a traditional part of Washington's night scene. Cavalry, foot soldiers, and marines were abroad; pacifists had gathered in groups, silently protesting. In the House were gathered Senators and Representatives, members of the Supreme Court, and, in the gallery, diplomats, newspapermen, and such visitors as could gain entrance. I was stationed just below the rostrum, to the President's right, facing one of the entrances to the chamber, with my gaze fastened on the door. My eyes only wavered once, when a figure on my left leaped into the air. I turned my head and unlimbered myself for action, but it was only Chief Justice White, carried out of his seat with enthusiasm as the President said, "We will not choose the path of submission."

Others who were present that night have written of the drama of the scene, the magnificence of the President's address, the perfection of his delivery. All I know is that I watched that door, and that no one came through it. A few years ago, when President Franklin D. Roosevelt went to the Capitol for a similar purpose, a photograph of the 1917 scene was reproduced in the newspapers, with an arrow pointing to a figure described as "Franklin D. Roosevelt, then Assistant Secretary of the Navy." Unfortunately for the camera historian it wasn't F.D.R. It was Starling, with his eye on the door.

The President, as I wrote to my mother, was tired. His face was ashen gray, and his step was heavy. He had wrestled with his conscience and he had done what he thought was right, but I did not blame him for leaning against me when I thought of the days ahead, and the casualty lists.

So we went to war. At the White House the effect was immediate. Soldiers were put at the gates, and my chief announced that the Detail would remain intact—any change requested by any of the men would not be considered. We were also told that taking care of the President was more important than being a soldier. "I guess I will stick," I wrote to my mother, "though I would like to carry the Stars and Stripes across the water."

My diary reads:

Wednesday, April 4

Arrived White House 1 P.M. At 4 accompanied President and Mrs. Wilson automobiling through Rock Creek Park. Returned at 5:30 P.M. At 8:15 accompanied President, Mrs. Alexander Galt, and Dr. Grayson to Belasco's, where we saw "Very Good Eddie." I did not appreciate it. Neither did the President. We should have gone to see "Twin Beds" at the National.

Thursday, April 5

Bad, rainy day. Did not leave White House.

Friday, April 6

Good Friday—Cold, dismal spring day. At 11 A.M. accompanied President and Mrs. Wilson walking. President would not wear overcoat, stepping out briskly and swinging a cane. Through Lafayette Park. Crowd at St. John's Church waiting for final Lenten service. To Scott Circle, up Massachusetts Avenue. Passed 1308 Twentieth Street. Both hesitated and looked at it. To Connecticut Avenue. Met Justice Oliver Wendell Holmes, out for constitutional. Chatted with him. On way back Mrs. Wilson stopped to look at dresses in shop window. Returned to White House at 12:20.

The diary tells too briefly what followed. The President ordered lunch served immediately. He and Mrs. Wilson were joined at table by Miss Bones. While they were eating word came from the Executive Offices that Rudolph Forster had received from the Senate the joint resolution for a declaration of war. He was told to bring it to the White House. The President hurried with his meal, and came out of the state dining room just as Rudolph came into Ike Hoover's office, where I was waiting.

The President came into the office with Mrs. Wilson and Miss Bones. "How are you, Rudolph?" he said. "You have the proclamation?"

"Yes, sir," Forster said, "shall I take it to your study?"

"No," the President said. "I'll sign it here."

He sat down at the Usher's desk.

"Give me a pen," he said.

"Use this one," Mrs. Wilson said.

She handed him a gold fountain pen, a gift to her from him.

"Stand by me, Edith," he asked.

She moved to a position just behind him and to his right, where she could look over his shoulder. By her stood Miss Bones. Directly behind the chair stood Rudolph Forster. I was at the President's left elbow. By me stood Ike Hoover, holding a blotter. Carefully the President read the tragic document, his jaw set, his countenance grim. Then, with a firm, unhesitating hand he wrote "Woodrow Wilson." When it was done he rose from the chair, returned the pen to Mrs. Wilson, excused himself, and went with the ladies into the corridor and to the elevator.

One of the first commands of the war was issued to the President by Dr. Grayson. The doctor insisted that his charge get more exercise, for the pressure of work doubled and tripled in the White House. Grayson suggested horseback riding, and to his surprise the President assented. The suggestion had been made before but nothing had come of it. Now I was despatched, with other members of the Detail, to Front Royal, Virginia, to secure horses, and stables were set up back of the Pan-American building. We made sure the mounts we brought back were safe for the President and Mrs. Wilson; for him we chose a particularly gentle but good-looking light bay named Arizona. He had a white streak on his face down to his nose, and two white feet. The President liked him, and rode him with the vigor of a cowboy breaking a broncho, but with none of the skill, since he had rather a "poor seat."

But he enjoyed himself and got plenty of exercise, and that was what

Dr. Grayson wanted. One afternoon as we neared the end of a ride in Rock Creek Park, he challenged me to a race from the ford to the Pierce Mill, where our automobiles were waiting.

Off we went, and before I came to my senses I was in the lead. I had the faster horse, and unless I did something to check his speed I would win, which would not only be bad etiquette and poor diplomacy, but dereliction of duty, since my job was to keep the President in sight and see that nothing happened to him. Giving every indication that I was straining to get more speed from my horse I slowly reined him in and let Arizona and his rider pass me. In the car, waiting for him, was Mrs. Wilson.

Frequently she rode with him, looking beautiful in her smart black tailored riding habit. She sat sidesaddle, and most of their rides together were along the bridle paths of the Ellipse, just south of the White House.

There one day, taking a short cut, her horse—a new one—stepped in a hole and threw her. The President and I reached her about the same time. She was stretched on the ground, her face very white, her eyes closed. Bending over her the President said in a voice full of anguish:

"Edith, my darling, are you hurt?"

Slowly she opened her eyes and smiled at him.

"No, Woodrow, I think I'm all right. Just shaken up."

We helped her up and put her back on her horse. At a walk we returned to the stables, the President anxious and fretful, his wife pale but smiling, her white face a contrast to the black of her habit and the shining jet of her boots. Fortunately she was uninjured, and the rides were not discontinued.

One of the interesting days of that spring was May 24, when General Pershing, who had just been made our commander-in-chief in Europe, called with Secretary Baker. I well recall how erect and vigorous he looked as he tramped in his glistening boots over the marble floor, and how he walked upstairs to see Mr. Wilson, refusing to take the elevator. We were given to understand that Baker and Wilson had promised Pershing complete freedom from all political interference. He would get orders from those two men and from no others. Another notable day was that on which Theodore Roosevelt, who wanted to raise a command of his own and lead it in France, called to see the President. I was not there and did not see him. But the correspondents—Dick Oulahan, Jack Nevin, and others—had known in advance that he would get nowhere with his request. The army was to be raised on strictly military principles, and precisely as the War Department and General Staff wanted it raised.

They still played golf, of course, but now, as they walked along the fairway laughing and joking, they had an unseen audience, of which they were unaware. The woods were full of Secret Service men, who took up their post before the couple arrived and remained until after they left, moving with them as they walked along the course, but always keeping out of their sight.

There were automobile rides, too, and the theatre, but in the summer it is necessary to leave Washington to get relief from the heat. Since it was impossible for the President to take a vacation that summer with the war on he used the *Mayflower* for weekend trips down the Potomac. With Mrs. Wilson he would go to the chart room and inspect the maps of Chesapeake Bay, selecting an islet or an inlet to explore to give zest to the trip. But often we could not get away until Sunday. On June 20 I wrote to my mother:

Sunday afternoon we enjoyed another trip down the river on the *Mayflower*. In the party were Mrs. Bolling, Miss Bolling, Mr. John Randolph Bolling, and Mr. Julian Bolling and wife.

I stayed on deck all the time, and only went below when dinner was served at 8 o'clock. Somehow or other I was more impressed this time as we passed Mt. Vernon. The bugler sounded taps and the band played the Star Spangled Banner while we stood at attention, heads uncovered —the usual tribute to Washington. It might have been that I was a bit homesick, or that I was a little off color because of thinking of our boys going across the water while I stay here and take things easy.

I know that I am doing the most important work that it is possible for a man to do. I know that our President and Commander-in-Chief must be protected, and well. How well, no one will ever know. Still I feel the pull to go to the front.

We are following our usual daily procedure—golfing, automobiling, and making occasional visits to the theatre. This week will be taken up with receiving and entertaining the Belgian and Russian commissions, which are now here.

One of the Chesapeake islands we visited that summer was Tangier, a small spot inhabited by fishermen and their families. It is a picturesque place, with neat, white houses set one after another on the streets, with a garden and a family cemetery in front of each, the whole surrounded by a white picket fence. There are no horses or automobiles, and no one was abroad on the streets when we landed on a Sunday morning. The only persons in sight, as we walked along, were an old man and a child. The old man was squatting on his haunches, holding the child. As I passed him I said, "Hi! Grandpa."

"Say, mister," he answered, "who is that feller with his woman?"

"That's Mr. Wilson," I said, "the President of the United States."

"Great lovin' hands o' God A'Mighty!" he said. "Everybody thought you was Germans and went to hide inside!"

"Grandpa!" the child cried. "You're hurting me!"

Unconsciously the old man had been squeezing the little one. Now he released his hold entirely and the child dropped to the ground and began to cry. The old man picked him up and headed into the house at what for him must have been a dead run.

When word got around that it was the President instead of the Kaiser's sailors the villagers came out and welcomed us. They explained that during the War of 1812 the British occupied the island, and used it as a base in preparing their attack on Baltimore. They were exhorted by Joshua Thomas, who was known as the "Parson of the Island." Thomas told them that they would fail in their attempt on Baltimore because the "God of hosts" was not with them. They did fail, and Joshua Thomas became Tangier's hero.

So they were expecting another invasion, now that we were at war again. The President assured them that this was not apt to happen, since the entrance to the bay was pretty well guarded. They listened attentively, and seemed reassured. Their simplicity and neatness, and the loveliness of their village, appealed to the President and Mrs. Wilson, and they stopped there frequently after that.

Letters to my mother reflect the heat and dullness of that summer with its long hours of work and lack of heartening news from the front.

July 8

Friday night we took in a show at the new National Theater, called "What Is Love?" It is supposed to be a musical comedy. It was hardly passable.

Last night we took in Keith's and saw a right good bill. As it was my night on I was glad of the opportunity to go. It broke up the long stay on duty at the White House.

This morning (Sunday) we rode about 25 miles to Pohick, about 8 miles the other side of Mt. Vernon, where George Washington attended services. It is laid out peculiarly on the inside, the pulpit being on the south side and the table for the collection plates and communion set being on the west side. The seats are not pews but enclosed boxes, and you can sit any way you like, facing north, south, east, or west. The President could not locate the pulpit, and when he did he had faced all four directions.

July 14

It is now 1:40 P.M. and we intend going to some boys camp near Annapolis, Md., at 2:30. On our way back we will stop on the side of the road and have a picnic. I am not on duty but it is so hot in the city that I will go along anyhow.

Thursday noon I had to dress up in cutaway and striped trousers and sit behind the President and Mrs. Wilson at the wedding of Miss Elizabeth Harding to a young soldier named Prince, of Boston. She is the daughter of W. P. G. Harding, Chairman of the Federal Reserve Board. I knew him in Birmingham.

Tomorrow morning we go down the river and will spend the entire day on the Potomac. We all enjoy these trips.

I was notified yesterday that my salary had been increased from $5 to $6 a day. As soon as I can clear up my tailor's bill I will start saving as much money as I can, for I am tired of living away from home.

July 22

Hampton Roads. We are here enjoying the ocean breeze, loafing on the deck of the *Mayflower*. We arrived at Yorktown yesterday morning and about 11 A.M. rode around part of our big fleet of battleships anchored in York River. We returned to the yacht at 12:30 and headed for this place. Hampton Roads is right at Fortress Monroe and Newport News, at which places I stayed during the Spanish-American War. I recognized several places.

I am beautifully sunburned this morning. Got up at 6 and had a salt water tub bath for half an hour. We leave this evening for Washington.

August 30

It now seems that I will be able to get away for my vacation as planned and I ought to arrive in Hopkinsville September 25th.

I want to impress upon you that I am very fond of country hams, peach cobblers, butter and buttermilk, fresh eggs, hot biscuit, homemade ice cream, and plain white cake.

We have been simply existing up here. There is nothing to do but automobile, play golf, and take in the shows. We will go down the river tomorrow and stay until Tuesday morning. Then in the afternoon we are to march in a parade gotten up for the boys who have been conscripted in the District of Columbia.

It is my private * opinion that we will have not less than one nor more than two more years of war. It is my opinion that this time next year will start the beginning of the end.

The other night we went to the National to see a comedy "The Country Cousin," by Booth Tarkington and Julian Street. Miss Alexandra Carlyle, an English actress, played the part of the cousin. She was excellent. I was backstage and enjoyed everything. It was the first night, and everyone was nervous and apprehensive. Miss Carlyle came over to introduce herself, brought me a chair, and insisted that I make myself at home.

* It must have been based on pretty good information because it was amazingly accurate.

September 3

At the mouth of the Potomac. We are now returning to Washington after a three day trip on the *Mayflower*. We left Washington Friday at 5:30 P. M. and arrived at Norfolk Saturday morning at 10.

There we transferred to a tug used by the Admiral of the Norfolk Navy Yard and took an exploring trip to the Dismal Swamp, going up the Elizabeth River to Albermarle Canal, then up North Landing River to the Dismal Swamp. We took our lunch and had four Filipino boys to serve it. We returned to the *Mayflower* at 5:30 P. M.

It rained all day Saturday but now, at 2 A. M., the weather is ideal. It is almost time for me to call my relief.

September 14

Long Island Sound. Execution Rock. Saturday morning.

We are anchored 25 miles out from New York. We will weigh anchor at 7:30 A. M. (it is now 6:30) and head for the 79th Street-landing, where we will probably stay until Sunday night, when we will board a train for Washington, ending a delightful cruise. We have had perfect weather, and nothing has happened to mar our trip in any respect.

On our cruise we have visited New London, Saybrook, Lyme, Gloucester, Woods Hole, Nantucket, and Siasconset. While at Siasconset— where the Sayres live—my partner and I were walking down a path toward a curio shop when we met two charming-looking young ladies coming up from the beach, attired in one-piece bathing suits. They looked very pink and healthy and it was all that I could do to step to one side and let them pass. But they guessed who we were and commenced a very animated flirtation with us. However, our time was limited and we had to leave them.

No automobiles are allowed on Nantucket Island. Two carriages awaited us at the dock. The President, Mrs. Wilson, and Mrs. Sayre rode in the first, and we occupied the second. Thus we drove to Siasconset, which is about 8 miles from Nantucket. We went to the Sayre cottage, and sat on the beach before it to watch the sunset.

I had dinner at a nearby inn, and there, where the most wonderful fish in the world are caught, what do you think was the leading item on the menu? Columbia River salmon! With a straight face I told the manager he ought to be ashamed of himself, and he actually hung his head in shame.

We left at 9 P. M. While helping the President and Mrs. Wilson into the carriage and arranging the lap robes for them, I tucked the ends securely under Mrs. Wilson, raising up her feet and putting the lap robe under them, so as to keep out the cold night air. Mrs. Wilson said, in her sweet Southern voice, "Thank you, Mr. Starling, you are certainly a good tucker!"

What I did not tell my mother was that as I bowed in gratefulness for this compliment I noticed the President staring straight ahead, his nose pointing, his jaws working. I was in bad again. But I didn't care. I was going home soon, to relax for a blessed two weeks in the luxury of my mother's company and Aunt Peggy's cooking.

When I returned it was deep autumn, and the winter schedule had begun. To my mother on November 6 I wrote:

We spent the day at Princeton, N.J., where the President went to vote. I should have said that we spent the day travelling to and from Princeton. We stayed exactly fifty-five minutes there.

The President and Mrs. Wilson visited the Bureau of Standards last Sunday after church. The visit was confidential. We had to go to a certain room to see a certain thing. However, it was Sunday, and the man who had the keys could not be located over the telephone, so the President and Mrs. Wilson had to step through a hole in a door. The upper part was glass, and this had been removed. We put a box in front of the door. Then I got through and placed a box on the other side. Mrs. Wilson stepped up on the box, then caught hold of my hand and arm, put one foot through the hole until it rested on the box inside, then brought her other foot through.

When asked whether she was willing to climb through she said, "I am willing if you-all don't mind." Well, I can truthfully say that I could help her through all day, for she had on a narrow skirt and owns a beautiful leg. She is a dear, gracious woman and I like her better each day.

So the year moved to its end, and the first winter of the war came to America. When I wrote to my mother on December 9th the gayety of my letters—usually a reflection of a similar mood on the part of the President—was gone, seldom to recur during the years ahead. The job of running the war and the moral responsibility for it weighed heavily on the President, and the task of guarding him grew constantly more complex.

Last night we attended the Gridiron dinner at the Willard Hotel. We were all opposed to the President attending it, but he is so d—— hard-headed we had to make the best of it and sigh with relief when it was over. Confidentially, we were a little uneasy about the food. I was placed in charge of it, and of his waiters. After I put him to bed this morning and was walking home about one o'clock I could not but be thankful to our Heavenly Father for a successful conclusion of the whole affair.

He is a hard man to handle, especially at this time. Please continue to pray that nothing ever happens while I am with him that can be attributed to negligence or oversight.

I honestly believe that our Heavenly Father is going to teach us a lesson, and will purge us with fire and make us a new people. It is already being accomplished.

That is the first reference I find in my records to outward evidence that the President was showing the strain. He was always hard-headed, but ordinarily he was not contrary or irritable, and above all he was reasonable and thoughtful. When he began to be otherwise I knew the load was telling on his strength.

One day not long after the Gridiron Dinner we were driving along Constitution Avenue. The watchman at the Munitions Building had a Stop and Go sign, which he used when government clerks were crossing the street in large numbers. Just as we came up he turned the sign to Stop. We, of course, kept on going. We had to—it would be unsafe to stop in the middle of a crowded street with the President exposed to full view in an open car.

As Robby drove past, the watchman, not recognizing the party, shouted, "What's the matter? Can't you read a sign?" The President told Robby to stop. I ran ahead to see what the trouble was.

"Tell that watchman to come here. I want to see him," the President said.

I went back and told the man the President wanted to see him. He turned pale and made the sign of the cross.

"I guess I'll lose my job," he said weakly.

"What did you say?" I asked. I had heard him shout, but had not understood the words.

He told me.

"Don't worry about your job," I said. "He won't have you fired. He's not that kind. Let's go back and see him."

The President fixed the poor man with a cold eye.

"What did you say?" he asked.

"I only wanted to know why you did not obey the sign," the man said. "I did not recognize you or I would not have turned it against you."

"It was a misunderstanding," the President said. "You may go."

He was sorry now, I could see, that he had created the scene. Moreover, he had defeated his justification for passing the sign by stopping of his own accord. He signalled Robby to go on. The watchman, fearful and worried, went back to his post.

The incident was not typical of Woodrow Wilson; he was not a petty man. But it was a forecast of things to come.

★☆★

The Armistice

THE NEW YEAR came in with a splurge of bad weather, red tape, and continued trouble with the railroads. The President worked hard, took his recreation where and when he could find it, and was constantly besieged by visitors of all sorts, including delegations from the minority peoples of Europe, who had taken hope from his pronouncements about the peace to come. A visitor who came quite often that winter was Bernard M. Baruch, Chairman of the War Industries Board, a tall, gracious, kind man whose friendly and humorous blue eyes went cold and gleamed like a polished gun barrel when he spoke about money, production, or any of the various aspects of finance. I used to wonder at such times how his eyes could ever grow warm again, but in a few minutes, when the subject had been dismissed, he would be laughing and his gaze would have the understanding warmth of a man of good will. He was a complex and fascinating person.

My diary and my letters to my Mother tell the story of those winter days of 1918 better than any reproduction my memory can fashion.

January 3—Thursday

Snow, clear, 8 above zero. At 3:30 P.M. accompanied President and Mrs. Wilson for a short walk down "F" Street to 11th Street, up 11th Street to "G" Street, then back to the White House. On reaching the White House the President and I walked through Pussyfoot Alley (passage from the basement of the White House to the Executive Offices). On our way over he laughed and said, "Starling, it stretches a fellow's legs to walk on the streets these days." Everything is covered with ice and both he and Mrs. Wilson slipped several times on their walk.

On returning to the White House from the Executive Offices the President stopped at the kitchen door and looked at a turkey in a crate. Then he asked me what kind it was, saying he had never seen its like before. I peeped into the crate and saw that someone had painted the turkey red, white, and blue. The President had a good laugh at me as I tried to figure out what had happened to the bird.

January 4—Friday

Clear, snow, zero. At 12:15 P.M. accompanied President to Capitol, where he addressed a joint session of Congress on railroad legislation. Dr. Grayson and Secretary Tumulty accompanied him, and both succeeded in getting in the way of the Secret Service men, who are placed in a very embarrassing position when so hampered. Mrs. Wilson, the Misses Maury of Roanoke, Virginia, and John Randolph Bolling preceded us and sat in the President's seats in the Gallery.

Colonel House arrived this evening at the request of the President, to assist in preparing a reply to German peace propaganda.

January 6—Sunday

Slightly cloudy, 25°. After work I walked down to the "Basin" where quite a crowd was skating. After watching them a while I struck out for a long walk, returning to the White House at 6:00 P.M. After dinner I went to hear Billy Sunday at the Tabernacle. Had to stand up, although one of the Police Lieutenants offered to get me a chair. The Tabernacle is immense and seats at least 15,000. His sermon was, "Why call Ye me Lord, Lord?" It was full of pep from beginning to end. The President would not attend the opening. He does not approve of Billy's methods.

January 7—Monday

Cloudy. Rained last night and then froze. Very slippery today. 25°. At 6:00 P.M. the President met and shook hands with the Finance Committee of the Red Cross. With them was Joe Hartfield, former Hopkinsville boy and school-mate of mine, now a prominent New York lawyer. He introduced me to Henry P. Davison, Chairman of the Red Cross and former partner of J. P. Morgan. I promised to have dinner with Joe and some of his friends who have leased a house here and are keeping bachelor quarters.

January 8—Tuesday

Clear, windy and pretty cold, about 25°. At 8:30 A. M. accompanied President and Mrs. Wilson golfing to Kirkside. Going out, a wagon suddenly turned, causing the President's car to stop and slide into another car. No damage. After the game I helped the President on with his overcoat. His fingers were so cold he could not handle the buttons. I put my right hand on his shoulder and with my left hand fastened the buttons. One was missing. I must tell the Chief Usher to have one sewed on.

Went to the Capitol unexpectedly this afternoon where the President addressed a joint session about peace terms.

An amusing incident happened as the ladies walked out on the front porch of the White House to get into an automobile to go to the Capitol. Miss Bolling slipped on the ice and fell, taking Miss Benham and Miss Bones with her. I rushed out to assist them, my feet shot out from under me, and I sat down in the middle of them. No one was hurt and we all had a good laugh.

January 11—Friday

Snowing, sleeting, raining. At 2:25 P. M. accompanied President to Executive Offices for a Cabinet meeting. On returning to the White House late in the afternoon, the President said to me, "Why, Starling, it is snowing!" I replied, "Yes, Mr. President, it has been snowing since 4:00 o'clock." He then said in a gloomy voice, "Well, this means more stalled freight trains and more suffering by the poor people for lack of coal."

About 8:00 o'clock it began to rain, a cold disagreeable rain, and when we returned from Keith's it was still raining and under foot it was slushy. As the President walked into the White House from the automobile he looked at me, shook his head, and said, "Some night."

January 14—Monday

(My diary has no more references to the weather or temperatures. I must have given up in disgust.) When the President came downstairs at noon to walk to the offices of the Shipping Bureau, I helped him on with his overcoat, got his fur-lined gloves for him, and selected his old gray hat. I handed it to him and said, "Mr. President, is this the hat you want to wear?" He sort of hesitated and then replied, "Guess I had better wear the brown hat, Starling, as that is the one I have been ordered to wear." I laughed right out and he grinned like a school boy.

January 17—Thursday

Mrs. Wilson had a tea this afternoon. The house looked beautiful, all dressed up in flowers.

Secretary Tumulty was over here in the Executive Offices with a committee of theatrical men, headed by George M. Cohan. They came to protest against the fuel order closing theatres on Monday. Secretary Tumulty is very much disgusted at the fuel order, aand said to Chief Usher Hoover and me, "That is what happens when you have a school-teacher for President. The order is worse than our losing 100,000 soldiers." I did not agree with him, as I deem it a wise move to shut down all industries until this traffic congestion is relieved. This must be done in order to get coal to ships and people.

January 18—Friday

At 8:10 P.M. accompanied President and Mrs. Wilson, Mrs. Bolling, Miss Bolling and John Randolph Bolling to the National Theatre to see "Toot, Toot!" I was on stage and it was my duty to examine about 25 guns and pistols that were used in the hold-up scene.

January 19—Saturday

At 8:15 P.M. accompanied President and Mrs. Wilson, Miss Margaret Wilson, Mrs. Bolling, Miss Bones and Dr. Axson (brother of the first Mrs. Wilson) to Belasco Theatre to see William Gillette in "A Successful Calamity." It was splendid. As Mrs. Wilson stepped out of the side entrance to get into the automobile she slipped on the ice and had a hard fall. The President was very uneasy until we reached the White House and found she was all right.

January 21—Monday

At 8:15 P.M. accompanied President and Mrs. Wilson, Miss Margaret Wilson, Mrs. McAdoo, Mr. and Mrs. Julian Bolling to the National Theatre to see Raymond Hitchcock in "Hitchy Koo." The show, as modern ones are judged, was good, but in expressing my humble opinion I thought the whole thing was about as crazy as the author and owner, Raymond Hitchcock. I was on duty just to the rear of the Presidential box.

Quite a lot of bitterness is being stirred up by Gum Shoe Bill Stone's political speech on the Senate floor this afternoon. Also the President's ire has been raised by Senator Chamberlain and the Military Affairs Committee favoring a Munitions Cabinet and universal training. The President actually charged that Chamberlain told an untruth when he stated in a New York speech that the War Department was inefficient. They seem to be after Baker's scalp.

January 23—Wednesday

Ex-President Roosevelt arrived in the city today and is staying at the home of his son-in-law, Nicholas Longworth. He says he is here to help speed up the war. He is in favor of universal training and a Munitions Cabinet. All classes of men are going to see him, Democrats, Republicans, Senators, Congressmen, et cetera.

January 24—Thursday

Ex-President Roosevelt speaks tonight at the Press Club, and his speech is eagerly awaited. The President went to bed early tonight as he was suffering with a bad cold.

During the afternoon I carried the diamond ring given to me by Mother—given to her by Father—and my watch to Julian Bolling at Galt Brothers (Mrs. Wilson's store). Ring is to have scroll work done and a new band so as to fit my third finger. The watch stopped running for some unaccountable reason.

January 30—Wednesday

Off this afternoon. Went to a moving picture show. Saw Harold Lockwood in a north woods scene. Not as good as the one I saw the other day, "A Red, White, and Blue Man," with Francis X. Bushman and Beverley Bayne. A heavy snow fell during most of the day, commencing at 9:40 A. M. After dinner went to Chief Moran's and Mrs. Moran and I went to the Knickerbocker Theatre to see Mae Marsh. It was a splendid picture. Mrs. Moran and I then walked back home where she had some gingerbread for me.

January 31—Thursday

On returning to the White House via 16th Street I met Mrs. Nicholas Longworth née Miss Alice Roosevelt. She was walking and had a good stride, although interfered with by a deep snow. She was headed towards Rock Creek Park.

At 8:15 P. M. accompanied President and Mrs. Wilson, Mrs. Bolling, Miss Bolling and John Randolph Bolling to the National Theatre to see "Lightnin'." It was a splendid play and I enjoyed it immensely. I was on stage and met Frank Bacon who was Lightnin' Bill Jones. I also met his daughter (supposed to be) Mildred Buckley. I had a handkerchief in my pocket which Kate sent me (the wife of my brother Guy). She pulled it out and admired it, saying it was beautiful work. She wanted to keep it, but I said, "No, my dear young lady, there are some things that a fellow does not care to part with." By this ambiguous reply I meant to convey the idea that my lady love had given it to me. Sorry I had to deny her, but she had not quite enough to offer.

February 1—Friday

At 8:15 P. M. accompanied President and Mrs. Wilson, Mrs. Bolling, Miss Bolling and John Randolph Bolling to the Belasco Theatre to see "Peter Ibbetson," played by John Barrymore and Constance Collier. The acting and scenic effects were wonderful.

Every writer on the subject of Wilson has mentioned his love for the theatre. It is regarded as something of a phenomenon, or at least a peculiar hobby for a President, particularly for such a determined intellectual. Perhaps the fact that I myself have been slightly stage-struck always caused me to accept our almost nightly visits to Washington's Rialto as natural. It seemed to me that if a man ever got to a point where he could do pretty much as he liked, he would go to the theatre often. When I saw the President rocking with laughter at a particularly good quip, or humming and tapping his feet while a vaudeville singer gave out with a new song, I considered that he was being very normal. I did the same things myself.

Looking back on it now I realize that the President got more genuine recreation from the theatre than he did from anything else. It entirely

relaxed his mind, and it is worth noting that he preferred musical comedies and good vaudeville to serious dramatic works. He was not interested in anything which required the use of his mind. He wanted to
laugh at the clowns, admire the pretty legs of the chorus girls—like
any normal man he had a deep and sincere appreciation of the female
form—and he loved good dancing, being himself an accomplished buck
and wing artist. He liked to tell dialect stories (English, Scotch and
Negro) and he found the stage a rich source of fresh material.

Often I took him back-stage to meet some of the performers, particularly the good-looking ladies. I knew he enjoyed the experience of
seeing them at close quarters, observing their charms, and inhaling their
perfumes. Seeing him walk into the White House after an enjoyable
evening at Keith's, the Belasco or the National, it was easy to observe
that his face was less careworn and his whole body was more vigorous.
The next day while golfing or automobiling he would be whistling or
humming the tunes he had heard the night before, chuckling again
over the jokes and remarking on the acting of the performers or the
beauty of the ladies of the cast. It was a genuine tonic for him, better
by far than eight hours of sleep or a pint of cod liver oil.

February 2—Saturday

At 8:30 P. M. the President sent for me and requested that I make
arrangements for him to secretly visit a gathering of some Ordnance
officers at the Army and Navy Club. I did so. I preceded him to the
Club and there met and escorted him to the room occupied by the
officers. We returned at 11:30 P. M.

February 3—Sunday

At 6:30 P. M. Mrs. Wilson sent for me and asked me to do some charity
work for her. It seemed that some woman had written to her, asking for
assistance. Her secretary, Miss Benham, had been sent to the Boston
Hotel, where the woman said she resided. She could not find her. Mrs.
Wilson wanted me to see if I could find her and give her $10. I asked
whether I should first ascertain if the case were a worthy one. Mrs.
Wilson smiled and said, "Oh, Mr. Starling, I believe I would rather
have you just hand her the money as I am sure she will need it and it

will be better to give her the money and make a mistake than not to give it to her and make a bigger mistake."

February 4—Monday

Visited Boston Hotel and after some questioning discovered that the lady who wrote to Mrs. Wilson was a dope fiend and that she had been taken to Emergency Hospital that morning. Also learned that the Y.W.C.A. had telephoned the hotel about her. I visited there and at the hotel and made a thorough investigation.

February 5—Tuesday

At 6:30 P. M. sent word to Mrs. Wilson that I would like to see her. She asked that I come right up. When I stepped from the elevator she and the President were standing at his bedroom door. She left the President and came to me and I told her what I had discovered about the lady she had asked me to investigate. I returned the $10 and she seemed sad that the case had turned out as it had. She thanked me graciously and I asked her to do me the honor of calling upon me whenever she needed help of any kind.

February 6—Wednesday

At 1:30 P. M. the President notified us that he was going on a shopping tour at 2:00 P. M. I quickly notified the boys. We went shopping for a pocketbook and had to visit several stores before finding one. An amusing thing happened at Woodward & Lothrop's. Two of our men stayed outside, thinking there was only one entrance to the store. After spending about thirty minutes in the store we left by the "F" Street exit, one block down from the entrance we had used. The two men stayed there until the store closed.

February 8—Friday

At 5:30 P. M. accompanied President and Mrs. Wilson and Colonel House, walked up 16th Street, across Massachusetts Avenue to Connecticut Avenue, and back to the White House.

Some friends of Miss Margaret Wilson arrived this morning from Atlanta, Georgia. Most of her friends look like Bolsheviks and Socialists. She is a little flighty at times, and causes a lot of disturbance by wanting everyone to wait on her at once. However, she is good-humoured about it, and often laughs at her own inconsistency.

February 9—Saturday

About 4:30 P. M. the President and Mrs. Wilson went down to the billiard room to play pool. He decided he wanted a fire so I put a match to the fire-place and the room was soon full of smoke. The chimney was stopped up.

February 11—Monday

At 12:15 P. M. accompanied the President to the Capitol where he answered peace notes sent by the Germans. I have reasons for believing that peace moves are being made public by the President in order to win over the Austrians. Also to make it known to the German people, who are not of the military party, that the President is making a bid for their support.

February 28—Thursday

During the afternoon an amusing incident occurred. The President was receiving the Minister from the Netherlands at 2:00 P. M., for his first visit. He should have been received at the door by the President's aide, Colonel Ridley, but as usual he was late. So Chief Usher Hoover stood at the door and received him. John Mays, the colored doorman, walked up to the Minister, bowed and extended his hand for the Minister's hat. John was arrayed in a fine uniform of blue, with gold braid and shining brass buttons. To his consternation the Minister bowed also, extended his hand, took John's hand and shook it cordially. The poor old colored fellow's eyes nearly popped from his head. Hoover and I hustled the Minister off to the elevator and then we went back and congratulated John on his new post as Minister from Haiti.

March 21—Thursday

The big drive by the Germans on the Western Front began with an attack on the English. To my mind they can never break through either the English or the French lines.

March 25—Monday

Drive easing up on the English and diverting towards positions occupied by the French. The Germans have failed in their drive, I feel sure.

Went to the Belasco Theatre for "Aida" by the San Carlos Grand Opera Company.

March 26—Tuesday

The English and French have occupied strong positions at Oise and are holding the Germans.

General Leonard Wood testified before the Military Affairs Committee today. May our Heavenly Father forgive these damnable politicians and grafters who have retarded our preparation for an Army and our supplies for it. Senator Lodge also broke over and spoke for salvation of the nation.

March 28—Thursday

Dear Mother: Yes, I do get careless sometimes and write letters that are cold-blooded and uninteresting. I sometimes wonder how it is possible for me to write a letter full of feeling and love after living the life I have led, a life that makes most men cold, suspicious and secretive. So many have told me, "Starling, you do not look like a detective or Secret Service man. Your face looks too open and serene." A certain distinguished educator who seems to admire me met me on the street the other day. I smiled and had a pleasant word for him. He said, "Oh, if I could look on the bright side of life as you seem to do, I would be happy. Yet, I know your responsibilities and I would not have your job for the world." I remember meeting a man some years ago who was an officer. I had worked with him on two or three occasions and in one place things were pretty close for both of us for a few minutes. I laughed and the situation was relieved. He asked me if I remembered our close call, and said he would never forget my laughing. He said he would always get out of the way when I commenced to laugh as he believed I could shoot and laugh at the same time.

Yesterday I met my dear friend Judge Eyster of Decatur, Alabama, at the Raleigh Hotel. We then went to the Capitol and got Judge Alman, who is now a Congressman. He brought Miss Jeannette Rankin with him and introduced her. She is from Montana, the first woman Congressman. She is very bright and rather good-looking. We then went to the Congressional Restaurant, had lunch, and talked to quite a number of Congressmen.

Colonel House is here now, having been sent for by the President. Lord Reading was here just before dinner. The big drive has ended its first offensive and we are now certain we can hold Germany at any point. It might be possible to end the War this year, or prolong it four or five years, depending on the United States. I believe we are going to strike hard and finish it as soon as we can. However, we are still dilly-dallying with red tape and unimportant details.

Our spring was early and pleasant that year (though on April 11th we had a surprise snow which stayed on the ground until the 15th) and the morning of Saturday, April 6th, found me picking wild flowers on the golf course while the President and Mrs. Wilson were playing golf. I was carrying a small bouquet in my hand when Mrs. Wilson noticed them. Of course I gave them to her, and later two of the caddies gave her some violets. I took all of the flowers then and made a small corsage for her. As I gave it to her I said, "These are not the prettiest flowers I have ever seen, but they do represent the admiration we poor fellows feel for our gracious First Lady." She blushed and said, "It is a pity about your being a poor little fellow."

That afternoon we went to Baltimore where the President reviewed a division of soldiers from Camp Meade, and I was pleased to see that Mrs. Wilson was still wearing the corsage. When we returned to Washington that night I was walking with her and the President on the depot platform. Turning to me she said, "Mr. Starling, see how fresh my flowers have stayed." Then it was my turn to blush.

There were all sorts of parades, rallies and demonstrations in connection with the war effort. One day that spring there rolled up to the Executive Offices the famous tank "Brittania" that figured in the English advance at Cambrai. It was a clumsy but impressive looking machine and it was well spattered with hits. The President rode in it from the Executive Offices to the front gates and then got out. He hesitated in the doorway, looking about for something on which he could lean or to which he could hold while descending. There were a lot of overhead pipes and one of the soldiers told him to grab one. He did, but unfortunately the one he chose was carrying the exhaust and was very hot. It burned the palm of his right hand severely and he had to go to the White House immediately to have it dressed and bandaged.

It was two weeks before he was able to use his hand again, but the insurance company showed little sympathy. He carried an accident policy, but the company held that he was not incapacitated, since he could sign bills with his left hand. On the day he burned himself my diary says, "During the afternoon the President saw Secretary of War Baker instead of having a Cabinet meeting. I talked to him for quite a while as he had to wait while the President had his hand dressed and bandaged. He seemed to be optimistic about conditions in France."

The White House acquired some sheep that spring. Eighteen of them were turned loose in the back yard and were the subject of a good deal of joking, but Mrs. Wilson had the laugh on all of us later when the sheep were sheared and she divided the wool equally between the 48 states, each of which auctioned off its portion for a good sum, netting the Red Cross a total of almost $100,000. On May seventh my diary says we went to the circus and "Secretary Lane of Interior gave the President a bag of peanuts and Mrs. Wilson kindly offered me some. We had a great time." From May 17 to May 20 we were in New York.

May 17—Friday

Arrived New York at 3:00 P. M. President staying at Waldorf Astoria. At 3:30 P. M. accompanied President and Mrs. Wilson, Col. House and Dr. Grayson automobiling. Returned at 5:30. At 6:00 the President appeared at his door, peeped out, saw me, grinned and said, "Starling, I want to slip out and stretch myself. Can I sneak out the back way? I am tired of policemen and preparations. I want to take a walk like an ordinary citizen." I said, "All right, Mr. President, go to it. I don't blame you. I can take care of you, but you know that more than one Secret Service man is supposed to accompany you." Well, we walked, talked, and laughed. He was like a kid, and he ran out in the middle of Madison Avenue ahead of a big dray, I right after him. An automobile was headed straight towards him. I grabbed his arm and jerked him back. One other Secret Service man finally caught up with us. We got back in about an hour, and then lost our way in the hotel.

Went to Col. House's for dinner. At 8:15 the President, Mrs. Wilson, Col. and Mrs. House went to the Globe Theatre to see Fred Stone in "Jack O'Lantern."

May 18—Saturday

At 10:30 A. M. accompanied the President, walking up Fifth Avenue to the University Club. Great crowds formed, and began cheering, and with the blaring of automobile horns it made a perfect uproar. At the Club I sat in the reading room while the President wrote his Red Cross speech, to be delivered in the evening at the Metropolitan Opera House. It was interesting to watch him compose on the typewriter.

At 2:30 P. M. we motored to 89th Street and Fifth Avenue where the President headed the Red Cross parade, down Fifth Avenue to 26th Street, to the reviewing stand. At 4:30 we motored up Fifth Avenue to 89th Street, reviewing the parade as we rode.

That night we went to the Metropolitan Opera House where the President delivered his address to tremendous applause. I sang my first song in the Metropolitan Opera House—"America." I was standing in the front row with the President on my right and Henry P. Davison on my left.

May 19—Sunday

At 10:50 A. M. accompanied President and Mrs. Wilson and Dr. Grayson, walking to the Brick Presbyterian Church at 37th Street and Fifth Avenue. After services we automobiled to Col. House's residence, where we picked up Col. and Mrs. House and then motored out to the home of Cleveland Dodge where they had lunch. Returned to the hotel by Pelham Camp.

At 6:00 P. M. accompanied President and Mrs. Wilson on a walk down Broadway, down 28th Street over to Madison Avenue, then back to 33rd Street and to the hotel. At 10:00 P. M. went to our private car at the depot.

Next morning found us in Washington and that afternoon we were at Poli's Theatre to attend a musical benefit for Italian soldiers. The performers were mostly Italian opera stars, among them Mme. Alda and Enrico Caruso. I was on duty on stage, and I was fascinated not only by the great tenor's magnificent voice, but by the energy of his whole body while singing. He perspired profusely, and as he stepped into the wings between bows, attendants, who stood ready with towels in their hands, wiped his face. Between numbers they put new make-up on his face and even changed his shirt. I have never seen anyone else perspire so much. He was, of course, nervous before the President, but the skill with which his handlers cared for him gave me the idea that this was a usual procedure.

When he had finished singing I took him to the President's box and introduced him. He was embarrassed and pleased, but it was the President who showed delight. His eyes were sparkling and he shook the singer's hand warmly. "You are a great artist," he said, with feeling, "a great artist. I have been thrilled." I still do not see how such incomparable music came from Caruso's short, thick body. Most tenors are tall and lean, but this man, who was the greatest of them, was a broad-shouldered little fellow with a short neck and a barrel chest.

Soon we were in the midst of another Washington summer, and during this one even trips on the *Mayflower* were curtailed. There was little recreation for any of us. June tenth was a typical day: "Accompanied President and Mrs. Wilson, Miss Margaret Wilson, Miss Bones, and Mr. and Mrs. McAdoo to Poli's to see D. W. Griffith's great moving picture, 'Hearts of the World.' Returned at 11:10. Midnight found me still on duty at the White House, the President, confound his hide, loafing in his study reading the *New York Evening Post*." June twenty-fourth also sounds uninteresting: "To Poli's to see 'The Chinese Puzzle.' I was on stage. This being the first night everything was upside down and everyone was nervous. The famous William J. Brady, who produced the play, was behind the scenes and was the cause of most of the confusion. The play was too long and the actors did not have the tone of the house. Therefore, the first act was heard only by the first ten rows."

On July fourth there was an elaborate program at Mt. Vernon. Diplomats from all the Allied nations gathered at the tomb of Washington and the President made a speech. Our hardest job that day was with the

Irish tenor, John McCormack. He was supposed to sing "The Star Spangled Banner"—and he did, magnificently—but he insisted that he could not perform without a piano for accompaniment, a grand piano. Where to put such an unwieldy piece of furniture was a mystery. McCormack wanted it set squarely in front of Washington's tomb, where he was to stand. We finally dissuaded him from this notion and succeeded in hiding the instrument behind some trees a little distance away. When he found that he could hear the notes clearly he was satisfied.

During the early days of August Mrs. Wilson was ill, and the President showed the strain of the load he was carrying, one day on the golf course. We were at Kirkside and I was carrying his clubs, since no caddies were available. He drove about 50 yards from the tee and I saw as he walked toward the ball that he was in an ugly temper. Generally he asked me what club he should use, but this morning he said, "Starling, give me my number two iron." As he was addressing the ball a boy at a house on the edge of the course cupped his hands to his mouth and tried to call like an Indian. The President stepped to one side, rested on his club, and said in a disgusted manner, "That boy must be training to be a Senator. He is always making a noise with his mouth and not saying anything."

He then hit the ball and topped it, rolling it ahead 25 yards. Then he asked me for a brassie—he should have been using a number six iron—and got a beautiful shot which landed 100 yards on the other side of the green. This tickled him, and his good humour was restored.

At the end of the summer the nation began its gasless Sundays, and on September first we rode to church in carriages drawn by horses. Getting a buggy for the President and Mrs. Wilson was not so difficult, but we scoured the city before finding something in which the Secret Service men could ride. We finally set off in an old-fashioned surrey, with plenty of fringe on top, most of it frayed.

I spent the first two weeks of October in Hopkinsville, on my annual vacation. When I returned to Washington the war was in its final phase and rumors of peace were as plentiful as sparrows. The President was happy, and was unusually cordial in welcoming me back. Mrs. Wilson reflected her husband's joyfulness. She asked about my mother and my family.

But a jarring note, one of many that was to appear in the peace melody, sounds in my diary for October twenty-fourth: "The President came out in the newspapers today with a plea to the people to elect only those who are Democrats to Congress at the elections to be held November 5. This action on his part has stirred up a hornet's nest and I am sorry he made such a plea. I really believe he made a mistake, as up to this time he has occupied a position far above that of a political one, and has been looked upon as one of God's chosen."

That mistake—for it was a mistake—was the handwriting on the wall for Wilson, but none of us recognized it as such at the time. There was an aura of good-will and happiness about the White House during those days as peace notes went back and forth between the President and the German government. We did not know that our allies were accepting an armistice on the basis of the Fourteen Points with tongue in cheek and the firm intention of getting around them at the Peace Conference. My diary reflects a jollity that never returned to the White House during the Wilson regime.

October 31—Thursday

I caddied for Mrs. Wilson. She was very gracious. Both she and the President are very happy on account of the probable peace. They saw a crawfish and did not know at first what it was. Finally, as I came up, the President laughed and said, "Oh, pshaw! it is a crawfish." Jervis said to Mrs. Wilson, "I wonder if I could put it in my pocket." I said, "Yes," and picked it up and handed it to him. Both he and Mrs. Wilson ran away from me.

Mrs. Wilson admired my diamond ring. I told her it belonged to my father and was given to me by my mother. She said it was the handsomest ring she had ever seen.

November 2—Saturday

I caddied for Mrs. Wilson and after the fourth tee she and I left the President and Dr. Grayson and played by ourselves, she doing the playing and I caddying and teeing her balls. She said, after I had teed a ball, "Mr. Starling, you make a good tee." I replied, "I got that manner of making tees from the President." She replied, "You can beat him." I said, "Well, I feel honored in knowing that I surpass him in one thing." After the game, while we were waiting for the President and Dr. Grayson, she said, "This has been a game that I have enjoyed, and I have you to thank for it."

On November 7 we had the false Armistice. The President stayed indoors but Mrs. Wilson could not resist the intoxication of the joyful crowds and went for a ride with her mother.

The next evening we went to Poli's to see "Atta Boy," a show given by soldiers from Camp Meade. Between the acts the boys sent word that they would like the President to come backstage and shake hands with them. He agreed to go and I accompanied him. After leaving the theatre I rode on the front seat of the White House car to the residence of Mrs. McAdoo, thinking to save myself a walk, as my room was just across the street.

In the car were Mrs. Bolling, Miss Bolling, Mrs. McAdoo and John Randolph Bolling. While John was taking Mrs. McAdoo to her door Miss Bolling said to me, "Mr. Starling, did you see the show?" I said no, I hadn't, being on duty behind the box, so that in order to see the stage I would have had to peep through curtains. "I was not interested in the show as much as in keeping my eye on the President," I said. She said, "I should have known that, and we all feel that way about it. Mrs. Wilson appreciates your loyalty. When the President left his box tonight I asked Edith where he was going and she replied, 'I don't know but Mr. Starling has got him and I know he will be safe.'" Mrs. Bolling then spoke up and verified the statement. I was happy, but I do not think these compliments pleased me as much as something that happened a few days later on the golf course, when the President called me "Murphy," and then, correcting himself, addressed me as "Will." It was the first time he had ever addressed me by my Christian name.

The real Armistice came on a day when, happily, a parade of United War Workers was scheduled. The President and Mrs. Wilson stood on the steps leading to the Executive Offices and reviewed it. After dinner they rode slowly down Pennsylvania Avenue enjoying the demonstrations of the crowds. It was the King of Italy's birthday and there was a ball at the Italian Embassy. Filled with enthusiasm the President decided to go to it, so we all climbed into white tie and tails and accompanied him.

It was days before things settled down again, and when they did, the ominous note crept back into the music. The President, we heard, was determined to go to Europe for the Peace Conference. Almost nobody seemed to think it was a wise thing. The Peace Commission was elected and neither a Senator nor a prominent Republican was on it. On November 25th McAdoo resigned as Secretary of the Treasury. My diary says: "Very much surprised at McAdoo's resignation. My first impression was that he and the President had come to an understanding that McAdoo would be the favorite candidate for President and that in order to make the candidacy stronger his resignation would be accepted and he would be appointed as a peace delegate. I am now of the opinion that McAdoo, finding that the President desired a third term, became disgusted, threw up the sponge, and decided to break loose while he was on top of an ascending wave of popularity, not taking a chance of impairing his health by working for someone else's glory."

On December 2d the President addressed a joint session of Congress on needed legislation and also announced his intention of going to France for the preliminary meetings of the Peace Conference. My diary says: "A very cool reception was given the President by Congress. Most of the applause was led by Congressman Heflin of Alabama. The Democrats are putting their all on the outcome of the President's trip abroad."

The next night we left Union Station for New York, to board the *George Washington* for Europe.

★★

CHAPTER EIGHT

Paris

WE BOARDED the *George Washington* at Hoboken shortly before noon
on December 4th, and soon thereafter were moving out to sea guarded
by the battleship *Pennsylvania,* flagship of the Atlantic fleet, and fifteen
destroyers. After seeing us out of sight of land five of the destroyers
turned back, while the remaining ten moved into positions on our right
and left. The *Pennsylvania* steamed directly ahead of us, acting as a
pilot boat, for there was not only danger of floating mines, but the
possibility that so soon after the Armistice we might run into a U-boat
which had been out of touch with its home base and was not aware that
hostilities had ceased. The destroyers and the battleship gave us all the
protection possible, but I was given an "abandon ship" list and informed
of the specific plans for taking care of the President if such an emergency
arose.

There were eight of us in the Detail: Murphy, Jack Slye, Arnold
Landvoigt, John Sullivan, Walter Ferguson, John Fitzgerald, Miles
McCahill and myself. Chief Moran and Jervis were already in Paris,
acting as advance men. The ship had been checked from bow to stern
and from keel to masthead, and members of the Secret Service all over
the United States had been busy investigating members of the crew.
They did not know it, but their names and home addresses had been
given to us when the ship was chosen for the President, and we had
sent the information to our various offices. There was not a fireman
or cabin boy whose family and background had not been thoroughly
looked into.

In addition the President was completely surrounded by trusted members of the White House Staff—Brooks, his valet; Ike Hoover, Chief Usher; and Charles Swem and Charlie Wagner, stenographers. Mrs. Wilson was attended by Miss Benham, her secretary, and Susie Booth, her maid, an amiable negress who referred to us as the "Silver Service." The President had a suite consisting of an office, a bedroom, and a bath. The office was equipped with two telephones, one a wireless instrument for keeping in touch with Washington. Mrs. Wilson had a suite of three rooms, a sitting room, a dining room and a bedroom and bath.

In the official party were the French Ambassador and Madame Jusserand; the Italian Ambassador and Madame Cellere; Secretary of State Lansing, a member of the Peace Commission, and Mrs. Lansing; and Mr. Henry White, the only Republican member of the Peace Commission, a veteran diplomat and one of the most engaging men I have ever met. The other members of the Commission—Col. House, and Gen. Bliss, were already in Paris, where headquarters had been set up at the Hotel Crillon. Also in Paris were Bernard Baruch, Herbert Hoover, and George Creel, who were unofficially members of the group.

Of Secretary Lansing I had already formed a distinct impression. He was a shrewd, sharp attorney, beyond question very learned in international law, but not broad in outlook, and extremely jealous of his rights. He was sensitive and easily hurt. From these traits arose some of his difficulties with Colonel House, for he felt the Colonel was entrenching upon ground that belonged to him. As Secretary of State he spent much of his time in safeguarding his office, and was continually suspicious. Henry White, with whom I became acquainted for the first time, was a man of broader and finer qualities. He was in fact one of the finest gentlemen I ever knew. Always cheerful, always thoughtful of others, always generous in outlook, he had a personality that was like a tonic. It was delightful to have him about. Of course he was a Republican, and we knew that he was a friend of Theodore Roosevelt and Henry Cabot Lodge. But he quickly became devoted to President Wilson and to Wilson's ideas, and he never wavered in his allegiance to both.

The trip was pleasant and the President enjoyed some rest and relaxation. Every night there were moving pictures, and members of the crew provided us with a home-made minstrel show. There were band concerts, and among the official party little dinners were given back and forth as if the ship were a miniature Washington. The moving pictures featured such stars as Marguerite Clark, Mae Marsh, Douglas Fairbanks, Charlie Chaplin, William S. Hart, Lillian and Dorothy Gish, Bert Lytell, John Barrymore, and Elsie Ferguson. There were also news reels and comedies, and an enterprising young photographer one night promised to show us some pictures he had taken of the President. The scene opened on a small promenade deck on top of the ship. A man in a dark overcoat and gray felt hat could be seen walking slowly around the deck, occasionally leaning against the railing. Finally he turned and walked toward the camera. There was a gasp of astonishment, then a roar of laughter, as the features of his face developed into the countenance, not of the President, but of myself.

The President and Mrs. Wilson turned and waved at me, laughing. The young photographer was embarrassed. He had taken the pictures shortly after we sailed, going up to the promenade deck and observing me as I walked about, testing the railing to make sure that it was safe. Thinking I was the President he had photographed me, and after grinding the crank as I came toward him had turned and fled before realizing his mistake. He knows better now, for Victor Fleming has become one of Hollywood's finest directors.

The *George Washington* was a sturdy ship, 700 feet long and capable of making better than eighteen knots. She had been the *Kaiser Wilhelm,* one of the German ships interned in our ports at the outbreak of the war, and confiscated by us. She had served as a transport, safely carrying 7,000 soldiers to France. We had trust in her, and in the destroyers and the battleship, but we could not help but be uneasy at the thought that directly beneath us lay several miles of cold water. We took every precaution. As I fastened the President's life preserver on him one day during boat drill, Mrs. Wilson, looking at the large collar which came up around his ears, laughed and said, "You look like Mary Queen of Scots!"

We travelled the southern route and sighted the Azores at dawn on the tenth. The next day two more destroyers joined our convoy. Early on the morning of Friday, December 13, at 4:20, lights were sighted on the horizon. At 7:25 nine battleships came into view: the *New York, Texas, Arizona, Arkansas, Florida, Nevada, Wyoming, Utah,* and *Oklahoma.* Each one came alongside and fired a salute of twenty-one guns. Then twelve destroyers were sighted. At 10:17 we saw our destination, Brest, France. Soon airplanes were flying overhead and a balloon was sighted.

At 11:00 o'clock two French cruisers and nine French destroyers passed and saluted. At 1:00 o'clock the shore forts saluted, and at 1:35 we anchored, surrounded by the biggest fleet of battleships I have ever seen.

Ceremonies immediately began, and it was 3:15 before the President and his party left the ship for shore. A delirious crowd awaited them, and they drove to the depot through a sea of human enthusiasm and joy which has seldom, I am sure, been equalled anywhere in the world. That day the President had Europe at his feet. He could have had a crown for the asking.

At 4:00 P. M. the Presidential special train left for Paris. At 7:00 o'clock Chief Moran and I, who remained behind, boarded another and faster train, in order to reach Paris ahead of the special and make arrangements for its welcome. As soon as we had passed the special we acted as its pilot train, getting into Paris two hours ahead of it, at 8:00 o'clock next morning. We found the preparations at the Gare Montparnasse agreeable, but when the President arrived we were horrified to discover that in the list of horse-drawn carriages that were to make up the procession there was no provision for the Secret Service. The list said that the President and President Poincaré were to occupy the first carriage; Mrs. Wilson and Madame Poincaré, the second; the Secretary of State and Ambassador Jusserand the third; Mrs. Lansing and Madame Jusserand, the fourth; Generals Pershing, Bliss, and Joffre the fifth; Admiral Benson and a French Admiral the sixth; General Harts and some French General the seventh; and Admiral Grayson and a French officer the eighth. Cavalry and members of the French Invisible Service on bicycles were to surround the procession and act as its guard.

Such an arrangement struck terror to our hearts. We never under any circumstances allow mounted men to act as guards. It takes all a man can do to manage a spirited horse; he has no time to watch a crowd and if danger should present itself his hands would be occupied and his body would be at the mercy of a nervous and unpredictable animal. As for bicycles, before a man could disentangle himself from such a machine and go into action a whole platoon of Presidents could be mowed down. Our system is to ride on the running board, one hand holding to the car and the other free to draw a gun. When the car is moving slowly through a crowd we trot alongside, both hands free and our eyes on the crowd.

There was nothing to do in this particular instance, since the French had charge of the arrangements and we were only guests. The best we could do was commandeer a carriage and tag along in the number nine position, chewing our nails and hoping that nothing would happen. Eventually we reached our destination, after passing under the Arc de Triomphe, and were able again to surround the President with our presence. The first thing we did thereafter was to inform the French police in no uncertain terms of our requirements and the place we were to occupy in any future parades or public affairs. We asked for a car with a chauffeur capable of speaking English, and designated the spot just behind the President as our reservation on any and all occasions. Our requests were met immediately, and during our stay in Paris the French police showed a great interest in the methods we used, so much so that on our second trip we noticed that the Invisible Service had somewhat Americanized itself.

The President and Mrs. Wilson were quartered at the palace of Prince Murat, a residence which completely lived up to its name. It was surrounded by a high wall and the entrances were guarded. We asked that these guards be American soldiers, and this request was granted. From our Military Intelligence we obtained interpreters to work with us twenty-four hours a day. The list of the President's engagements for the day was checked each morning, first by us and then by the Military Intelligence.

At the French Foreign Office, the Quai d'Orsay, where the meetings of the Peace Conference were held, I was stationed in the room next to that in which the meetings were held—the Holy of Holies, as it was called. Only one entrance to the building was used, and we always travelled the same street route, which was guarded and checked.

The President had come to Paris with the idea of getting down to business immediately and returning to the United States with a peace treaty before the adjournment of Congress. It was obvious that his colleagues from France, England, and Italy, had no such notion. They were inclined to talk a lot and put off anything definite to the indefinite future. It was suggested that the President visit England and Italy to give the people of these countries an opportunity to see him. This he was willing to do, for his whole plan was for the welfare of these people, but if things had been done his way the Conference would have been held first and the triumphal tour staged later. However, since he had come to cure Europe of its political faults, he was inclined to put up with its social foolishness. Thus at midnight of Christmas Eve we found ourselves on a special train headed for Chaumont, General Pershing's headquarters, where we were to spend Christmas before going on to London for a visit with the English king and queen.

We arrived at Chaumont at 9:00 in the morning and were met at the depot by General Pershing and his Staff. We then rode to the City Hall, where the President was welcomed and Mrs. Wilson was presented with a box of gloves. After that we automobiled to the point where the President was to review our troops, and where he made a speech to them. We drove on to Matigny, where we had our Christmas dinner with the soldiers. It was a traditional meal, consisting of turkey, celery, creamed cauliflower, mashed potatoes, salad, pumpkin pie, coffee and fruit. We then drove through several small places and inspected detachments of troops billeted in stables, barns and like quarters. To my mother I wrote, "It made my heart heavy to see the boys putting up with such hardships, especially on Christmas Day."

In the evening we returned to our train and the next morning at 9:30 were at Calais, where we boarded a channel ship to Dover, arriving there at 11:00 o'clock. At 2:30 we were in Charing Cross Station, London, where King George, Queen Mary, Princess Mary, Lloyd George, Mr. Balfour and others welcomed us. The ride to Buckingham Palace was a victorious passage, the people cheering the President as if he were their own hero. I liked London and the English people, and my fickle heart wavered in its fancy when I walked into Charing Cross and saw the reception committee. "On my honor I have fallen in love with Queen Mary," I wrote to my mother, "she looks like a thoroughbred."

I could not enjoy London for long, for I had to hurry off to Manchester and Carlisle to arrange for the President's visit to those cities. I went first to Manchester, where Mr. Wilson was to be the guest of the Lord Mayor and other dignitaries. He had a special regard for Manchester as a center of liberal reform, and a city connected with two of his heroes, Cobden and Bright. The place struck me as un-British, for in those days just after the Armistice manners had become free and easy. Going up in the elevator in the hotel, one of the British army officers hugged and kissed the elevator girl; and the corridors seemed full of women in kimonos, wandering from one room to another as if they were at home in all of them. Perhaps it was a large family party!

Carlisle, a beautiful border city, was a smaller place, and much more like the decorous English towns that I had imagined. In fact, the men I met there were just like those I had known at Hopkinsville in Kentucky, and I immediately felt at home. Hunting up the town clerk, I made all the arrangements for the President's visit with him. Next morning the President and the press men arrived. Mr. Wilson was taken to the Presbyterian Church of which his Grandfather Woodrow had been pastor, and made a brief speech from the pulpit. I watched him as he spoke, and it was clear that he was deeply moved by the occasion.

In the afternoon we went to Manchester, staying there the night. The next day we left for London, where the President and Mrs. Wilson again stayed at Buckingham Palace. The next day the King and Queen saw them off at Victoria Station, and we crossed the Channel again. The members of the Detail who had remained in London could give me little information about life at the Palace. The only member of the party, other than the President and Mrs. Wilson, to reach terms of intimacy with royalty was Susie, Mrs. Wilson's maid, who made a hit with the Queen. Susie also made a hit with the London newspapermen. I remember a cartoon of the President and his party which showed Susie bringing up the rear, her feet pointing east and west while she grimly headed north, her hat perched on her head in just the unexpected way which, it seemed to me, the English ladies wore them.

We were back in Paris at 7:00 that night. The next day we played golf at Saint Cloud, and at 7:00 P. M. boarded the King of Italy's royal train. When I woke up we were in the Alps, and I sat staring out of the window, devouring the beautiful scenery. All day we descended through snow-covered peaks until we were in fertile valleys where oxen were plowing, while above them grape orchards glistened on the slopes. We had left Paris on New Year's Day. At 10:30 on the morning of January third we arrived in Rome.

The reception in Rome exceeded anything I have ever seen in all my years of witnessing public demonstrations. The people literally hailed the President as a god—"The God of Peace." They paved the streets with flowers, so that the cobble-stones were not visible for blocks. I have never seen such roses, great white beautiful things that showered down upon us as we went slowly through the hysterical mob of shouting, singing, weeping people. Few men in history have known such adulation as was the President's in that hour when King Victor Emanuel and Queen Helena escorted him to the Quirinal, the Royal Palace. It was the same wherever we went in Italy—Genoa, Milan and Turin.

This attitude of the people was of practical use so far as we were concerned, for it lessened our anxiety about the President's safety. It was impossible to keep the crowds from pressing close to the automobiles and carriages, but we felt reasonably sure that no one meant harm to our precious charge. Moreover the plans for this trip had been handled in our own manner. We had in the Service an Italian who had specialized for years on work in his native country. He accompanied Chief

Moran as advance man for the party, and as a result the precautions in Italy were identical with those which would be made for a comparable trip through the United States.

In Rome the President attended a state dinner, addressed the Italian Parliament, visited the Pope, toured the historical spots, and at 9:00 o'clock on the evening of the fourth, left by train for Genoa.

Here the next morning we were greeted by the usual array of distinguished officials, including the American Consul and his wife. The automobile set aside for the Secret Service had been appropriated by some of the members of the reception committee. There was nothing to do but trot alongside the President's car, hopping a ride on the running board when necessary. Looking about for help I spotted an Italian Naval Officer in a big Packard touring car. I spoke to him, discovered that he understood English, and explained our situation.

"You shall have my car," he said, with a smile, "and I will be delighted to act as chauffeur for the White House Secret Service."

Gratefully Jack Slye and I got in with him and rode through the streets of Genoa in our accustomed position just behind the President's car. We had the best-looking chauffeur in the whole parade, and we were almost tempted to bow when some of the avalanche of roses thrown at the President's car overshot their mark and landed in our laps.

We drove to the Christopher Columbus monument where the President was to place a wreath. By that time it was raining. I got out of our car and went to the side of the President's automobile, waiting patiently for someone to produce the wreath. After a while the President lowered a window and whispered to me, "Starling, what are we waiting for?"

"We are waiting for the American Consul and for the wreath," I said.

I went over to General Harts and told him of the delay. He explained that the wreath was in the Consul's carriage and probably the horse had been unable to keep up with the pace set by our automobiles.

At this point Murphy and Jervis, who had been missing from our group, came running up, almost out of breath. Unable to commandeer a Packard with a Naval Officer for chauffeur, they had captured instead a carriage drawn by a fat and sleepy horse. They had taken forcible possession of the vehicle, over the protests and lamentations of the driver, who could speak no English but who had screamed and shouted about something that sounded like "flowers."

"Is there a wreath under the seat?" I asked.

"Yes," Jervis said, "there is. We started to throw it away but Joe decided to keep it for the owner."

"Get it out," I said, "that's the wreath the President is waiting to lay on the monument. You two robbers stole the American Consul's carriage." Jervis got the wreath, handed it to the President, and the ceremony was performed, while buckets of rain poured down on our uncovered heads.

We had another such ceremony just ahead. I don't remember now who the celebrity was, but I wanted to be sure that we were ready for him. After the President had returned to his car, I looked about, saw that everyone was rushing for shelter, and quickly stole the wreath away from Christopher Columbus and took it back to our car. It was still raining when we got to the next monument, and just as I feared, no one was ready with a wreath. I produced my trophy, handed it to the President, and he laid it on the tomb of another distinguished Italian.

That little adventure taught us a lesson. Since then, whenever a President sets out on a similar expedition, we carry a duplicate wreath in the Secret Service car.

At 11:00 A. M. we were on the train for Milan, where we arrived at 2:30, paraded through an immense crowd to the Royal Palace, and in the evening attended a performance of "Aida" at the Opera de la Scala. At 11:30 we were on our way to Turin. We arrived there the next morning, went through a series of ceremonies, and departed at 5:00 in the afternoon for Paris, arriving there at 10:00 the next morning.

Suggestions for all sorts of other trips were awaiting the President, but he was determined to get down to business, and meetings actually began at the Quai d'Orsay, though from what I could gather a great deal was said and very little was done. On January 15 I wrote in my diary: "As we were leaving Quai d'Orsay it fell to my lot to put a lap robe on the President's knees, and he said to me in an undertone, 'I am glad to get away from them. It is nothing but a talk shop.'" Still, the meetings were being held, and the delegates were committed to the President's program, by their own act of the Armistice—made on the basis of the Fourteen Points—and by public opinion. On January 20 I wrote to my mother:

Our time for the last ten days has been completely taken up with preliminary peace conferences and the President has been in fine fettle. Of course it is interesting to see all those big men come walking into the conference room, each accompanied by an aide who carries his chief's portfolio. I had the President's portfolio today. I am stationed in the adjoining room to that in which the conferences are being held. All persons who enter the conference room must pass by me. I, therefore, daily see such men as President Poincaré, Clemenceau, Marshal Foch, Lloyd George, Balfour, Lord Cecil, Hughes, Barnes, Orlando, Sonnino, and Venizelos. They are all big men and are certainly interesting to study.

Morning sessions commence at 10:00 and end at 1:00. Evening sessions commence at 2:30 and generally end about 6:30. The doors between all rooms are soundproof and are actually double doors. No one is allowed in any room adjoining the conference room but those passed upon by the commission. There are some wonderful paintings and statues in the rooms. The favorite subject for all artists it seems is the nude form of woman.

I am comfortably situated at the Hotel Crillon, a French hotel run by Americans. I was fortunate to draw a room with bath and I enjoy the warm water. The hotel is headquarters for the American Peace Commission. Our meals are excellent and I have developed into a real tea drinker. One has to drink something over here as the sun hardly ever shines. It is a mystery to me how the French people keep so bright and cheerful and I do not blame them for drinking wine. This afternoon I had to visit the French Opera and make arrangements for the President's visit there Friday night. I will be sitting in his box.

. . .

Paris was still a war city. Food coupons were in circulation, and the making of pastry was prohibited. The streets were filled with captured German cannon, about which the children played, shouting and imitating their soldier fathers and brothers. Most of the men were still in uniform, and they still sought pleasure in the manner of men on a furlough. Paris is Paris, of course, and to a Kentucky boy it seemed pretty fast. I wrote to my mother:

Last night I took in a show called "Folies Bergère." This theatre as well as a great many others is a semi-restaurant, containing tables where one can sit and order drinks. Between acts one walks around a promenade and soon is approached by one of several young ladies who asks in a soft kind of pleading tone, "Monsieur, won't you buy me a drink?" Or, "Won't you please give me a cigarette?" If you yield to her entreaties you can be prepared to go the limit. These places are, of course, well patronized by soldiers, and I am informed that they have been running full blast during the war. These French people are wonderful and simply can not be downed.

The Prince and Princess Murat were in their home today—now occupied by the President and Mrs. Wilson. Both are very good-looking and I understand are very democratic in their ways and manners. Last night I caught the President in the reception room of the palace trying a skirt dance while waiting for the Japanese Foreign Minister. He looked up when I walked in and laughed heartily. He seems to be well satisfied with the way things are going but he is also very tired and looks a great deal older than he did two months ago. In addition to meetings at the Quai d'Orsay in the mornings and afternoons there are League of Nations' meetings every night beginning at 8:30.

The President was being entreated constantly to make a tour of the devastated battle areas but he contended that he was working to see that such a thing did not happen again and had no time to look backward when he was trying to get the world to face forward. He finally agreed to spend a Sunday automobiling through some of the regions. We left Paris at 8:00 in the morning, six automobiles being in the party. We went first to Château Thierry, by way of Belleau Wood, and after lunching there drove to Rheims by way of the Champaigne sector along the Marne River. We got to Rheims at 3:00 in the afternoon in the midst of a heavy snow storm.

The destroyed city seemed even more desolate under a blanket of snow. At the famous Cathedral, still standing but smashed and battered, the snow drifted through great holes in the roof. Cardinal Mercier himself showed us through the historic building and told us that of an original population of 200,000 there now remained in Rheims some 3,000 half-starved people. The city was a terrible sight, lonesome and broken, each sidewalk still lined with barbed wire and pitted with shell holes.

Among the members of that party was my old friend Eddie Jackson, the photographer, now a Lieutenant but still carrying his camera. Eddie was never content with an ordinary shot. He had to have an unusual angle, and wherever we stopped he could be found diligently climbing a tree or mounting the ruined walls of a shattered building. At one place the destruction was so complete that not a thing was left standing. There was no tree, no wall, not even a rubble heap. The President looked around and said, with a twinkle in his eye, "Well, Eddie, how are you going to take a picture? There is nothing for you to climb up on." Eddie blushed and stammered and the President laughed. "As soon as we come to a spot with a tree or a good high wall we will stop and let you take a picture," he promised.

It was now accepted that we would have to return to Washington and come back again to complete the Peace Treaty. The President had managed to whip the Covenant of the League of Nations into shape, and it was presented to the public. On Friday February 14 we left for Brest. Before taking the train the President talked for an hour and a half to newspapermen. Much of it was off the record, and I find in my diary that he said Clemenceau was doing a lot of objecting but that he would no doubt acquiesce to the majority. He said Hughes of Australia was impossible, was stone deaf and would not read papers furnished him on the subjects under discussion. Early the next day, while people all over the world were reading the text of the Covenant, we boarded the *George Washington*. Midnight found us out of the harbor and on our way. Behind us we left a quagmire of misunderstanding, doubt, fear, suspicion, jealousy, and greed.

It is difficult at this distance and time to separate what I then knew from what later was revealed. I talked a good deal, during my idle hours in Paris, with the American newspapermen—Roy Howard of the United Press, Dick Probert of the Associated Press, and Jack Nevin of the International News Service; and we all voiced theories, opinions, and prophecies about what was taking place in the Holy of Holies. Certain facts were beginning to seem true in spite of all the evidence that was cast against them. The European members of the Conference were more against Wilson than for him. They looked upon him as a highhanded interloper who was taking too much power into his own hands, considering how little, in their judgment, his country had done to win the war. They had their own ideas of how the peace should be made and they wanted no interference from an impractical idealist, which was the polite phrase they used to describe him.

Years later, of course, these very things were admitted by the men themselves. In their autobiographies and memoirs, Clemenceau, Balfour, and Lloyd George confessed that they never sincerely subscribed to the Fourteen Points, and that they plotted to sidetrack as many of them as was possible. Lloyd George was to wear the President down and to deceive him about their intentions. They had made secret treaties among themselves which provided for dividing the spoils of war, and it was Lloyd George who invented the scheme of mandates to cover up this steal. The President accepted the idea of mandates, though in actuality there was never anything but complete possession of the helpless territories and countries by the powers to which they were given in trust.

Thus the President was surrounded at all times by a set of high class connivers, each intent on getting what he wanted for his country while using the President as a front man who would cover the whole dirty business with an aura of international morality and good will. There was Clemenceau, with his bulldog face, his strange animal eyes, and his cotton gloves to cover his eczema. He hated Germany, had no faith in the future of peace, and was determined to smash Germany so that she would not rise again.

There was Lloyd George, with his piercing blue eyes, who was willing to nail the world to a cross for the sake of his re-election at home. There was Orlando, the kind of Italian who could weep over the plight of his country; and with him was the pig-eyed Sonnino, a strawberry blonde with a hooked nose who was not to be trusted.

Against these the President had left Colonel House, a man whose weak spot was his vanity—a weakness administered to by his son-in-law, Gordon Auchincloss. With House, but opposed to him because he was jealous of the fact that House had somewhat pre-empted his position, was Lansing, a fine lawyer with a handsome face that betrayed a slight weakness. The others were able men, but they were handicapped by their honesty: rugged old General Bliss; understanding, intelligent Admiral Benson; diplomatic, gentlemanly Henry White. I could not imagine them hitting below the belt, which seemed the only way to get any place at the Quai d'Orsay.

Thinking of all these things as I stood at the rail that night, I was glad to be going home. Europe was not to my taste. The people were too weary and cynical. Even the royalty, I reflected, had been disillusioning—mild King George, with his sloping and peaceful face, dominated by the majestic Queen Mary; and little Victor Emanuel, a miniature man striding beside the tall elegance of his wife. I wanted to get back to a country where a man could look his wife in the eye without climbing up a ladder, and where, when a friend slapped you on the back, he did not have a knife in his hand.

On the *George Washington* there was published each day a miniature newspaper called *The Hatchet*. The issue of Sunday, February 16, listed the members of our party, which included Franklin D. Roosevelt, Assistant Secretary of the Navy, and Mrs. Roosevelt. There was a long story about the Covenant under the following headline: PRESIDENT AND HIS COMMITTEE SUBMIT MARVELOUS DOCUMENT IN CONSTITUTION OF LEAGUE OF NATIONS BEFORE LEAVING PARIS. A week later, side by side with the story of the celebration of Washington's Birthday by the Presi-

dent and his party, was this headline: IN SENSATIONAL SPEECH BORAH
ATTACKS LEAGUE. I read with uneasiness what Borah had said: "I can
state my position in a single line. There is not a supernational tribunal
nor a supernational government which can be created by wit of man
so well calculated to take care of the public as the conscience and wisdom
of one hundred million people to whom a loving God has entrusted its
keeping and its destiny."

Still, ex-President Taft was continuing his speaking tour in favor of
the League, and such other Republicans as Elihu Root and Charles
Evans Hughes, who had almost beaten the President in 1916, were en-
dorsing it. And the next day when we landed at Boston a great crowd
welcomed us and poured into Mechanics Hall, where the Republican
Governor of Massachusetts, a slight, unimpressive man named Calvin
Coolidge, said:

"We have welcomed the President with a reception more marked
even than that which was accorded to General George Washington;
more united than could have been given at any time during his life
to President Abraham Lincoln. We welcome him as the representative
of a great people, as a great statesman, as one to whom we have entrusted our destinies, and one whom we are sure we will support in
the future in the working out of that destiny, as Massachusetts has sup-
ported him in the past."

The audience cheered wildly, and I looked at the little man with
new interest. The people on the platform were applauding him too,
especially the young Assistant Secretary of the Navy, Mr. Roosevelt.
The President was smiling, happy. He had come home and he had
been received with as much affection by his own people as by the people
of Europe. What could any set of politicians do against the united will
of the masses of the world? He would have his way, and theirs would
be the triumph.

★☆★☆★☆★☆★☆★☆★☆★☆★☆★☆★☆★☆★☆★☆★☆★☆★☆★☆★★☆★★

CHAPTER NINE

Versailles

WE RETURNED to the *George Washington* on the night of March 5, after a week in Washington. We entered the Capital as conquering heroes; we departed playing quite a different role.

February 27—Thursday.

At one P. M., accompanied the President to the Peace Monument, where we headed a parade up Pennsylvania Avenue to the White House, where the President stood to review it. The parade was in honor of the soldiers returned from France. Mrs. Senator Warren on the stand asked me to come to see her before I returned to France. She has a message to send to her brother General Pershing. She intimated she would send him a kiss by me if she dared presume. I assured her the message would be delivered. I feel as if I should call on her as she is a very handsome woman. Very handsome. Lawsy me! These women!

March 4—Tuesday.

At 10:45 A. M., accompanied the President to the Capitol where he occupied his room on the Senate side. The 65th Congress adjourned. No bills signed. Republican filibuster. Serious break with the President on account of the League of Nations being put through by the President without first consulting the people through Congress. Republicans claim President consulting no one but himself and his party, making it possible to claim it as a party asset put through by his administration.

The President brought about these conditions himself, has no one to blame. His letter to people of country to vote only for Democrats was a serious blunder. His failure to appoint men like Taft or Root on

Peace Commission another blunder, and also served to antagonize Republican party. He should have stayed in background and worked in that manner.

At Philadelphia 5:15 P. M. Visited Mrs. Sayre and young baby. Departed 6:15. Arrived New York 8:15. Spoke with Taft at Metropolitan in favor of League. Wild reception. Boarded ship at 10:15.

This time we followed the northern route. The weather again was pleasant and the President enjoyed himself walking the decks. During the first few days he remained in his rooms, resting from the strain of his stay in Washington. An incident which happened after his speech in New York seemed to have upset him a good deal. A committee of Irish-Americans had asked to see him for the purpose of presenting a paper relative to Ireland's claims at the Peace Conference. He agreed to meet them providing they came without their leader, Daniel F. Cohalan, who had been a trouble-maker during the war.

After finishing his speech at the Metropolitan he went to an upstairs room to receive the committee. When Tumulty came in to announce them he admitted that Cohalan was present. The President was angered. He took out his watch and said, "I will wait five minutes. If the rest of them want to come in I will meet them. If not, I will leave." Tumulty pleaded with him, but to no avail. He delivered the ultimatum and the members entered, minus Cohalan. Whatever their mission was it failed, for they were embarrassed and the President was cool and detached, though seething with irritation.

The sea air soon revived his energy and restored his good humor. One day Mrs. Wilson came to the door of his sleeping room and asked me how many entrances there were to his suite. I walked through both suites with her to make an examination, and the President joined us. When we came to his bathroom we discovered a balcony overlooking it. The President asked Mrs. Wilson why a balcony should be built in such an odd spot.

"I have no idea," she said, "unless it was made for the *George Washington* band to occupy so it can play while you are taking a bath."

They laughed together, and they seemed at the moment as happy and as carefree as they had been in the days before the war.

Again we were scheduled to arrive at Brest on the thirteenth, in deference to the President's superstition. He considered thirteen to be his lucky number, and when it fell on Friday, as happened on our first arrival, he believed it to be doubly potent.

It was 8:30 when we dropped anchor, too late for the party to make the night train to Paris. An official party of Frenchmen came aboard, accompanied by Colonel House and his son-in-law, Gordon Auchincloss. When the President saw House he excused himself to the Committee and took the Colonel to his suite. I followed them and took up my watch outside the door. There I was discovered by Jack Nevin of the International News Service, who gave me the news and gossip of the Conference. Rumor had it that Colonel House was letting the water out of the dam which the President had erected. He was collaborating with Lloyd George, Clemenceau, and Orlando, who were using reports of the Senate opposition to the League as ammunition in their attack on the Fourteen Points. England, of course, was hammering away at the second point—freedom of the seas. France was crying for reparations and restrictions on Germany which would keep her weak. Italy wanted all she could get of anything which was being handed out.

As I listened my disgust with Colonel House increased, while I felt increasingly sure that the President would have done better to stay in Washington and let others do the fighting in Paris, preferably Republicans. In this way he would have received credit for everything that was won, while the Republican delegates would have been blamed for anything that was lost.

Jack left me, and after what seemed like a long time Colonel House emerged from the suite, looking disturbed and walking rapidly. As I stepped inside to close the door I saw the President standing, his eyes fixed on me but showing no recognition, his arms hanging loosely at his side. Something in his appearance made me pause for a moment. His face was pale, and seemed drawn and tired. His whole figure expressed dejection. I closed the door, mentally cursing Colonel House.

Next day we were in Paris, and the President and Mrs. Wilson took up residence in a new home, the Château Bischoffsheim, at 11 Place des États-Unis. It was considerably less splendid than the Prince Murat palace, but it was more suited to the President's taste, and he used it more and more as the location of meetings of the Big Four. I returned to the Hotel Crillon, where the Peace Commission was still housed.

The President got down to business immediately, and refused all social appointments. He may have felt already that he was fighting a losing battle in the tricky business of the Peace Treaty, but he kept on working for all the details of his plan, putting more and more emphasis on the League as the means of solving problems which at the moment seemed insoluble. He felt that whatever mistakes were made in trying to settle the European puzzle now could be rectified at future meetings of the League. To see that the League was put into the Treaty and accepted by all the participants was the strategic objective of his whole campaign. He got plenty of opposition.

Colonel House, of course, had played into the hands of this opposition. In fact, from the beginning his peculiar reaction to his position as Peace Commissioner had been troublesome. He was supposed to be an undercover man, an adviser who kept his presence and his personality in the background. This was the role he had played at home. In Paris he succumbed to the temptation of the first of the Seven Deadly Sins— Pride—and began to drink the champagne of fame and publicity.

On our first visit there was trouble because Lansing resented the fact that meetings to discuss the League of Nations were held in the Colonel's suite instead of in his. He was right, of course, since he was Secretary of State. Someone told the President about it, and he immediately changed the scene of the meetings to Lansing's rooms, where thereafter they were held. Now Jack Nevin came to me and said that the Colonel was holding press conferences, which he was not authorized to do. When the newspapermen came to the hotel seeking information, they were led to the Colonel's suite by Gordon Auchincloss, his son-in-law.

There was plenty of evidence that something of this nature was going on, because many of the newspapers and magazines which arrived from home contained articles praising Colonel House and hailing him as the genius of the American delegation. The same idea was popping up in the British and French papers. In a sly way the President was being discredited.

"Why don't you tell Grayson about it?" I said. "I don't want to carry the tale second-hand."

Jack told the doctor, who was skeptical. A day later the two met, and Jack offered to prove his statement.

"Come up on the roof with me," he said.

They got into the elevator and went to the top of the Crillon where they found Colonel House with a group of newspapermen, with whom he was being photographed.

Grayson was convinced, and related what he had seen to Mrs. Wilson. They decided not to tell the President, first because it would seem like tattling, which he would resent, and second because there was no need to warn the President further in the matter. The Colonel through weakness had betrayed his trust and given in to the foreign delegates, and this, to a man whose only weakness was that he would give in to nobody, was unforgiveable. From the time of our second arrival in Paris the President had little use for Colonel House's opinions or advice. The disillusion and sorrow he experienced after talking with the Colonel at Brest turned slowly into an icy contempt, which was obvious to anybody well acquainted with the Wilsonian character.

This was the genesis of the famous "break" between the two.

On the night of April 1 I was standing outside his door when the man from our Embassy in Paris who had been acting as confidential go-between for the President and Clemenceau, called to deliver a paper. The door was left ajar and as it closed I heard the President say vehemently:

"I will not stand for it. Not another minute! I will put a stop to all proceedings and go home first! Tell that to Clemenceau!"

Two days later, on the third, he took to his bed with a bad cold. His fever went up and his chest was affected. Still he went on talking with Clemenceau, Lloyd George and Orlando, who visited him in his room.

Mrs. Wilson and Dr. Grayson—he was now an Admiral, having received the promotion just before our first trip abroad—protested against the meetings, but the President insisted on holding them. He was sick, but more afraid than sick—afraid that he would be by-passed or blocked out or in some way flimflammed if he took the rest he deserved and got out of touch with the Conference.

Mrs. Wilson hovered over him like an anxious mother. Several times at night, when I was on duty, she called me in to help her in shifting his bed or raising the heavy windows. He did not stir as the bed moved or the windows rattled, sleeping deeply and peacefully, but looking more like a dead man than the living hope of the world.

On the seventh it was announced that he had sent for the *George Washington* to come immediately to Brest. The reaction was immediate and violent. Next day Lloyd George, Clemenceau and Orlando, came to see him in the study. The day after that the President was able to get up and take an automobile ride. The following morning his three pals were again at his study door, and from then on things moved with reasonable speed, and our hope of getting out of Paris before the beginning of the next war seemed possible of realization. Our plan, as I wrote to my mother on March 18 was to "return to the United States about June 1 or even sooner, call an extra session of Congress say for July 1, and in the meantime make a tour of the Western states in the interest of the Peace Treaty and the League of Nations."

But the President remained spent, exhausted and haggard. His prostrating illness had left him very weak. He never did regain his physical strength, and his weakness of body naturally reacted upon his mind. He lacked his old quickness of grasp, and tired easily. It was noteworthy, too, that he now saw Colonel House much less frequently, and that their relations were strained. Once the Colonel had called once or more daily; now he seldom appeared, and when he did his reception was chilly.

The next eruption was in Italy. Orlando and Sonnino insisted on Italy taking Fiume, which was scheduled to go to Yugoslavia, giving this new country an Adriatic port. Orlando left the Conference and returned to Italy. Almost overnight the attitude of the Italian people toward the President changed. From being a God he changed into an emissary of the devil. In Fiume an insulting cartoon depicting the President wearing a German helmet and faced by a question mark, was plastered on the walls of public buildings and on shop windows. The representative of our Army Intelligence in Fiume, Major Charles Wellington Furlong, reported that when he protested to General Grazioli and asked that they be removed at once the General smiled sarcastically and said, "I assure you they will all be removed within twenty-four hours."

"That's twenty-four hours too late," Major Furlong said.

Grazioli bowed. "I will give orders for their removal shortly."

Two hours later not a single poster had been removed. Major Furlong then toured the town in a Fiat and did the job himself.

Orlando finally returned to Paris and the meetings proceeded.

One day a representative of our State Department came to me on a confidential errand.

"Tomorrow or the day after tomorrow the Japanese situation will be discussed," he said. "When the President goes to the Quai d'Orsay tomorrow he will have all the information on the Japanese in his briefcase. It's very hot and the Nips would give anything to get their hands on it. I want you to keep your eyes on it and see that it doesn't get out of the President's hands even for a moment."

The next morning the President emerged with his briefcase and I watched it carefully until it disappeared into the Holy of Holies, still safely under his arm. As soon as the session was over and some of the members came out I stepped inside the door and looked for the President. He was standing by the little school-type desk at which he sat during the meetings. There was one for each of the political giants, and it amused me to see them sitting there, like children waiting for the teacher.

The President was engrossed in conversation with Lloyd George. The briefcase lay on top of his desk. Still talking to Lloyd George, the President walked off and left it. I was so surprised that for the moment

I did nothing. The President had a genius for detail, and he was always catching others in such misdemeanors. My job was to follow him, but before doing so I had to get the briefcase. Standing not four feet from it, with their eyes glued to it, were two members of the Japanese delegation. I walked to the desk, picked up the precious portfolio, and bowed to the two Japs, who bowed and smiled in return. "So sorry, you bastards!" I said.

I caught up with the President as he was getting into his overcoat. I put the briefcase on the table in front of him, where his hat was resting. Still absorbed in his conversation with Lloyd George he picked up his hat, put it on and turned away without noticing what I had done. Lloyd George, however, watched me as I picked up the briefcase for a second time, and gave me something between a knowing look and a wink. It was a telltale sign that the President was no longer at his peak, and was tiring fast, and since it was Lloyd George's task to wear him down he must have felt a twinge of triumph at this indication of success.

The two separated and I got into the President's automobile with him. I rode in front with the chauffeur. Just before we reached the Place de la Concorde the President suddenly leaned forward and said to me, "Starling, we will have to go back to the Quai d'Orsay. I have left my papers on my desk."

"I beg your pardon, Mr. President," I said. "You gave them to me to keep for you when you put on your coat. I have the briefcase here on my lap."

With a quick sigh of relief he said, "You had better give it to me. I must not let it out of my hands."

What was in the briefcase I do not know, but before we entered the war the President told many of his intimates that one reason America should not enter the conflict was that she would be weakened for her eventual struggle with Japan. He was sure it would come some day.

The Drafting Committee was now at work and we were all impatient, standing around in small groups, waiting for the mail pouches and discussing news from home. One day Admiral Grayson, Ray Stannard Baker and I were together, and the Admiral was trying to get a rise out of me by asking Baker what he thought of a Presbyterian Elder who was blessed by the Pope. He said that Arthur Krock of the Louisville *Courier-Journal* had written an article about the Pope and me which had put me in bad at home. To answer him I produced a clipping from the Hopkinsville *New Era* entitled, "Three Fine Americans." There was a photograph of the President, General Pershing, and me, walking together. Actually, I was a step behind, in my accustomed position, but in the picture I appeared to be abreast of the other two. The text was by my friend Tom Underwood, and was to the general effect that the President and the General were in good company. Grayson ran off with the clipping, saying he was going to show it to the President, which he did. Brooks reported to me that the President laughed when he read the story and told the Admiral that the men in Starling's country were the most amazing creatures he had ever seen, and that he was proud to be considered their equal.

On the seventh of May the terms of the Treaty were handed to the German Peace Delegates in the dining room of the Trianon at Versailles. The Germans were ill at ease. Clemenceau handed the document to Count Brockdorff-Rantzau and told him in a few words that he and his colleagues would be allowed a maximum of fifteen days in which to make their answer, and that all comments and pleas must be made in writing.

The President now allowed himself some relaxation. He attended the horse races and went to the theatre. One day I accompanied him on a tour of the battlefields, along with Admiral Grayson and Bernard Baruch. I wrote in my diary: "I notice that Frenchmen take extraordinary care of their horses. They are all fat and well groomed. Male horses are never cut, yet they remain gentle, fat and easy to handle."

On May 29 the Germans submitted their reply. They refused to accept many of the points in the Treaty and demanded immediate membership in the League of Nations. They were given more time to think it over. Then the delegation was recalled to Berlin, and another took its place. When these men arrived the haggling continued. It seemed that we would never get home.

The seventeenth, eighteenth and nineteenth of June were spent in Belgium, where the President and Mrs. Wilson, along with the official members of their party, were the guests of King Albert and Queen Elizabeth. A letter to my mother describing the trip says:

We then rode to Ypres and its horrible battleground. I shall never forget this scene. Not a brick left, everything mowed down. Everything is just as it was after the Germans were last driven back. I stood up in our automobile and looked over several miles of country, seeing before me overturned British tanks, wrecked cannons, smashed airplanes, bones of dead horses, shells still unexploded, shell cases, wrecked pill-boxes, and stumps of dead trees. At one point southeast of Ypres not even a stump was left, and the shell holes overlapped each other.

I never expect to see such desolation again, and yet it inspired me with admiration for the English. It is proof of the British soldier's bravery and doggedness. At this point five hundred thousand of them were killed.

Returned to Brussels at 6:30 P.M. and left the President and Mrs. Wilson at the Palace, where they attended a state dinner. At 10:20 I rode to the Palace from our hotel, arranged the cars, and then looked at the Palace and watched the guests walk back from the dining room to the King's private wing. It reminded me of ancient times, as I remembered them from Sir Walter Scott's novels. First came President Wilson and Queen Elizabeth, then King Albert and Mrs. Wilson, then the officers in attendance upon them, each with a lady on his arm. The beauty of the procession was improved by the architecture of the palace. The main building is square and massive. On each side is a narrow wing, enclosed in glass and illuminated with soft lights. It was down one of these wings that the party walked as I watched.

Bernard Baruch told me he had a beautiful woman as his partner. He said she was so pretty he forgot to eat and actually missed two courses of the dinner.

At last the Treaty was ready to be signed. On the afternoon of Tuesday, June 24, the President went to Versailles to inspect the Hall of Mirrors, where the signing was to take place. Clemenceau and Balfour met him there, and after looking at the hall they made a tour of the palace itself, going through secret doors and up and down concealed stairways. The President seemed to enjoy this part of it, and also showed interest in the Chamber of Deputies, where the guide pointed out the seat occupied by Victor Hugo, and the one in which Clemenceau sat forty years before.

On Saturday the twenty-eighth I dressed in my cutaway, to the envy of the other members of the Detail. Early in the week we had been told we would not be allowed to enter the Hall of Mirrors. I refused to accept this ruling, at least for myself, and after a lot of wire-pulling and some tall talking I got a special pass which allowed me to enter the room as the President's attendant. I stood behind him during the whole ceremony.

What happened was this. During the long weeks of the spring while the meetings dragged on interminably and my boss was badgered on every side by what I came to regard as a bunch of crooks in silk hats, my Kentucky blood rose slowly in temperature. When I was told that I could not enter the Hall of Mirrors I got mad. To certain influential members of the French government with whom I had become friendly I spoke in frank disgust. This outburst gained for me the permission I sought. But I was still mad when I jammed my silk hat on my head, purposely tilting it to a blue grass angle to look as little like the rest of the peacocks as possible.

As soon as we arrived at Versailles I went to the Hall of Mirrors and inspected the entire room. It is oblong in shape, fronting on the East, where the wall is composed of immense French windows. The entrance is on the North side, and here the distinguished guests sat, flanking the main passage. On the South side the press was seated. The Delegates framed the center of the room on three sides. At the center of the long table on the West side sat Lloyd George, Clemenceau and the President. In front of them, in the very center of the room, was the table containing the Treaty. At the end of the table of delegates, near the entrance passage, sat the Germans.

As I took up my stand behind the President I noticed a Frenchman staring at me. Finally he came over and spoke to me. I gathered that he wanted to know what I was doing there, and that he was telling me to go away. My blood began to move toward the boiling point. I took him aside and asked him if he spoke English. He said he did.

"Then get this," I said. "I am an American, and I am damned sick and tired of the way we Americans have been treated over here. I am a member of the Secret Service and it is my job to watch the President. That's why I am here and that's what I intend to do, and I don't intend to let any snivelling little pipsqueak in a hired suit interfere with me.

"Now you get the hell out of here and let me alone or I will break you into pieces and hand you around for souvenirs!"

While I was emptying my wrath over him his eyes grew bigger and bigger and the points of his moustache curled slowly downward. Without a word he turned and left me and went back to his place, and all during the ceremony he kept his eyes on me. I do not know whether he was trying to figure out who I was or whether he was afraid I would go after him. He was also wearing a cutaway and perhaps he thought this would impress me. It didn't. I knew he was superintendent of buildings for the palace.

Just before three o'clock the delegates entered and took their seats. At three the Germans were brought in. There were only two, Mueller and Doctor Bell. Mueller was tall and raw-boned, with light hair and eyes sunken and weary with anxiety. Doctor Bell was slender and dark, with a small neck and a large head, his hair cut short and worn in a pompadour. The eyes of both were downcast. They wore spectacles, celluloid collars, and black bow ties. At 3:07 they were brought to the table in the center of the room and shown where to sign. Nobody had risen when they entered; the atmosphere was one of grim hostility. They might as well have been brought in handcuffed, allowed to put down their names and then handcuffed again. The spectacle, gratifying as it was to the vengeful French spectators, did not appeal to me. Long afterward I had the opportunity of telling Franklin D. Roosevelt, during the Second World War, that I hoped there would be no immediate peace treaty and that the passions of war would be allowed to cool off first.

Now President Wilson rose and went to the table, followed by the American delegates. When they had signed, the British, headed by Lloyd George, put their signatures to the document. The French were next, then the Italians, then the Japanese, and then the smaller countries. At five minutes after four it was finished and the seal of each delegate had been affixed.

As we left the building Clemenceau, elated, took the President's arm and walked him, along with Lloyd George and Orlando, through the gardens, where immense crowds were gathered. The people could no longer be held back, and they crowded around the Big Four. I fought to keep my place and managed to stay between the President and his well wishers, but it was a dangerous and uncomfortable situation. The other members of the Detail worked as hard as I did to keep a small space open around the four men as they walked. Finally we got our charge safely back to his car and returned to Paris.

We were packed and ready to leave, and after the banquet that night at the Elysee Palace, where President and Madame Poincaré were hosts, we left by train for Brest. At two o'clock the next afternoon the *George Washington* steamed out of the harbor, escorted by four French destroyers. The President stood on the bridge, his head bared, while the band played the Star Spangled Banner. Thus we said good-bye for the second and last time to France, and sailed home with the Peace Treaty of Versailles, which contained the Covenant of the League of Nations. Everyone of us hoped and prayed, and at the moment believed, that at Paris an end had been made of war, and an age of peace begun.

The next day we were well at sea, in pleasant weather. I walked around the deck with the President and Mrs. Wilson. The President stumbled against one of the iron rings set into the deck and used for lashing the life boats in heavy weather. Next time around he stumbled against it again, although it was in plain sight. When it happened a third time Mrs. Wilson looked at me questioningly. As we approached it on the fourth turn I stepped ahead of him and forced him to turn out from it. Mrs. Wilson followed my example the next time, and so on, the President not suspecting. He was pale and haggard, a tired man, and it seemed to me that since his illness in Paris he lacked the co-ordination of both mind and body which always before had been his outstanding characteristic.

The ship was crowded with returning soldiers, many of them wounded. There were French war brides aboard, too, and the talk among every group was of the country we were approaching, not the one we had left. But it was not going to be quite the place we had left. The ship newspaper, *The Hatchet,* carried a gloomy obituary in the issue of July 1. John Barleycorn was dead. Prohibition was in effect. When we docked at Hoboken the country would be dry. We spent July 4 at sea, and the President addressed the soldiers and sailors. They swarmed about him, perching on every available spot, while he delivered an inspiring address that sounded like his old self.

"I was thinking today that a new freedom has come to the peoples of the world out of this war," he said. "It has no date. It has no Fourth of July. There has nowhere been written a Declaration of Independence. The only date I can think of for it is the eleventh of last November . . . and perhaps some of these days we shall date the freedom of the peoples from the eleventh of November, 1918.

"The laws of freedom are these: accommodate your interests to other people's interests, that you shall not insist on standing in the light of other people but that you shall make a member of a team of yourself and nothing more or less, and that the interests of the team shall take precedence in everything that you do to your interest as an individual.

"That is freedom . . . it takes a lot of intelligence to be free . . . that is what makes you free, and my confident ambition for the United States is that she will know in the future how to make each Fourth of July as it comes grow more distinguished and more glorious than its predecessor . . . this is the most tremendous Fourth of July that man ever imagined, for we have opened its franchises to all the world."

While he was speaking Jack Dempsey was battering down Jess Willard at Toledo, and all over America bootleggers were delivering their first orders to the back rooms and cellars which had taken the place of the condemned saloons. The nurses on the *George Washington* still wore skirts to their ankles and let the sea breeze put color in their cheeks, but ashore dresses were crawling toward the knees, and grandmothers tried out their granddaughters' lipsticks. The jazz age had begun.

Our last night on board was a happy one. Before the picture show the ship's quartet, which included Chief Moran as bass and myself as baritone, sang three songs, "Carry Me Back to Ol' Virginny," "Good Night Ladies," and "Love's Old Sweet Song." Then I sang "Kentucky Babe." When the moving picture was over we all stood and sang, softly, "God Be With You Till We Meet Again."

The next morning, Tuesday, July 8, I stood on the upper bridge of the Captain's deck with the President and Admiral Grayson, watching the escort of twenty-two destroyers and four battleships, and the assortment of yachts and tugs loaded with members of the various reception committees. Our voyage of crusade was almost over, and I thought of something I wanted to say to Admiral Grayson.

"I want to thank you for your kindness and thoughtfulness in looking out for the Secret Service men," I said. "You have been more than nice to us and we appreciate it."

"You got no more than you deserved," he said. Then, lowering his voice he continued, "In fact your good work and faithfulness has so pleased the President and Mrs. Wilson, and they are so grateful for your loyalty, that in a few days you will get some good news."

We were met by Vice President Marshall and Governor Alfred E. Smith, among others, and the ceremonies of reception took most of the day. It was ten-thirty at night before we got to Washington. The summer heat had already begun. It struck us as we walked out of Union Station.

A few days later Chief Moran sent for me. He seemed very happy about something.

"Star," he said, "the President has sent word to me by Admiral Grayson that he wants you substantially promoted. I am more than willing to recommend you for a raise, and it will be from six to eight a day."

Then he added, smiling, "In all my thirty years experience here I have never known an agent to be promoted two dollars at a time, nor have I ever known a President to ask for and insist upon the promotion of one of our men."

On July 10, two days after his return, the President put the Treaty before the Senate and the trouble began. The battle lines had been drawn already, and the same old series of conferences, meetings, memoranda proposing changes and modifications which had plagued the President in Paris began all over again. He contended that he had no moral right to alter a single phrase of a document he had signed in full faith with other nations. The Senators had decided that they were the cooks and that they were going to have a hand in the preparation of the broth, even though it already had been set on the table for them to drink.

July passed, and August, with the heavy heat of Washington taking its toll of energy and nerves. The Western trip was now on, now off. Doctor Grayson and Mrs. Wilson opposed it on the grounds that the President's physical condition was not up to so strenuous an effort. Grayson, in fact, was convinced that his patient would not survive the ordeal. But the President was determined. He saw no other way of defeating the Senators. He was a man of the people, and to the people he would go, asking them to insist that the freedom he had won for them be accepted by Congress.

We left Washington on the evening of September 3, and our schedule said that we would be in Louisville on September 29. There I was to leave the train and go to Hopkinsville for my annual vacation. My mother was ill, and I was anxious to see her.

The trip began smoothly, with speeches at Columbus, Indianapolis, St. Louis, Kansas City, Des Moines, Omaha, Sioux Falls and St. Paul. The crowds were large and enthusiastic, and the President was in top form. Swinging up through the colorful Bad Lands of South Dakota we stopped to enjoy a particularly beautiful view. As usual we of the Detail took a look under the train before starting again, and discovered that we had picked up three passengers, Knights of the Road, with "bindles" and shaggy beards. They were the most happy, carefree men I have ever seen. They bowed and apologized profusely for getting on the President's train. They wondered, politely, whether he would shake hands with them. He was glad to do it, and offered them a lift. They declined, saying they would wait for the regular train. As we moved away they lifted their hats and bowed again. I think the President envied them, for he smiled wistfully as they disappeared in the distance.

From Bismarck we went to Billings, where a group of small boys carrying flags crowded around the rear platform to hear the President. As the train began to move away one of them handed his flag up to Mrs. Wilson and said, "Give it to him!" She accepted the flag, and I noticed one of the other boys, obviously thinking fast, plunge his hand into his pocket. Looking up he caught my eye, and pulling his hand out of his pocket he began to run after the train. We were moving rather quickly now, so I hooked my leg through the railing and leaned down to him. He reached out until his hand touched mine, running as fast as he could. "Give him this!" he gasped. His hand put something into mine and I straightened up. Turning to the President I opened my fist —lying in it was a dime.

We went to Helena, Coeur d'Alene, Spokane and Portland, where one of the newspaper correspondents, Ben F. Allen, of the Cleveland *Plain Dealer,* was killed in an automobile accident while we were sightseeing along the Columbia River. We did not see the accident—it happened at the end of the procession—but it made us jittery, and from then on nothing seemed to go right.

We went to Tacoma and then to Seattle, where the President reviewed the Pacific fleet. We were to go to the *Oregon,* and the Admiral's barge was to take us there, but it did not arrive and a naval launch was used instead. Our party was too large for such a small boat, and when we shoved off it heeled over until the rail was almost under water. Then we rammed another launch, and I was certain we would all be pitched into the water. Finally we reached the *Oregon,* but while more than a hundred ships passed in review I and the other members of the Detail spent every minute making sure that the arrangements for our return to shore were safe.

Now we went down the coast to San Francisco, San Diego, and Los Angeles. At Los Angeles the mysterious Mrs. Peck came to visit the President. She turned out to be a drab, faded woman of middle age, and how anyone could have cast her in a romantic role was more than I could imagine. From Los Angeles we went to Reno, then to Salt Lake City, then to Cheyenne, and from there to Denver. By now the President was on his last legs. Nothing but courage kept him going. In his speeches he had begun to repeat himself a little, and several times I noticed that he lost the thread of his thought and wandered into a new subject.

The crowds were tremendous and the applause thunderous. But behind us, in every city where the President had spoken, his enemies also were making speeches—Senators Reed, Borah, and Johnson. They were pointing out to the same people who had listened to the President's inspired pleas, that the Treaty was not a good one, that the Fourteen Points had been twisted and blunted, that such things as heavy reparations and questionable boundaries were certain to produce trouble, and that the Covenant of the League required us to send our soldiers to fight in any squabble that might arise in the future, however petty and remote from our interests. The crowds which gathered for these speeches were growing larger, and their response more enthusiastic.

Even the President knew that much of this criticism was justified. He knew it better than anyone else, in fact, for it was the measure of his defeat in Paris. He knew that he had been tricked, that he had been preyed upon, that he had been beaten down until the peace was tailored to Britain's theory of the "balance of power," France's desire for a weak Germany, and the general notion that the Wilson plan was too idealistic. But he had his main objective. Outpointed in every round, he believed he had won by a knockout in getting the League into the Treaty itself. He was far too intelligent to suppose that all the arguments could be settled once and for all at the Peace Conference. The League was to be a perpetual conference, shifting and rearranging the details of the body of the peace as time and occasion demanded. If only he could get the Treaty ratified, the League would take care of all the points under discussion.

On the morning of Thursday, September 25, the President spoke in the auditorium at Denver. At eleven o'clock we left for Pueblo. As we neared the city the President, sitting on the rear platform, asked about the arrangements for the afternoon. Tom Brahaney, Rudolph Forster's assistant, told him that he was to make a visit to the Fair Grounds to greet a crowd of people before going to the auditorium for his speech. The idea seemed to enrage him.

"Who authorized such an idiotic idea?" he demanded.

Brahaney explained that the appearance at the Fair Grounds was included in the original plans approved in Washington by the President himself. The President contradicted him.

"Send for Tumulty," he said, "and tell him to bring the original program."

Brahaney went to get Tumulty and the latter brought the document in question, which included the Fair Ground's visit. It was signed "Okeh, W.W." The President snorted.

"Any damn fool who was stupid enough to approve such a program has no business in the White House," he said.

Then he turned to me and told me to send word ahead to Dick Jervis, the advance man, that under no circumstances would he go to the Fair Grounds.

When we got to Pueblo the reception committee pleaded against the change in plan. Some ten thousand people were assembled at the Fair Grounds, and to disappoint them would create a bad impression. They begged the President at least to ride around the track and wave his hand. Reluctantly, and perhaps thinking of the enemies who were hot on his trail, he agreed, and that is the way it was done. When we returned to the city and stopped at the auditorium I walked beside him from the car to the entrance. There was a single step. He stumbled on it, and I caught him. I kept my hand on his arm, and almost lifted him up the steps to the platform. He made no objection. In the past he had refused any suggestion of physical assistance from me, even when we were battling our way through large crowds.

While he spoke I stood close behind him, afraid he might collapse at any moment. Much of his speech was mumbled; he mouthed certain words as if he had never spoken them before. There were long pauses. He had difficulty following the trend of his thought. It was a travesty of his usual brilliant delivery and fine logic. His voice was weak, and every phrase was an effort for his whole body. Once he wept. We left at five o'clock, bound for Wichita. In the cool of the evening the train stopped, and I was called to go with him and Mrs. Wilson for a walk. Doctor Grayson thought the exercise in the open country would do him good.

I followed the two down a dusty country road, until they reached a wooden bridge over a stream. There they paused, staring at the water. Then they returned, the President walking slowly, lifting his feet that were once so light, as if they were weighted and shackled.

Back on the train I crawled into my bunk and slept until early next morning. In the corridor I met Brooks. He told me that during the night the President had suffered what appeared to be a stroke. He was in a state of collapse.

"It's all over now," the faithful valet said gloomily.

I hurried back to the President's car and found Mrs. Wilson, Admiral Grayson, and Tumulty in conference. The rest of the trip was to be abandoned. The train was to proceed to Wichita, but was to stop on the outskirts. There we were to meet with the local committee and explain the situation.

This was done, and Jervis was told to cancel the remainder of the engagements. The railway officials arranged an immediate run direct to Washington. With drawn blinds we raced through the city and headed East.

We would be in St. Louis late that night or early the next morning, but I did not now expect to leave the train there, taking it for granted

that I would go on to Washington. During the evening Mrs. Wilson
sent for me.

"Mr. Starling," she said, "I don't want the President's illness to interfere with your visit to your Mother. We both want you to leave us at
St. Louis as you had planned and we want you to stay at home until
you are assured your mother is well. Before you leave the train we want
you to come back and see us. We both have little tokens that we wish
you to take to her."

When I went back to the car the President was reclining on a couch,
wrapped in a dressing gown. Otherwise he was fully dressed. The left
side of his face seemed to have fallen a little, but he was so wan and
tired that I could have been mistaken in this. He offered me his right
hand. I pressed it, but did not give him a handshake, for he looked as
if such a vigorous treatment would be painful.

"I want you to know how sorry I am," I said. "I will be praying for
you until you recover, and I am sure it will be soon."

He smiled, and now I saw for certain that only the right side of his
face responded to his command.

"Thank you, Starling," he said. "I want you to take something to
your mother for me."

His gift for her was a beautiful shawl. Mrs. Wilson added two large
boxes of candy. I was unable to speak. The fact that they in their own
grief should remember me and my trouble filled me with a sense of
gratitude. I shook Mrs. Wilson's hand and departed.

It was half past three in the morning when we arrived at St. Louis.
In the yard I met R. S. Mitchell, Chief Special Agent for the St. Louis
Terminal. He was an old friend, a native of Bowling Green who had
served with me in the Spanish-American War. He took me into Union
Station, to the Chief Despatcher's office. I had four hours to wait for my
train.

I sat and looked at the big board, watching the little red light that was
the President's train moving out of the yards and on to the main line.
Suddenly I felt Mitchell's hand on my shoulder.

"What's the matter?" he said.

"What do you mean what's the matter?" I answered.

"You're crying, you damn fool!" he said. "Come on with me. You need a drink!"

With the shawl over one arm and the boxes of candy tucked under the other, I followed him down the stairs.

CHAPTER TEN

Wilson—The Tragedy

WHEN NEXT I saw the President it was spring of 1920. The Treaty and the League had been defeated, the Prince of Wales and the King and Queen of the Belgians had come to the White House and gone, Secretaries Lansing and Lane had resigned, and the hostile Senate had sent Senators Fall and Hitchcock to the White House on a spying expedition, to ascertain the truth of rumors that the President was mentally unsound.

I remember the day the two Senators came. I knew Senator Fall well; he was a dramatic old fellow with far too much sweetness and light to be genuine. When he came down on the elevator after the visit I asked him how he had found the President. "If there is something wrong with his mind I would like to get the same ailment," he said. Brooks reported gleefully to me that the President was never more witty than with the Senators. When Fall told him they had been praying for him, he said, "Which way?"

Lansing resigned at the President's request, after violating good taste and the law by calling unofficial Cabinet meetings in his office. Bainbridge Colby replaced him. Lane resigned after the President refused to approve his idea of leasing government oil lands to private companies, something which had been made possible by a recent law. During this period also the President vetoed the Volstead Act. Considering the history of the next ten years these two decisions alone should prove that there was nothing wrong with Woodrow Wilson's judgment at this time.

He had suffered a second stroke soon after the first, and now when we saw him his left side was badly affected. He could walk but a few steps, and these with the aid of a cane. For longer journeys he used a wheelchair, and in this he made his first appearance before us on a warm day in April. We took him in the elevator to the basement, then rolled the chair through a door which leads to the New England garden on the East side of the grounds. There he sat in a protected corner formed by the jutting end of the East Wing. The spot was usually warm and sunny, and commanded an excellent view of the vista to the South. Soon we built a platform in the driveway at the South Entrance, so that the wheelchair could be pushed up it to a position level with the floor of the tonneau. Then the President would stand, and we would lift him into the car and place him in the right hand corner, arranging his cape and adjusting his cap, so that when he appeared on the streets there was no indication that anything was wrong with him.

When the first circus came to town in May, we made arrangements to have the parade leave Pennsylvania Avenue at the south end of the Treasury and come north on East Executive Avenue, returning then to Pennsylvania Avenue after passing by the portico of the East Wing, where we seated the President. With him, in addition to Mrs. Wilson, was little Gordon Grayson, the Admiral's son, who had become his playmate and companion. Gordon wanted a balloon so I went and got him one. In a few minutes he managed to burst it and I had to get him another. After that we made the same arrangements with every circus that played Washington, and the clowns and other performers made a habit of waving to the President and performing a few of their tricks for him in the street. He and his little friend Gordon were enthralled.

A moving picture machine was installed in the White House, and this helped to atone for the theatre, which he missed a great deal. As soon as he was strong he began to attend it again.

We conspired in every way to give him comfort and solace. When he was to go for a ride some of us organized a group to stand at the gate as he returned, and we told them to cheer as he passed through.

The first time it happened, when we went to lift him from the car after driving around to the back, there were tears in his eyes.

"You see," he said to Mrs. Wilson, "they still love me!"

But however sound his mind remained, his temper was the worse for the defeat he had suffered and the illness he was undergoing. Frequently he was irascible, and we had trouble evading his unreasonable orders without embarrassment. He got the idea that no automobiles should pass us while we were driving, despite the fact that we proceeded at a very moderate rate of speed, frequently going at fifteen or twenty miles an hour so he could enjoy the scenery. Whenever a car passed us he would order the Secret Service car to pursue it and bring back the driver for questioning—a repetition of his conduct of a few years before with the watchman at the Munitions Building.

We always told him that the car was going too fast to be overhauled. Then he decided that he wanted to be a justice of the peace so that he could arrest these drivers and try their cases. We told him it would not suit the dignity of the President.

This may sound as if he were concerning himself with petty affairs, but sick as he was and defeated as he had been he was plotting to get the Democratic nomination for a third term. He actually sent Bainbridge Colby to the convention at San Francisco with instructions to have his picture thrown on a screen at a psychological moment, for the purpose of stampeding the delegates in his favor. Colby carried out instructions, but the ruse failed. When he was told of it the President unleashed a tornado of masterful profanity.

When I heard, by way of Brooks, of this magnificent effort to win a battle that was already lost, I could not but think of the last square of French soldiers at Waterloo, as described by Victor Hugo in *Les Misérables*. They stood at the foot of Mont St. Jean, and they were commanded by an officer named Cambronne. Hugo wrote of them:

"When this legion had become only a handful, when their colors were but a rag, when their ammunition was exhausted, and muskets were clubbed, and when the pile of corpses was greater than the living group, the victors felt a species of sacred awe, and the English artillery ceased firing . . . an English general . . . shouted to them, 'Brave Frenchmen, surrender!'

"Cambronne answered, 'Merde!' "

Cox and Franklin D. Roosevelt won the nomination. At Chicago Harding and Coolidge were named by the Republicans, Harding coming to the front during the deadlock between General Leonard Wood and Governor Frank Lowden of Illinois. Cox and Roosevelt came to Washington and visited the President. He gave them an inspiring talk on the meaning of the League of Nations, and the absolute necessity for its success if the world was to be kept from destroying itself. Both were deeply impressed, and neither ever forgot the President's words. I know this because in later years they told me so, and one of them, Roosevelt, kept constantly before him the vision of what was intended for the League, as he fought the terrible results of its failure.

They promised to support the League, and they did, but their campaign was foredoomed to failure. The Republicans were riding a wave of reactionary feeling, and so easy was their success that they could hardly believe it themselves. The only thing that rose to trouble them was a charge that Harding had negro blood. The President himself squelched this report; he refused to allow it to be circulated.

The visit of Cox and Roosevelt, and the promise they made him, improved both his spirits and his health. I find that I noted this in a letter to my mother, and that I also added:

The President and his family were talking about the Secret Service men, and someone remarked that they were always looking at him when in a crowd, instead of looking at the crowd. The President spoke up and said, "Starling never looks at me, he looks at the crowd." I am glad he feels that way about it for he is observant and exacting. He knows when you are doing all that you can. He has taught school so long that he knows only his way, and it is just this that has caused him to break down. He has tried to do the work of four men, because he knew that if he did it, it would be done well. I am glad to say that he is slowly but surely improving. In the meantime Mrs. Wilson is as sweet and gracious as ever. She is a darling.

We stayed in Washington through all of the summer, taking our recreation by way of automobile rides. Because he had determined to endure the heat the President thought that all of his official family should do likewise. There is no doubt that he was cantankerous. When Admiral Grayson said he wanted to take his family up to New Jersey for a few weeks, the President replied gloomily, "All right. I suppose Tumulty will be going next. Everyone is leaving me."

There was no reason why Admiral Grayson should not take a vacation, since the President was now in the hands of specialists. The incident was in keeping with his reaction a little later when his car had to be overhauled. Mrs. Wilson arranged for the President to use our car, and we were to follow in an extra Cadillac that was available. But when the President learned that these arrangements had been made without first consulting him, he quietly said that he was going to ride in a horse-drawn carriage. So we had to procure an open victoria for him and we followed in an electric car. Back of this, where he would not notice it, was the regular Secret Service car ready for an emergency.

Those who are prone to believe that Mrs. Wilson made the President's decisions for him during this period will do well to ponder. Woodrow Wilson was the most independent person and the most incorruptible character I have ever known. He worshipped Mrs. Wilson, but she could not have made him change his mind about taking another bite of toast.

It is true that Mrs. Wilson and Admiral Grayson stood between the President and the rest of the world while he was ill. How much they kept from him will never be known. They were concerned with his health, and strictly speaking, that was their first loyalty. It is claimed that a compromise might have been brought about between the Senators and the President if certain people had been allowed to see him. In this connection it is said that Colonel House's letters to him were unanswered. Probably they were, for by then the President himself had as small an opinion of the Colonel as had Mrs. Wilson and Admiral Grayson. The notion that a compromise might have been effected is rubbish. It is an attempt to whitewash the men who killed the Treaty and the

League. The only compromise they sought was the President's utter defeat. They got it.

A constant hazard on our automobile rides was the danger of blow-outs. We kept our tires carefully inspected and were generally lucky, but that summer of 1920 found us left behind the President's car several times while we labored with jack and lugwrench. I therefore organized the men into a team and we practiced changing tires for speed, each man training himself in a certain task. The first time we had a chance to try our skill was on the Speedway. Immediately I grabbed the lugwrench, the driver took the jack, while the third man unlocked the tire case and got the new tire ready. When we had finished and again caught up with the President's car we found that the entire time consumed by the operation was five minutes.

The President's rides were the subject of a great deal of speculation on the part of the newspapermen. Covering the White House had become a drab assignment, and the only news of importance was the President's health. Everyone was waiting for the announcement that he could again walk. One day we returned to the White House and instead of going around back drove up to the front door. This was because the ride was not ended. The President and Mrs. Wilson were going to Union Station to meet Mr. and Mrs. Sayre, and they stopped by the White House to find out how the train was marked up and on what track it would arrive. After finding this out we drove off again. The Associated Press man, Deacon Simpson, happened to see us drive away from the front door, and assumed that the President had walked out to get into the car. This was the news he had been waiting for and he rushed off to send out the story, which unfortunately we had to deny.

There were two Simpsons at the Associated Press that summer, Deacon, who is now with the *Tampa* (Florida) *Tribune,* and Kirke, now the association's military analyst. Deacon, who came to the White House, was a South Carolinian, and spoke in a soft voice. He was the soul of courtesy. Kirke, who worked on the desk at the office, was poetic and moody, and often sounded irritable and curt. Tumulty, who spoke with Deacon during the day, often talked by phone with Kirke at night.

He would ask for Simpson, and Kirke would answer. Tumulty was puzzled. He feared that Deacon was a Jekyll and Hyde, perhaps because of liquor; a courtly Southern gentleman by day and an unhappy misanthrope by night. He began to regard Deacon with a suspicious eye. Finally one day he took him aside and gave him a long, roundabout talk on the evils of drink. Deacon agreed with him, and said that he was glad that he personally was unable to drink, since he suffered with stomach trouble. Tumulty then suspected a worse ailment. It was months before he discovered the truth and the amiable Deacon was cleared of the charge of possessing a split personality.

One day Chief Moran called me to his office and with a sour look on his face handed me a small newspaper clipping. It was from a question-and-answer column, and it read:

I have seen recently many photographs of President Wilson, taken while he was touring the country previous to his illness, and in almost every picture of Mr. Wilson taken in his automobile there is a good-looking man standing there smiling. Is he a Secret Service man? He seems always to be smiling, that's why I don't think he is an S.S. man.

Thank you very much for your kindness in answering this question.

M. C. V.

Yes, the "good-looking man" is a Secret Service man, but even an "S.S." man smiles, though probably in a mysterious and inscrutable manner, for one never could be certain at what a member of the Secret Service department is smiling.

It was Edmund Starling who stood on the running board of the President's car while he toured the country. Besides carefully guarding the President Mr. Starling skillfully caught the many hundreds of bouquets of flowers that were thrown at the President by his admirers. So you see a Secret Service man's duties are many and varied!

"Where did this come from? What newspaper was it in?" I asked. Chief Moran stared at me glassily. "I don't know. I don't remember," he said.

Thus does the Secret Service encourage romance. It is no wonder that I remained a bachelor.

In November Harding was elected. With his career in the White House definitely ended the President seemed suddenly more cheerful. Now that there was no more he could do to promote the League of Nations he became interested in what he could do for himself and Mrs. Wilson. Only once did I see him show feeling over the election result. That was when I delivered to him a message sent by Charlie Barker.

"Mr. Barker wants you to know that he is still with you," I said, "and he says he will still follow you anywhere you want to go."

He was sitting in the car, and he looked away from me quickly, for tears had leaped to his eyes. He tried to smile, and when he turned to me the tears had been blinked back.

"Tell Barker I thank him," he said, "but there is nowhere now to go."

It would seem, indeed that there was nowhere to go, as we wandered about the city looking for a suitable house for the couple. They had decided to remain in Washington. It was Mrs. Wilson's home, and the President wanted to use the Congressional Library for his research. He planned to do some writing. Mrs. Wilson had sold her Twentieth Street house, and finding a place that was suited to both their needs, with sufficient library space for the President's thousands of books, was not easy.

They finally settled on a house in the 2300 block of S Street, Northwest, and purchased it. It had been built for bachelor living, and with the addition of some shelves there was sufficient book room. A garage had to be built, and a street level entrance leading to an electric elevator. While these things were being done we rode by every day, and the President was as eager as a bridegroom about getting back to private life and resuming his studying and writing. He seemed to gain new strength as he shed the idea of responsibility and assumed the freedom of a civilian. But he did not forget his dreams. One night at the theatre after Mrs. Wilson and I had walked into the box ahead of him, to screen him while he took his seat, he insisted on being helped to his feet to acknowledge the cheers of the audience.

March 4, 1921, was a fair day. The President-elect and Mrs. Harding came to the White House, where Cabinet members, aides and official guests had gathered. Senator Philander C. Knox was sent by the Senate as escort, and Uncle Joe Cannon represented the House. Brooks brought the President downstairs and he and Mrs. Wilson met the Hardings in the Blue Room. The President was determined to walk that day, and to go out through the front door. He made it all right, and got into the car with Mr. Harding. Mrs. Wilson and Mrs. Harding followed in the next official car, directly behind the Secret Service car. On the way to the Capitol I was at times close to the crowd that lined the way, close enough to hear such remarks as, "Poor President Wilson! This will kill him." "Doesn't the new President look fine and healthy?"

It was traditional for the President and his successor to walk together up the Capitol steps. The President could not attempt it, of course. Harding was informed of this, and chose to walk up alone. After he had left the car it drove to a side entrance, where a platform had been built, and where Brooks awaited the President with his wheelchair. We went through the lower corridors to a private elevator, which discharged us near the President's room. When he was seated behind his desk the ritual went forward. He signed bills, offered congratulations, and then, suddenly there was a hush. Into the room walked the spade-bearded Henry Cabot Lodge, implacable enemy of the League, who more than any man had brought the President's dreams to ruin. As Chairman of the Foreign Relations Committee it was his duty to inform the President that Congress had completed the business before it and stood ready to adjourn unless there was a further message.

The President listened to this formal report. Then he said, simply, "I have no communication to make; I appreciate your courtesy. Good morning."

He did not go into the Senate to see Vice President Coolidge sworn in. It would have taxed him too much. When word was received that Harding had taken the oath of office we left, going by the same route we had followed in entering. In the car now were the ex-President and Mrs. Wilson, Admiral Grayson, Tumulty, Brooks and I. Swiftly we drove to the S Street house, where we found a group of spectators waiting, and Miss Margaret Wilson and Miss Bertha Bolling. We helped

Mr. Wilson out of the car and through the street level entrance. Tenderly we placed him in his wheelchair and rolled it into the elevator. Then we said goodbye to him. He thanked us for our service to him, and for our loyalty.

Turning from him I met Mrs. Wilson. She shook my hand and thanked me. Miss Margaret and Miss Bertha, both weeping, kissed me. I returned to the car, and Robby the chauffeur and I drove back to the Capitol, there to serve another President, if he wanted us. At the moment we did not care whether he did or did not. Our hearts were behind us, where we had left a great man and a great woman.

★☆★☆★☆★☆★☆★☆★☆★☆★☆★☆★☆★☆★☆★☆★☆★☆★☆★☆★☆★

CHAPTER ELEVEN

The Harding Honeymoon

THE NEW PRESIDENT was making his Inaugural Address when we returned to the Capitol. Robby put the car in position at the head of the line, ready for its new owner, and I entered the Secret Service car and inspected the line of parade back to the White House. I then went back to the Capitol plaza and joined the procession, which was about to get under way. The crowds cheered Harding just as they had cheered Wilson—just as they will cheer any President, I discovered as the years went by.

The White House was full of politicians, Republican Senators and Congressmen, job-seekers, friends of the new Presidential couple, and the usual riff-raff of official Washington. The afternoon was spent in a reviewing stand in front of the White House, watching a parade. Heading one of the contingents was a negro drum major, dressed in a white uniform trimmed in gold, wearing a highly decorated helmet. He kicked his feet almost as high as his head, and handled his baton with amazing skill. The President noticed him, and I was sent to bring him back so that he could perform again in front of the stand. That was my first mission for Warren Gamaliel Harding, whom I had not yet met.

The next morning I was presented to him formally. He was a handsome man, friendly and cordial, with sympathetic and gentle eyes. His mouth was weak, and I noticed that he had a "high stomach"—his paunch sat way up, crowding his breast bone. It was several days before I met Mrs. Harding, who was eight years her husband's senior. She seemed well-groomed, neatly dressed and highly marcelled when in public. She had a determined mouth, but her eyes lacked decision. They reflected ambition, but they had a clouded, puzzled look, rather than the clear brightness which is associated with an active and logical mentality. Like her husband she appeared to be in excellent health, but in the way which such news has of getting around we soon were informed that she had only one kidney. The President called her The Duchess, and showed her deference in every way, as did his friends.

The other members of the new official family were George B. Christian, the President's secretary; Dr. Charles B. Sawyer, Mrs. Harding's physician, a homeopath; and Captain Joel T. Boone, the physician assigned to the President by the Navy. Christian was a life-long friend of the President and his neighbor in Marion. He was a friendly, personable man, and he helped us a great deal in getting acquainted with the habits and peculiarities of our new boss. I asked him what exercise the President took, and what sports he enjoyed.

"He loves to play golf," Christian said, "and if he can get into the low nineties he's tickled to death. He might be interested in horse-back riding; I don't know. He enjoys any sport so long as it is not brutal or painful to the players.

"He loathes prizefighting, for instance, and hunting. He is sensitive to the infliction of pain on anybody or anything.

"One day I was sitting with him on his front porch when I noticed some ants crawling along the balcony rail. I folded my newspaper and swatted them. He protested. 'Why do you kill those harmless insects?' he asked. 'Have they ever injured you?'"

This was my first insight into the character of a man who could not bear to believe that there was evil in any man or selfishness behind any plea for help. To the boys at the Press Club he said, "It is a good thing I am not a woman. I would always be pregnant. I cannot say no."

So much criticism, scandal and gossip has been circulated and written about the Harding administration that the public has come to accept his name as a symbol for corruption in public office and a shining example of the depths to which machine politics can descend. Looking on those tragic few years after nearly a quarter of a century it is easy to see the truth. Harding was ruined by his friends, just as Wilson was ruined by his enemies. But the main point is that he should never have been President of the United States.

He did not want to be President. He was happy as editor and publisher of the Marion *Star*. His friend Harry M. Daugherty—who was reported to have said when he first glimpsed Harding, "What a President he would make!"—maneuvered him into a seat in the Senate. That was a little further than he wanted to go, but he found enjoyment in the job and he learned to perform it as well as his colleagues (which is damning him with faint praise). He shrank from the first mention of his candidacy for President in horror. But Daugherty was persistent, and he had the backing of Mrs. Harding, who was always ambitious for her husband. Daugherty studied the situation which would prevail at the Republican convention in Chicago as if it were a chess problem, and he came to the conclusion that Harding could win. He was right. The two leaders closed in a deadlock, and every compromise candidate had something against him—except Harding. He was nominated, he was elected, and then inaugurated: into Washington thronged the "Ohio Gang," which had elected more Presidents than any other state but Virginia, and which had come to town to collect the spoils of war. Daugherty was designated to dispense the patronage, but a lot of people got to see the President, and if they did not get precisely what they wanted, they got something. It was a complete change from the Wilson way of running things.

It looked for a while as if patronage was going to extend to the Detail. Not long after the inauguration Tumulty got hold of me and said he had confidential information that the Hardings were going to ask for my transfer. It had been reported to them that I was a Southerner, a Democrat, and inclined to be officious.

"I have some friends I can approach who will intercede for you," Tumulty said.

I asked him not to. I was gloomy over the fate of the Wilsons, and my homesickness was so intense that I had decided my only chance of happiness lay in returning to Hopkinsville to live with my mother. I would welcome dismissal.

A few days later another friend of mine, A. B. Bayliss, a thirty-third degree Mason who had railroaded with me in Alabama and whose life I had saved in the yards at Birmingham, came to me with precisely the same information.

"I have some friends high in Masonic circles who can reach the President," he said.

I thanked him, but repeated that it was my intention to return to Kentucky. Shortly afterward I met Tobe Hert, Republican National Committeeman from Kentucky. He said he was glad to know there was a Kentuckian at the White House, and I told him I did not expect to be there long. When he inquired why I told him what I had heard.

"Forget it!" he said. "You'll be at the White House as long as Harding is President."

I didn't believe him and I didn't care, but in a few days his prediction was confirmed. Mrs. Harding sent for me to come to the West sitting room.

"Mr. Starling," she said, "I owe you an apology. On our arrival in Washington we were given information about you which was entirely untrue. I am sorry for that and I want to make a request of you. I want you to stay with my husband as long as he is President, and go with him wherever he goes. I know that he will be safe with you."

If she had asked me a few weeks before I would have declined. But now spring had come, and my melancholy had lifted. I had been getting out on the golf course, and I had taken the President for his first ride on Arizona. (He had a worse "seat" than President Wilson.) Life seemed good again, and livable, even in Washington. I thanked Mrs. Harding for her candor and her trust, and said I would do my best to fulfill the obligation she had asked me to undertake.

Christian had meant exactly what he said when he described the President's feeling for golf as "love." He played as if his life depended on every shot, and he made so many bets that sometimes he was betting against himself. His most usual companions were Senator Frank B.

Kellogg, Secretary of Agriculture Henry C. Wallace, Senator Fred Hale of Maine, Senator Joe Freylinghuysen of New Jersey, Speaker Frederick C. Gillett, Ned McLean, Christian, and any well-known golf professional who happened to be in the city. The President and his partner would bet their opponents six dollars Nassau; meaning six dollars out, six dollars in, and six dollars across. Then the President would bet his partner on low score, and as they went along he would bet on individual holes and on individual shots. I had to keep accounts, and it was a job for a Philadelphia lawyer. The President insisted on being treated without respect for his office. No matter how bad his lie, he played it, even when his opponents begged him to pick it up.

"Forget that I am President of the United States," he would say. "I'm Warren Harding, playing with some friends, and I'm going to beat hell out of them."

He played most often at the Chevy Chase Club, and used the house set aside for the President. I kept the key to the desk drawer where three or four bottles of Scotch and Bourbon were stored. When we returned to the house the colored man in attendance, Taylor, brought set-ups, and while the players drank highballs I calculated the results of the bets and announced the winners. The President took a single drink, and when this was finished and the bets were settled he would say to me, "Telephone the Duchess and say I am on my way home."

He did the same thing when he played cards at night. Exactly at eleven forty-five he would say, "All right, boys, we will wind up now. Starling, telephone the Duchess that I am on my way home."

At the card games he drank one highball, then switched to ale. His playing companions were usually the Secretary of the Treasury, Uncle Andy Mellon; Senator Charles Curtis, afterward Vice-President; former Ambassador to France, Hugh Wallace; Henry P. Fletcher, Under-Secretary of State and Chairman of the National Republican Committee; and the various members of his golfing company. The stakes were modest, since these men played purely for the sport of it. How could Andy Mellon, for instance, get a kick out of winning money in a poker game? They played with great zest and good humor, drank moderately and sociably, and smoked—all in the best tradition of the Elks Club. They took turns at being host, and usually there was a dinner beforehand. I attended all of these gatherings and I have yet to see the slightest sign of debauch. So far as the President was concerned he could not have drunk more if he wanted to. He suffered from stomach trouble, and was allergic to alcohol in any but small doses.

He chewed tobacco a great deal, and I wondered at the time whether this might not be the source of some of his digestive disturbances. He smoked, too, but I have seen him tear open a cigarette and empty it into his mouth when he was nervous and wanted a chew. Considering the opinion in which most people hold the habit of chewing tobacco I wonder how President Harding ever got the reputation of being a ladies' man. He wasn't, of course, but the legends about him would make Casanova blush.

He fulfilled not one requirement of a great lover except that he was handsome. He preferred the company of men; he liked to play golf and poker and sit around swapping stories and making bets. He chewed tobacco, was friendly and easy-going, and made no pretensions to a cultural or artistic background. He would no more have read poetry to a woman than he would have appeared in silk pants. In fact if he had known anything about women, or had been expert in handling them, he would never have gotten into trouble with them, if get into trouble with them he did. He may have, but not while he was at the White House. That I know for certain.

He had not been President for long when a man who was close to him approached me and asked me to act as a go-between for some correspondence with a certain young lady, unnamed, in New York. I declined, pointing out that it was not my job and was a private matter which the President would have to handle himself. Later I understood that one of the other members of the Detail accepted the assignment, and on one occasion brought the young lady to the White House for a brief meeting with the President. This I suppose was Nan Britton, who later wrote the book *The President's Daughter,* in which she gave details of the affair and admitted that she did the courting. This at least is plausible—the idea of Harding pursuing her is something no one who knew him would believe. But with his twin inabilities—to say no and to hurt any living thing—the parapets of his virtue were probably not insurmountable. After all, he was human. But this is the one thing which people will not forgive in a President, though frequently it is the reason for elevating him to the office.

The Nan Britton affair, if it happened (and I would be foolish to say that I am certain it did, for I am not), began while Harding was in the Senate and ended before he entered the White House. From the moment of his election until the hour of his death he was never free from our surveillance. His acts are things to which I can swear. He never did anything more reprehensible than cuss mildly at a golf ball and play poker with his friends. He was the kindest man I ever knew. But he was weak, and he trusted everyone.

The easiest way to visualize the predicament of Harding and clear up the "mystery" about him is to pick out a citizen prominent and well-to-do in your community and imagine him suddenly transported to the White House, with all his faults and virtues intact and his wife trailing along, clutching an armful of roses from the Tuesday Afternoon Bridge Club. You have known these people for a long time—let us say their names are Joe and Susie. You have learned to love them for their virtues and to bear with their faults. Joe is an amiable fellow who hates to get dressed up, and whose greatest joy is the Saturday night poker game at the Country Club. He puts ten dollars in a side pocket and when that is gone he buys a round of drinks for the boys and goes home. He runs a successful business, doesn't send bills to people he knows can't pay them, and can always be counted upon to make up the deficit in the minister's salary. Susie likes to play bridge, and is sometimes very good at it. She spends a lot of money on her clothes but always manages to look a little dowdy around the edges. She belongs to the Mission Society and devotes one afternoon a week to the Red Cross.

How do you suppose Joe and Susie would stand up under the incessant glare of publicity which beats down pitilessly upon the occupants of the White House? Not very well, you admit. Not as well, probably, as the Hardings, and they were prominent people from a small town. There was only one Harding tragedy. He should not have been President.

The man responsible for this was Harry M. Daugherty, who became Attorney-General in the Harding Cabinet. Daugherty was a corporation lawyer who was fascinated by the idea of national politics. He longed to make a president, after the style of Mark Hanna, and from the day he met Harding he felt that he had his man. He dreamed of putting him in the White House just as a prizefight manager dreams of putting his man into the championship. He succeeded, and from then on he was a little bit like the small boy who asked the small girl for a kiss. When she said yes he was stumped. "Now I got it what I gonna do with it?" he asked.

Daugherty rented a house on H Street from E. B. "Ned" McLean, the young publisher of the Washington *Post*. Ned's father, John R. McLean, had been publisher of the Cincinnati *Inquirer,* and an old friend of Daugherty's and Harding's. Daugherty used the house as a residence, and opened an office on the ground floor for the reception of people who came to see him about patronage. So many of these people came and so much talk went on about them, that Daugherty gave up the house and moved to the Wardman Park Hotel. While he was at the H Street house the President and Mrs. Harding went there to dine with him several times. I mention this only to differentiate the H Street house from the "Little Green House on K Street," where the President never went.

This latter establishment, so far as I know, was run by lobbyists, and was frequented by people of the same ilk. All sorts of stories were circulated about it, one being that a woman was killed there when her throat was pierced by slivers from a shattered champagne glass, which was thrown at her by another woman. The fact that such a case was never recorded or investigated by the Washington police is proof enough of its non-existence. You can't get away with murder, even in Washington.

A person who probably did drop in at 1625 K Street was Jess Smith,

Daugherty's man Friday, a simple soul with the same friendliness which distinguished Harding but none of the President's grace and polish. Daugherty had known him for many years, and because Mrs. Daugherty was an invalid he accepted the doglike devotion which Smith offered him and made him his companion. In Washington Smith looked after Daugherty's household and took care of his personal business. He turned out to be one of the weak links in the chain of friendship which the new administration forged in the Capital. The others were Senator Fall, Colonel Thomas W. Miller, whom Harding appointed Alien Property Custodian, and Charles R. Forbes, whom we made head of the Veterans' Bureau. One of the strong links, by comparison, was little Doctor Sawyer, a shrewd and capable man. His main reason for being in Washington was his familiarity with Mrs. Harding's condition. Whenever her single kidney was affected she was in danger of death, and the doctor's experience in pulling her through these crises was indispensable. The President made him a Brigadier General, and the little man insisted on all the trimmings. He was quite a figure when mounted on his horse, his epaulets shining in the sun. Harding, a little to his surprise, found him a capable and valuable adviser.

Another strong link was Christian, the secretary. His appointment was a real act of friendship, for this old Marion neighbor was a Democrat. The tact and good taste which he showed in discharging the delicate office of buffer and intermediary for the President were of inestimable help. As a secretary he could hardly have been improved upon.

In selecting his Cabinet Harding swung away from partiality. He got the very best men available, and if two of them happened to be old friends from the Senate no one disputed their ability. Senator Fall was expected to make an excellent Secretary of the Interior, and former Senator John W. Weeks was a first rate Secretary of War. Daugherty accepted the post of Attorney-General, a job he claimed he did not want, and whether he failed or was cut down by enemies is still a matter of dispute. There could be no better man for Secretary of State than Charles E. Hughes, and the remainder of the Cabinet was near him in ability: Herbert Hoover, Secretary of Commerce; Andrew W. Mellon, Secretary of the Treasury; James J. Davis, Secretary of Labor; Henry C. Wallace, Secretary of Agriculture; Edwin Denby, Secretary of the Navy; Will Hays, Postmaster General.

From these men Harding gladly took advice, and he also sought the counsel of such men as Senator Oscar Underwood, Senator Frank B. Kellogg, Senator Lodge, Budget Director Charles G. Dawes, and Vice President Coolidge. Richard Washburn Child was at the White House now and then, and George Harvey came frequently until he went to Great Britain as ambassador. In fact, Harvey would often play poker in a late night session with the President. Nicholas Murray Butler was an occasional visitor and a valued adviser.

The President needed advice, for at first the country was in a mess. The Harding years are remembered vaguely as a time of peace and prosperity, but this did not come until later. In 1921 there was an unemployment problem, a national debt problem, a credit problem, an agricultural problem. The war taxes had not been repealed, government expenses were sky high, the cost of living was still beyond reason, and business was in trouble. We had not yet made peace with our enemies, having refused the Wilson Treaty, and we did not know how we stood toward the rest of the world. When the new President called Congress into session there was plenty of work to be done, and it was a year and a half before it was able to recess.

The President worked hard. He also played hard. He was vigorous in whatever he did. On week days he went to the Chevy Chase Club for eighteen holes of golf. Sunday morning he rode horseback, and it was my duty to see that he got back to the White House in time to attend Calvary Baptist Church with Mrs. Harding. He was not much of a church-goer, but the Duchess insisted that he put in an appearance. One morning he said to me, "Colonel, let's take that path." I said, "If we do we won't be back in time to go to church." He said, "I know it—your memory is too damn good!"

On evenings when he did not play poker or go out to dinner he liked to attend the theatre. Sitting in the box with him I could not help contrasting his manners with those of President Wilson. Between the acts of George M. Cohan's "Mary" I saw him put his program to his mouth and from behind it call out to an old crony in the audience. "Hey, John," he said in a stage whisper, "how do you like the girls?"

On the other hand, he fraternized with the rich, which Wilson would not do. He quickly made use of the President's house at the Chevy Chase Club, and he was often at the enormous *Friendship* estate of Ned McLean and his diamond studded wife, Evelyn Walsh McLean, on Wisconsin Avenue. On my first visit to their town house I wrote to my mother, "I remained inside during the President's stay and enjoyed looking at the wonderful paintings and tapestries.

"On entering you walk up a short flight of steps to a ballroom. Crossing this room you enter an indoor garden containing a large pool. Turning to the left you reach the dining room. Coming back toward the front door you run into a large sitting room. If you turn to the right there you enter the music room. Turning again to the left you are in a waiting room at the foot of a magnificent stairway. You then go back to the entrance."

Harding's first journey as President was to New York, for the dedication of the statue of Simon Bolivar. It was an important trip for me, for I was now advance man for the Detail, Murphy having gone to Service Headquarters as Assistant Chief, and Jervis having been named to succeed him. This was the first schedule for which I was solely responsible, and as might have been expected, something went wrong.

I left Washington on Sunday, April 17, and worked steadily until the Presidential party arrived on Tuesday afternoon. As usual Harding had a large crowd with him. It took ten automobiles to transport them and I had a difficult time getting them started—this one wanted to ride with that fellow and that fellow wanted to ride with somebody else, etc. I finally got them all to the Waldorf-Astoria, and after the President had received the South American diplomats we started for the statue, this time with thirty-five cars in the procession. Swinging into Broadway below Columbus Circle the forward cars suddenly stopped. I ran ahead to see what had happened, and found John F. "Red Mike" Hylan, the

Mayor of New York, assisting the President from his car to plant a tree.

This arrangement had been made entirely without consulting me, and the President was being exposed to a crowd at a place where no stop had been anticipated and no precautions were in effect. I was mad and scared, and I bawled the Mayor out.

"You have not kept faith with me," I said. "We agreed upon a program, but regardless of the President's safety and comfort you arranged this halt in the procession without consulting me. You have endangered the President's life"—I turned to Mr. Harding—"and I want him to hear me say it."

They both looked ashamed as I hustled them into the car. The rest of the program went off without trouble and we were back in Washington that night.

Our next trip was in June, when we motored through Maryland and Pennsylvania to Valley Forge, where the President was a guest at the home of Senator Philander Knox. The Senator's home was beautifully situated in a country used mainly for stock raising. It was a treat for me to be in such an environment, and the morning after our arrival I was up at five o'clock, enjoying the dew on the grass and the mist that hung over the bathing pool and the spring, which furnished the house with drinking water. Leaning against a tree, inhaling the clean air, I heard someone come and lean against the other side of the tree. Soon there were deep sighs of satisfaction and sounds of simple human happiness. I went around to see who it was and found Senator Knox, in his pajamas and bare feet, staring with dreamy eyes at the scene before him.

"Dammit, Starling, this is why I like to come up here!" he said, "I like to come out here in the morning and feel the wet grass on my feet and let it run up between my toes and just lean against a tree and commune with nature!"

That afternoon we communed at the three hundred acre estate of Mr. E. T. Stotesbury in Philadelphia. The contrast was painful, and I was all for the Senator Knox type of nature. The trees and flowers on the Stotesbury estate were too pretty and too well pruned to be real.

In July we spent a week-end at Harvey Firestone's camp on the Licking River near Hagerstown, Maryland. We arrived on Saturday afternoon, July 23, and before dinner went for a horseback ride—the President and Mr. Firestone, Russell Firestone, Henry Ford, Edsel Ford, Secretary Christian and myself. We rode again the next morning, but otherwise the camp offered little recreation. I was amazed that so rich a man had such a poor establishment. I decided that it must be ignorance. Perhaps he believed that camping had to be uncomfortable.

The place was located along the road, which took away its privacy. The ground was low and looked like a small island. The river was sluggish, with mud banks. The tents were badly arranged and the flies were terrible. The eating tent had been up all day and when we sat down to lunch all the heat in that part of the country had succeeded in getting into it. There was only cold water for shaving, no arrangements for a bath, and a player piano for entertainment. With a jack knife and ten dollars I could have built a better camp.

In August we went to Plymouth, Massachusetts, for the Tercentenary celebration. An account of what I did there before the President arrived will give an idea of the duties of the Detail's advance man. The President was to arrive on the *Mayflower,* and there was to be a luncheon, afternoon exercises, a dinner, and a pageant. To prepare for this I did the following:

Procured and numbered the automobiles for the procession; selected the persons who were to ride in each; arranged the seating of guests at the luncheon and dinner tables; laid out the line of march and selected those who were to participate actively in the parade; designated the time to be consumed by the parade, the luncheon, and each of the speeches; organized the program for the afternoon exercises; set the time of arrival at the Plymouth Hotel and the time to be consumed by the President before dinner; listed the line of march for entrance into the dining room; designated the time to be consumed at dinner and the time the President was to leave for the pageant; checked the program of the pageant and the arrangements for proceeding to the dock; arranged for a baggage car and for an automobile for Brooks and Mrs. Harding's maid; procured bronze badges for the President's seventeen guests; went down the harbor and met the President.

Everything went off according to schedule.

In September we made a trip on which nothing went off according to schedule.

The President accepted an invitation to go to Atlantic City as the guest of Alexander P. Moore, afterwards Ambassador to Spain, and his wife, Lillian Russell. He decided to go on the *Mayflower,* and since the yacht drew too much water to permit docking at the resort I arranged for a submarine chaser to meet us off shore.

Heading up the coast after leaving Chesapeake Bay we ran into heavy weather, which slowed our progress. It was dark when we reached our destination, and a heavy sea was running. Our captain, Commander Ralston S. Holmes of the Navy, was worried.

"Starling," he said, "I think it is dangerous to attempt to transfer the President to a small boat in this sea, but I am not willing to take the responsibility of keeping him aboard alone. Will you back me up?"

"If you think it is dangerous that's enough for me," I said. "I am responsible for his safety. We won't transfer. I suggest that you fail to find the submarine chaser because of the darkness."

While we cruised about the weather grew steadily worse. Finally Holmes decided to head for the open sea. During the night he gave up the fight to maintain his position and headed south. When the President came on deck the next morning with two of his guests, we were heading into Chesapeake Bay.

I was on the bridge, and he headed straight for me. I heard him say, "I'll bet that's the fellow responsible for this."

When he reached me he said, "Did you have anything to do with our failure to land last night?"

"I'm afraid I did," I said, "but I'd rather you ask Commander Holmes about the reason why."

He turned from me and went into the Commander's quarters. After he came out the Commander told me that we would land at Norfolk for a game of golf, and that he was radioing Admiral Hugh Rodman, Commandant of the Norfolk Navy Yard, to meet us at the dock with automobiles.

The President wasn't speaking to me as we made ready to land. As soon as I got ashore I took Admiral Rodman aside and told him my predicament. When a Kentuckian gets into trouble it seems there is always another Kentuckian around to get him out of it. Admiral Rodman was not only a native of the blue grass but a life-long friend of the Starling family.

"Don't worry," he said, "I'll fix it."

He climbed into the car and sat next to the President. I sat in the front seat. As we drove off the Admiral opened fire.

"Mr. President," he said, putting concern and solicitation into his voice, "I was greatly relieved by your wise decision last night. I cannot tell you how glad I was to hear that you would not try a landing at Atlantic City. My reports indicated a dangerously rough sea up the coast. I sat up until I received the information that you would not land. I was mighty pleased to hear it."

The President snorted. "Well," he said, "that makes two damned Kentuckians who were pleased!"

A round of golf restored his good humor. When he called me into the lounging room of the *Mayflower* after dinner that evening to give an accounting of the bets he was smiling and affable. With him were the other members of the foursome: Secretary Hughes, Speaker Gillett, and Director of the Budget Dawes. The President rubbed his hands together gleefully and said:

"Now, Starling, give us the bad news. We will start with our friend Dawes. How does he stand?"

"Mr. Dawes owes the Secretary of State thirty-three dollars," I said.

"Fine," the President said. "Charlie, fork over the money."

Mr. Dawes counted off the amount, rose from his chair, and with a profound bow offered the money to Mr. Hughes.

Mr. Hughes' face turned red. He stuttered as he tried to explain his situation to the President.

"I cannot accept this," he said, "I have never gambled in my life."
"Take it!" the President boomed. "You won it!"

Reluctantly the Secretary of State accepted the money. I am certain that later he turned it over to some charity, providing he was unable to get Dawes to take it back.

We made the Atlantic City trip successfully a few weeks later.

Early in October we went one week-end to the Battle of the Wilderness field, to watch the Marines in sham battle. We slept in tents, and it was the coldest night I ever experienced. When I was ready for bed I found only two blankets on my cot. I went foraging and found another, then went to the Secretary of the Navy's tent and commandeered two more. With five of them wrapped around me, plus a heavy bathrobe, I nearly froze. Next day I left for my annual vacation in Hopkinsville.

While I was at home our Republican Governor, Edwin P. Morrow, visited in town. I was invited to play golf with him, along with two of my friends. A few days later I received a letter from the Governor's mansion informing me that I was now a Colonel, the honor having been bestowed in recognition of the service I had performed in guarding President Wilson, particularly during his two trips abroad. Coming from a Republican who had been elected in the Harding landslide I appreciated the courtesy.

The story was sent to Washington and the President greeted me on my return with, "Hello, Colonel." That settled it. There had been a lot of confusion about my name. The family called me Will. Some of my friends called me Ed. My chief called me Star or Starlight. Now everyone but the family followed the President's cue and the division of opinion ended. I was Colonel to them all.

One of the first things I did on my return was visit the Wilsons on S Street, carrying some preserves as a gift from my mother. Mrs. Wilson received me, as lovely and gracious as ever.

"I am sorry Mr. Wilson is not available," she said. "He is not dressed yet."

Just then we heard a familiar voice calling down the stairs.

"Is that Starling, Edith? If it is send him right up. I want to see him."

I went up the stairs and found him seated before a mirror, shaving. One half of his face was clean and he was working diligently on the other half.

"Sit down," he said. "How is everything at the old homestead?"

We talked about the White House, he asking me questions about his friends there, I answering and giving him little tidbits of news which I thought would please him. When I left he said to Mrs. Wilson:

"Edith, whenever Starling comes, send him right up. I do not stand on ceremony with him. I consider him an old friend."

"So do I," said Mrs. Wilson.

That same night as I stood in front of the Willard Hotel waiting for the President to arrive at a charity ball I heard a man's voice shout, "Hello, Colonel!" Then a woman's voice repeated, "Hello, Colonel!" I turned quickly around and got a glimpse of Admiral and Mrs. Grayson, all dressed up and trying to scamper into the hotel before I spotted them. Later I saw both of them inside and they congratulated me with straight faces, inquiring about my uniform and my horse.

This was the honeymoon period of the Harding administration, and the social season that winter was rich and full. In mock seriousness I wrote to my mother:

Our Diplomatic Reception was very gorgeous and pretentious. Beautiful women, scantily gowned, very much to my delectation, helped to make the long hours pass quickly and brighten my tired eyes. In the line were diplomats in full dress, their costumes containing all the colors of the rainbow—looking well on some and ridiculous on others.

Some were cads and others were thoroughbreds. Some were at home, gracious and thoughtful; others were ill at ease and afraid to speak to anyone but the President—these were the most gorgeously dressed, in lace and gold. Some had on old shoes and were suffering with bad feet. Some had on shoes that were too small and they could hardly walk after standing in the long line waiting for the chance to be seen in the Blue Room shaking hands with the President and Mrs. Harding.

I was on duty at the door leading from the Red Room into the Blue Room. It was my duty to pass each guest from one room to the other.

Mrs. Cornelius Vanderbilt had on about four million dollars worth of diamonds. Mrs. E. B. McLean had on about two million dollars worth of the same stuff, and the others followed suit according to their means and borrowing capacity.

The Harding receptions were always large, and it was not too difficult to get an invitation to one of them. Everyone spoke of the democratic manner of the new President, and they freely predicted that he would be in the White House at least eight years. He was handling the railroad strikes—which were bedeviling the whole country—in a firm manner, and the Disarmament Conference, which had been in session in Washington since he called it to meeting on November 21, was turning out to be a great success. There was not a cloud on the horizon.

Jervis and I were a little bit uneasy about something which had happened to us, but we were sure it had no direct connection with the President. Daugherty had appointed William J. Burns head of the Federal Bureau of Investigation, and through Burns we two were offered jobs in the bureau at much higher salaries than we were getting. It looked like an attempt to get us off the Detail, but for what purpose we could not conceive, since the appointment of our successors would be up to Moran and Murphy, who could not have been reached with a hundred foot pole plastered with thousand dollar bills. We turned down the offer, naturally, and nothing more was heard of it. It was about this time that Burns hired Gaston B. Means, a man who would not have been caught dead telling the truth. His engagement as a G-man was a fatal mistake; later he smeared the President and the administration with vicious and scandalous lies which are still quoted as truth by most of the public.

I think people like to remember the Harding administration as having been abandoned to liquor and sex because the country itself at the time was in such a state. The Roaring Twenties were beginning to howl. There was a mass demonstration of disrespect for the Eighteenth Amendment, and the White House itself joined in this rebellion— plenty of liquor was served there, although the President, as I have said, was a one drink man. Skirts had now reached the knee, and women were going to the barber shop to get their hair cut. On the occasion of the signing of agreements at the close of the Disarmament Conference I wrote:

Our Disarmament Conference ended in success. It was quite different from the Peace signing at Versailles. This meeting radiated good feeling and renewed confidence. The one at Versailles was held amidst strained surroundings, with a feeling of passing sentence on the condemned. Of course conditions there were quite different. The war was hardly over and there were still bitter feelings in the air.

I sincerely hope that the nations are determined that another war shall not come to pass. Look at us now. This country is heavily burdened and the people are dissatisfied. England and France are at odds and are saddled with debts and unsettled labor conditions. Germany was crushed, but is fast rising again. Russia is coming to the front. She is raising a large army, while thousands of the poor are starving to death.

What we need is Christianity. In my opinion there is more for the church to do now than ever before. People are money-mad and pleasure-drunk. They only think of their soul's salvation at the last moment. What Paul wrote to the Romans is true now:

"And even as they did not like to retain God in their knowledge, God gave them over to a reprobate mind, to do those things which are not convenient;

"Being filled with all unrighteousness, fornication, wickedness, covetousness, maliciousness; full of envy, murder, debate, deceit, malignity; whisperers.

"Backbiters, haters of God, despiteful, proud, boasters, inventors of evil things, disobedient to parents,

"Without understanding, covenant-breakers, without natural affection, implacable, unmerciful:

"Who knowing the judgment of God, that they which commit such things are worthy of death, not only do the same, but have pleasure in them that do them."

★☆★

CHAPTER TWELVE

Disillusion

At the end of January Washington had a blizzard. It began snowing on a Friday night, and by midnight was ten inches deep. The President and Mrs. Harding were at Senator Hale's for dinner and did not leave until twelve-thirty. The automobile managed to get through to the White House, and I was able to go home on a street car, but the next morning I had to walk to work. It snowed all Saturday and Saturday night, and by Sunday morning the fall was two feet deep. The street cars, which had to give up early Saturday morning, were not able to resume until Monday night, and then only on certain streets. On Saturday night about nine o'clock the roof of the Knickerbocker Theatre caved in under the weight of the snow and more than one hundred people were killed. Twice that number were injured. A young lady I had once courted was there with her husband, a groom of five months. She escaped with a few bruises, but he was killed. The whole city was shocked and grieved, and the White House cancelled all social engagements for a week.

It was a cold winter. In March we went to Florida. We returned to the White House to find spring beginning. Soon the President was out in the backyard practising golf shots. He had an old carpet put on the ground and from it drove dozens of balls all over the south grounds. Laddie Boy, his dog, did most of the retrieving.

You never knew what to expect when you went around back in those days. One day I found Bill Tilden, Little Bill Johnston, R. Norris Williams, and Dick Washburn, playing tennis on the White House courts, while the President watched. Once I brought the car around to the front door to take him golfing, and he appeared with two utter strangers, one of them a dark-visaged man who looked like a Balkan spy. He was Ring Lardner. The other man was Grantland Rice. One day he turned up with a pair of very pretty girls. They were Hope Hampton and Viola Dana, two of Hollywood's brightest stars at the time.

All during the winter there had been talk of a trip to Alaska during the summer, but as the weeks slid by and Congress showed no signs of getting its work done the possibility faded. There were the railroad strikes too, which had not been settled. The President had to reconcile himself to the prospect of another summer spent largely in Washington. In the spring someone presented him with an automobile, and he conceived the notion of going in it to Marion, doing the driving himself. He even thought it would be a good idea to drive back and forth during the hot months, just to relieve the monotony.

By the time we got through talking him out of the notion we had compromised by agreeing to a motor trip to Marion in which he would ride in the regular White House car. Even this was bad enough, from our standpoint. In 1922 automobiles were none too trustworthy. Tires blew out easily, axles broke, and things happened to the motors.

Most of the main roads were paved, but little had been done to remove sharp curves and steep grades. The roads were narrow and the shoulders were unprotected. Most of them were slick and dangerous when wet.

I picked what seemed to be the safest route through Pennsylvania and West Virginia to Ohio, and prayed for good weather. I got it both ways, and the trip was without accident. In Marion I had no trouble with the arrangements for the President's visit. Everyone was possessed with pride for this friend who had made good, and agreed to anything that would make his homecoming more pleasant and restful.

Those brief days in his home town were the happiest of President Harding's career, I think. He was at the peak of his national popularity, and the enthusiasm of his fellow townspeople was a reflection of the way the whole country felt about him. A man who loved all people, and who wanted all people to love him, could have asked for no more. His cup was filled.

On the itinerary of the trip was a pilgrimage to the birthplace of General Grant at Point Pleasant, near Cincinnati. There was to be a boat ride on the river, and when I arrived in Cincinnati I found that the committee had chartered an old Ohio River side-wheel excursion steamer for the purpose. It was called the *Island Queen,* and the committee was selling tickets at five dollars apiece to anyone who wanted to ride with the President. I disliked the idea, naturally. There would be a large crowd, and the ship looked none too safe. I withheld my approval pending an investigation of the *Island Queen.*

I put on a pair of overalls and went over her thoroughly.

There was a top deck to which ticket holders would be admitted. On the deck below this a place had been fitted for the President and his party, equipped with wicker chairs and set off from the crowd.

The ship was old and rickety, and the whole proposition was reckless and foolhardy. I told the committee they could put all the people they chose on the *Island Queen,* but the President would ride in another boat. I requisitioned the War Department tug *Cayuga* for him.

The committee reacted violently. The tickets had been sold and the people could not be disappointed. The chairman of the committee called Washington and talked to George Christian. Christian talked to the President. The President said he would abide by whatever plans were made by the Secret Service. The committee decided to run the *Island Queen* parallel with the *Cayuga* so the ticket holders could get the view they had been promised.

The cruise of the *Cayuga* was uneventful; not so that of the *Island Queen.* The *Cayuga* was on the port side of the big boat, and all the ticket holders rushed over to see the President. The *Island Queen* tipped, and suddenly there was a tremendous crash. The upper deck collapsed, just over the place allotted to the President. A mass of tangled timber and bodies crushed the wicker chairs in which he and his party were supposed to sit. Scores were injured.

Shortly after our return to Washington Mrs. Harding became seriously ill. Her one kidney locked and for several days she was on the verge of death. She did not convalesce rapidly, and all through that fall was ill, so that the President remained at the White House, journeying no farther than the golf course. One day I went with him to *Friendship,* the McLean estate, and he sat out in the garden talking to Bernard Baruch.

They were discussing politics and I was paying little attention to the conversation. It was necessary for me to be within earshot, but I had trained myself not to eavesdrop. Gradually, however, I became aware that they were discussing me.

"He would be just the man," Mr. Baruch said. "We'll send him back to Kentucky and groom him for Senator."

"He'd make a good one," the President said. "The Colonel is all right wherever you put him."

I stepped over to them and said, "Excuse me, but I think I heard my name taken in vain. Who is going to put me where?"

They laughed and Mr. Baruch said, "Wouldn't you like to be a Senator?"

"No," I said. "I would not. I feel exactly as General Sherman did. If nominated I will not run; if elected I will not serve."

"Are you sure?" Mr. Baruch said.

"Absolutely," I answered.

He turned to the President. "You see why I think a lot of this man," he said.

The President smiled ruefully. "You have chosen better than you know, Colonel," he said.

One day during a round of golf on the private course at *Friendship* Ned McLean asked me to find for him a reliable man of middle age who could be assigned to guard his young daughter (now the wife of Senator Robert Reynolds).

"I want a man you can absolutely vouch for," he said.

A few days later I told him I had secured Elridge P. Wilkins, a Christian County man who years before had ridden deputy sheriff with me. His character and courage were beyond question, and he was a staunch Presbyterian. I speculated, when he came to Washington to take the job, whether the McLeans and their environment would influence him, or whether his austere ways would have an effect upon them. It was, I discovered later, a stand-off. Each was impervious to the other.

At Christmas time the President called me into his office and handed me a stack of new ten dollar gold pieces, one for each member of the Detail. After passing them out I found that the one which remained in my hand was old and worn. For a moment I thought it was a matter of not being able to get enough new ones to go around. Then I recalled President Wilson's curious feeling for the number thirteen. Somehow this gold piece looked as if it belonged to someone. I decided to risk embarrassing the President in order to make sure. I went back into his office.

"Was this piece meant to go with the others?" I said. "It is not like them and I thought it might have been put in by mistake."

The President looked at it, then snatched it from my hand. He seemed frightened.

"That is my personal good luck piece," he said. "I would not lose it for a million dollars. I have carried it ever since the day I became owner of the Marion *Star*. I take it with me to every poker game. I had the other gold pieces in my pocket and it must have gotten mixed up with them."

He was so disturbed that he shook my hand in gratitude.

"Thank you for bringing it back, Colonel," he said. "Thank you very much."

That same afternoon we stopped on our way back from the golf course at the home of a Mr. Sewell, just across the street from the Wilson residence on S Street. I was walking up and down on the sidewalk trying to keep warm when a man approached me and said, "Isn't this Mr. Starling?" I recognized Doctor Axson, brother of the first Mrs. Wilson.

"I thought it was you," he said. "Mr. and Mrs. Wilson are in their car over there and they sent me to ask if you would come over and speak to them."

I crossed the street with him and shook hands with my old employers. Both looked fine and Mrs. Wilson giggled when her husband called me Colonel.

"Oh," she said, "I forgot all about calling you Colonel. Now you are the one with the title."

The sight of Mr. Wilson's face, so free now from care and flushed with the vigor of the winter afternoon, haunted me for days, for I could see in the face of President Harding the same care and weariness which once had marked the countenance of his predecessor. Now it was Harding who looked sick.

One day Brooks took me aside and said:

"Colonel, something is going to happen to our boss."

"What's the matter?" I said.

"He can't sleep at night. He can't lie down. He has to be propped up with pillows and he sits up that way all night. If he lies down he can't get his breath."

The "high stomach," I thought. No wonder he tired so quickly on the golf course. One day that winter after playing the twelfth hole he sent me back to the eleventh tee for a club he had forgotten. When I rejoined him he said:

"Colonel, why after playing eleven or twelve holes do I drag my feet and feel so tired?"

"You are working too hard," I said. "You need a vacation. Why don't you confine your game to nine holes until you rest up?"

"Hell!" he said disgustedly. "If I can't play eighteen holes I won't play at all!"

After Christmas the McLeans went to Florida. When the McLeans left, Wilkins told me that he was going to Hopkinsville to visit his sister, Mrs. Charles B. Lacey, and that he had told Mr. McLean to get in touch with me in case he was needed in a hurry. McLean soon wired me from Palm Beach, and I in turn wired my brother Guy. In view of the false importance attached to the message later I give it here in full:

GUY STARLING 320 NORTH MAIN STREET HOPKINSVILLE KENTUCKY TELEPHONE E. P. WILKINS AT MRS. CHARLES LACEY'S HOME AND HAVE HIM REPORT TO MCLEAN'S PALM BEACH FLORIDA FIRST TRAIN.

(SIGNED) E. W. STARLING

Early in March the President decided to take a rest by going to Florida. It was to be a barnstorming golf tour, beginning at Ormond Beach and proceeding by way of the Inland Waterway to Palm Beach, with a houseboat for transportation. Murphy went with me to make the arrangements. We borrowed a Department of Commerce boat at Miami and went over the route carefully, getting a blueprint of each golf course, talking with the officials of the various clubs, and examining the landing facilities.

We met the President's train at Ormond Beach, and the first golf was played there. An amiable drunk fastened himself to the party and decided to keep the President entertained. I dropped back to keep him company and prevent him from interrupting the game. After a while I noticed a group of players on the opposite fairway who seemed to be in some sort of trouble. I suggested to the drunk that he go over and find out what was wrong. He was back in a few minutes, shaking his head woefully.

"This is a terrible thing," he said. "How the poor people will suffer! It is a great tragedy. Tomorrow the price of gasoline will go up two cents a gallon all over the country."

"That's too bad," I said. "How do you know?"

"It is inevitable," he said. "Old man John D. has lost his golf ball!"

Next day we boarded the houseboat and left the Rockefellers behind.

In the party were the President and Mrs. Harding, Mr. and Mrs. McLean, Henry P. Fletcher, Speaker Gillett, and Attorney-General Daugherty. Jervis and Harry Barker of the Detail were also aboard, while I remained ashore, along with Arnold Landvoigt, Walter Ferguson, and Charlie Fredericks, our driver. We had two cars and it was our job to keep the boat spotted and bring the mail and telegrams to it. Our communication office was in Palm Beach, under Agent Jim Haley. When the boat anchored at night Jervis would go ashore and call Haley. I would also call Haley, and after getting the location of the boat would proceed there with whatever was to be delivered. I would get a list of things needed, return with them in the morning, and during the day pick up the mail pouches.

At New Smyrna I drew alongside the waterway and walked to the bank. The President was the only person on deck. He was leaning on the rail smoking a cigarette.

"Where are you going to play golf tomorrow?" I asked.

He took the cigarette from his mouth and flipped it toward me. Then, after slowly exhaling the smoke he said, "None of your damned business!" and turned to enter his cabin. As he opened the door he turned around and laughed at me. I raised my cap and bowed, laughing back at him.

He did not resent our constant attention; he was just sorry it had to be that way. One day at the White House visitors detained him so long that he did not have time to eat his customary sandwich and drink his usual glass of milk before going to the golf course. When we got there he sent me to the club house for a bottle of mineral water and some bread and cheese. He thought he would have time to eat this snack before joining the others at the first tee, but while he was biting into the first sandwich one of the caddies came to say that the others were waiting for him and he was holding up the game. He rushed out, the sandwiches in one hand, the bottle of mineral water in the other. As we walked toward the first hole he suddenly stepped behind a tree.

"Colonel," he said, "I am afraid it wouldn't be dignified for me to walk out there in front of those people eating my lunch. Let's stand here until I finish.

"Damn it, Colonel, that's the trouble with being President. You can't do the things you want to do, and what you can do you can't do your own way. It has to be somebody else's way."

While we were in Florida Secretary Fall resigned. Nothing was thought of the move. Fall was going abroad to act as agent in the merger of some oil companies, and had to be free of his official position to do so. As yet there was no public hint of wrongdoing anywhere in the Harding administration. Congress had made a good record, and that summer we were to have our promised trip to Alaska. Already I was working on the itinerary.

But privately the talk of scandal had begun to circulate. Colonel Charles R. Forbes, head of the Veterans' Bureau, had gotten himself involved. The President knew about it; Doctor Sawyer had warned him, and investigation had proved the little homeopath was right. Forbes, a high-living gentleman with a taste for fast friends, was a veteran of the World War who had met the Hardings in Honolulu and become one of their favorites. The President could not bear to see him disgraced and prosecuted, and had sent him abroad on an official mission, asking him to resign when he was safely out of the country. The resignation was received on February 15, and on March 2 the Senate began an investigation of the Veterans' Bureau. On the fourteenth Charles F. Cramer, legal adviser to the bureau, committed suicide. It was this news which was received by the Presidential party in Florida with misgivings. One of the weak links in the chain had given way. The President had been betrayed.

Still, it was a thing which could happen to any President. He might have chosen a man solely on his merits and gotten the same result. At least that was the attitude of the members of the official family. And as yet nothing had been proved; Forbes had not been indicted. But more trouble was ahead.

The President was playing golf at the Chevy Chase Club one day when a retired army officer of my acquaintance drew me aside. I had done a favor for him some time before, and he said he wanted to repay me.

"I have a letter from a friend of mine out West," he said. "I want you to read it. It may be something you can pass on to your boss. If you think you want to do that I will let you have it."

I read the letter. It told my friend that a scandal was brewing over some leases of naval oil lands, a scandal which might reach the President and involve his whole administration. The writer was advising my friend to look around and see that he had no social connections which might in any way prove incriminating.

"I'd like to take this with me," I said, "I don't know whether to show it to the President or not. May I have it?"

"Do as you like with it," my friend said.

All during the golf game I walked behind the President, debating what to do. The letter was not in the class of rumor or gossip. It seemed to be authentic information. Perhaps the President already knew it. He seemed so tired and listless, so suddenly old. If he didn't know it why should I add to his troubles? Yet the situation might still be in a stage where he could do something about it.

As we rode back to the White House I made my decision. I waited until he was upstairs in his room and the others had dispersed. Then I followed him and knocked at the door. He asked me to come in. I stepped inside and handed him the letter.

"Perhaps I am doing wrong in giving this to you," I said. "A friend of mine gave it to me and asked me to use my judgment in passing it on for your examination. I decided to bring it to you."

He read the letter, his face turning ashen as his eyes scanned the lines. When he had finished he stood with his hands hanging at his sides, much as I had seen President Wilson standing that night in Brest after Colonel House left him.

"I am glad you brought it to me," he said. His voice was flat and far away. "It is something that I should know."

"No one else will be informed of it," I said.

He nodded his head automatically. I went out, leaving him with the letter and wondering whether I had done good or harm. In either case I wished the job had been someone else's.

★★★

CHAPTER THIRTEEN

A President Dies

THE ALASKAN TRIP, though primarily a vacation, had a business angle. In Washington thirty-five different federal agencies were arguing over control of the various sources of natural wealth in the territory: timber, mineral, and fishing rights were involved in a maze of supervision. The President had been urged to put an end to the chaos and he promised to do so after the trip, during which he planned to visit the spots under discussion.

I was to leave Tuesday, the twelfth of June, stopping at St. Louis, Kansas City, Hutchinson, Denver, Salt Lake City, Idaho Falls, Butte, Helena, Gardner, Spokane, Portland, Tacoma, and the following places in Alaska: Juneau, Seward, Fairbanks, Sitka, Anchorage, Matanuska, Moose Creek, Chickaloon, Talkeetna, McKinley Park, Kobe, and Cordova. Returning I was to land at Seattle and proceed to San Francisco, going from there to Yosemite, Los Angeles, and San Diego. There was to be a little visit to William Wrigley's home on Catalina Island, and a return trip through the Panama Canal with a stop over at Puerto Rico.

Moran, Murphy and I were discouraged at the way preparations had been handled up to the time of my departure. Walter Brown, who succeeded Will Hays as Postmaster General, went in a private railroad car to each of the stops in the states, and worked with local committees on programs for the President and his party. In each place the President's friends and those with the most political influence were chosen to do the entertaining. When the list of ceremonies was complete Brown sent it to Washington for the President's approval. He was to pass it

on to me. Up until the day I left I had only one program in my possession, that being for St. Louis, the first stop. Before I left the office,
however, the President sent for me.

"Brown is making a circus out of the trip," he said. "He has booked
me for from eight to ten hours of constant activity every place we are
to stop. I won't get a minute's rest.

"I want you to go out and cut every program to the bone. I'll back
you up. I want to do as little work as possible on this trip and I am
depending on you to help me out."

It was the first time I had heard him express the slightest concern for
his own comfort in any matter whatsoever. He had been completely
the slave of his office and his friends. But now another blow had been
delivered to his theory that all men are good. On May 30 Jess Smith,
Daugherty's companion and personal secretary, had committed suicide,
shooting himself with a pistol while in the apartment of Daugherty at
the Wardman Park Hotel.

Just before this Daugherty had told the President that Jess had apparently "gone bad," and was running with a wrong crowd. Smith's
name had been removed from the list of guests for the Alaskan trip.
What would follow as the result of his suicide nobody knew. It depended on what Jess had been up to. There might be a scandal.

That was what the President now feared above all things. He had
not wanted to be President, but once in the position he had conceived
an ambition. He knew that he could not be remembered as a great
President, but he set himself to the hope that he might be remembered
as a respectable one. Now even that was lost, if Forbes and Smith were
as guilty as they seemed, and the oil scandal broke.

He looked more weary than I had ever seen him. The Sunday previous, Mrs. Harding had called me aside at the Baptist Church. We
arrived late and were waiting for the opening prayer to finish before
taking our seats.

"You are leaving soon to make arrangements for the trip?" she asked.

"On the twelfth," I said.

"I want you to promise me something," she said. "Wherever we are to stop I want the doctors, General Sawyer and Captain Boone, as close to the President's room as possible. If they can be put in the adjoining suite I would appreciate it. At any rate, I want to be informed of their room number in each place. I am also taking a trained nurse with us."

She looked at me steadily. "You understand?" she asked.

"Perfectly," I said.

"Are you *sure* you understand?" she said. "It is not for myself that I want this done"—she was only then recovering from her long and serious illness—"but for Warren."

"I understand," I said. "I will follow your instructions."

This I did, and I was glad to find that the naval nurse assigned to the party was Miss Ruth Powderly, a brilliant and efficient young lady, who had nursed President Wilson during his long illness in the White House and won the love and admiration of her patient and Mrs. Wilson.

I had also promised the President that I would do as he asked. Nothing pleased me more than the prospect of cutting the speech of a pompous windbag from an hour to five minutes, or telling a safety pin manufacturer that the Presidential procession would not pass his factory on its way to the hotel. (I would sometimes find the automobile route zigzagging all over the city in order to pass property owned by the committeemen.) I left on schedule and arrived on the coast on June 29, exhausted from fifteen days of guerilla warfare with the pride of the Republican party. Next day I sailed for Alaska.

The Presidential party left Washington the twentieth of June, and on the fifth of July boarded the U.S.S. *Henderson,* a naval transport, at Tacoma. They landed at Seward on Friday the thirteenth.

Meanwhile I was on my way back to the states, arriving in Seattle on the twentieth and proceeding to San Francisco, where I first called on Daniel J. O'Brien, the Chief of Police. The Palace Hotel had been chosen for our party, and O'Brien, a fine Irish gentleman whose son George was a movie actor, went with me to make the arrangements. We met William J. Shepherd, one of the assistant managers, and accompanied him to the seventh and eighth floors, which I selected for our use. We examined all the rooms, and I assigned them to various members of the party. Room 8064 I designated as the President's, ordering the twin beds removed in favor of a large comfortable double bed. The adjoining room I reserved for Mrs. Harding. Rooms 8051, 8053, and 8055, directly opposite the entrance to the Presidential suite, I assigned to the Detail. Our reservations were to go into effect on our return from Yosemite.

The next day at noon, as I was leaving for the Park, I followed a hunch and got hold of Shepherd.

"There's always a chance of plans being changed in a hurry," I said. "These rooms may be needed sooner than we think. I believe we had better put all the arrangements into effect immediately."

Shepherd sent for the head housekeeper; we made a final tour of inspection; the double bed was moved into the President's room; then all the rooms were locked.

"Hold them until you hear from me," I said.

The next morning at two o'clock I was asleep in an upper berth enroute from Merced to Yosemite. The train conductor woke me and gave me a telegram marked "Urgent." It was from George Christian and read:

ARE ROOMS READY AT PALACE HOTEL? SCHEDULE HAS BEEN CHANGED. PARTY GOING DIRECT TO SAN FRANCISCO. ARRIVING TOMORROW MORNING.

Across the envelope I pencilled a reply and handed it to the conductor:

ROOMS READY PROCEED.

While that was being sent I wrote out two more messages, one to Shepherd and one to Chief O'Brien, advising them of the change in plans. At Yosemite I went ahead as if nothing untoward had happened, selecting cabins, allotting them to the members of the party, and arranging for a buffet luncheon. This was on Sunday the twenty-ninth of July. I went on to Los Angeles and worked with the local committee and with Mr. Wrigley, who was putting his yacht at the President's disposal. I telephoned this news to the captain of the *Henderson*.

Some time after midnight I was awakened by a long distance call from San Francisco.

"Hello, Colonel," Doc Smithers said. "The boss is sick. Christian wants to talk to you."

Christian told me that on the advice of the physicians the President had decided not to complete the itinerary of the trip.

"Cancel everything," he said. "But leave it open. We may be able to resume."

I began working at six o'clock the next morning. I called the captain of the *Henderson* again—the ship was in San Diego—and told him the trip through the canal was off. I met with the local committees and helped them word the announcements of cancellation. That evening I took the train for San Francisco.

It was three o'clock the next afternoon when I reached the Palace and reported to Christian and Chief Moran, who was in San Francisco acting as witness in a counterfeiting case. They both told me that the President was better. He had been suffering from bronchial pneumonia but had passed the crisis. They told me to get some rest. I followed their advice, for I was worn out, largely from lack of sleep. I went to bed early and slept until almost noon the next day.

It was now the afternoon of Thursday, August 2. Christian had gone to Hollywood to read the speech which the President had prepared for delivery at a meeting of Knights Templars. Mrs. Harding sent for me and I went to her room. She assured me that the President was much improved but said she wanted me to make arrangements for an immediate return to Washington.

"Please don't mention your plans to Mr. Christian," she said. "He is so worried about the abandonment of the trip, and he is so faithful to Warren. I don't want you to mention it to Warren, either. I know he would like to see you. Will you go in?"

She took me into the President's bedroom. He was sitting up in bed, bolstered by many pillows. They were arranged just as Brooks had described them to me.

"Well, here's the Colonel," he said. "I am glad to see you back. I want to thank you for the marvelous arrangements you made for me on this trip. You carried out my wishes to a T."

He was in good spirits, though pale and obviously weak. He talked about the details of the Alaskan journey, telling me the things which had impressed him. His only regret was that his luck at fishing had been bad. He had not caught a single one.

"But I'll get some down at Bill Wrigley's place," he said. "We'll spend ten days down there and get in some good deep-sea fishing. That's a good spot, isn't it?"

"Wonderful!" I said. "You can catch anything you want down there."

"You make the arrangements," he said. "I'll leave everything to you."

I left him after a few more minutes, wishing him a quick recovery and assuring him that I would carry out his instructions. Mrs. Harding went to the door with me. I had now sworn fealty to both of them.

The rest of the afternoon I spent riding about the city with Chief O'Brien. In the evening I travelled far out into the residential section, beyond the Fairmont Hotel, to have dinner with Tommy Foster, head of the Secret Service in San Francisco. He was a Springfield, Tennessee, boy and an old friend. As we finished our dessert about seven-thirty the telephone rang. Tommy answered it.

"It's the Chief," he said. "He wants to speak to you."

I put the receiver to my ear. Moran was talking.

"Star," he said, "your boss—the President—is dead."

I could hear him weeping. He was a sentimental man. When he could control himself he said, "Come to the hotel as quickly as you can and take charge."

As I hung up the receiver I heard sirens. Chief O'Brien had sent his own car and a motorcycle escort for me. We went down the San Francisco hills at a speed which would have frightened me into a coma at any other time. In no time we were at the corner of Market and Geary Streets and I was walking through the lobby with Shepherd, who had been waiting for me. We took the private elevator to the eighth floor, where I found Moran, Chief O'Brien, and Commissioner of Police Rossi, now Mayor of San Francisco.

"Star," Moran said, "I want you to take charge and clear the hotel."

I assigned policemen to each elevator, instructing them to allow no passengers to stop at the eighth floor unless so instructed by Chief O'Brien. All callers were to be announced to me. With Doc Smithers, who had charge of the telephones as well as the telegraph lines, I went to work on arrangements for the funeral train to Washington.

Meanwhile I tried to find out what had happened. The President had seemed well. Mrs. Harding had been reading to him. Suddenly she had rushed from the room, calling for the doctors. He had stiffened, then relaxed. When they got to him he was dead. I asked Dr. Sawyer if he knew the cause.

"Cerebral hemorrhage," he said.

"Do the other doctors agree?" I asked.

"Yes," he said.

But they had not, I discovered, signed a certificate to that effect. Though it was now past midnight I told Doc Smithers to assemble them for such a ceremony. There were, in addition to Sawyer and Boone, Dr. Ray Lyman Wilbur, now president of Stanford University, and Dr. C. M. Cooper, a San Francisco heart specialist who had been called in for consultation.

The four came to the anteroom adjoining the President's bedroom and signed a statement that death had resulted from a cerebral hemorrhage. I talked with them, trying to reduce medical terminology to terms I could understand. They explained that what had happened to President Wilson partially, had happened to President Harding completely, and had struck him at the base of the brain.

From Jervis, Smithers, Miss Powderly, and Steve Early, who was covering the trip for the Associated Press, I got pieces of the story. Mrs. Harding had been reading to her husband an article about him appearing in the *Saturday Evening Post*. It was entitled "A Calm View of a Calm Man," by Samuel G. Blythe. The President liked it. "That's good," he said. "Go on, read some more." Then he stiffened, shuddered, and relaxed.

Steve Early happened to be in the corridor when Mrs. Harding came out and called the doctors. He realized that something was very wrong and ran down the steps to the next floor to call the San Francisco office of the Associated Press. He told them to get ready for a bulletin.

Jervis and Smithers, meanwhile, were in the dining room downstairs having dinner. They were paged and went immediately to the eighth floor. Entering the anteroom they saw Miss Powderly standing by the bedroom door. She nodded to them in a gesture of finality.

The door was open. They could see Mrs. Harding sitting by the bed, sobbing and saying to herself over and over, "Warren, Warren, Warren!" The President lay back on the pillows. There was no doubt that he was dead. His face was relaxed and his expression was peaceful.

Early, pacing up and down the corridor, saw Jervis and Smithers when they came out. Their faces told him the news even before they could speak. Again he raced down the steps and telephoned his office. Thus the Associated Press got a beat of twenty-five minutes on the story.

The President died at seven-twenty P. M. Twenty-four hours later, on the evening of August 3, the funeral train left San Francisco. I shall never forget that journey. The nation was grief-stricken. Every town and city through which we passed was in mourning. People stood by the side of the tracks singing hymns while we went slowly through. Masons in full dress uniforms, with helmets and plumage, waited at each stopping place on the long three-thousand-mile journey.

Sometimes it was the middle of the night when we crept slowly into a station, the bell of our locomotive clanging dolefully. From either side of us out of the misty night would come the flicker of white garments, then the low, rolling tones of thousands of men softly singing "Lead Kindly Light," or "Nearer My God To Thee." Across the breadth of the continent there seemed to be no sound but the beating of our bell and the voices, rising up and washing over our train like a tide.

On the morning of Tuesday, August 7, we arrived in Washington. That day and night the President lay in state at the White House. In the evening Mrs. Harding sent for me.

"Colonel," she said, "I have one last request to make of you. You have done everything that I asked, and I thank you with all my heart.

"When the services are over in Marion and he is taken to the cemetery, I want you and Mr. Jervis to walk along beside him—one on each side. When the receiving vault is reached, please stand at the door, one on each side, and stay until the entrance is sealed.

"Warren loved you both. He appreciated your loyalty and faithfulness. I know that this request I am making will please him."

I promised her that we would do as she asked. Both Jervis and I had been busy, he on the preparations for the ceremony at the Capitol and I with the schedule for the train to Marion. Neither of us expected to play a part in the funeral procession, and we found ourselves without proper clothes. At the moment neither of us possessed a dark suit or a black hat. The stores were already closed and would not be open during the following morning. I finally had to call my friend Donald Woodward and get him to take me to his store, Woodward and Lothrop's, so I could be properly outfitted.

Next morning the casket was put on a caisson and started slowly for the Capitol. Never have I travelled that mile of Pennsylvania Avenue so slowly or with such an ache in my heart. The Marine Band was playing "Onward Christian Soldiers." Then above the music I heard a wave of high-pitched sound. Hundreds and hundreds of school children were singing, "Nearer My God To Thee," and as the caisson moved toward them they threw flowers on the street for it to roll upon.

The ceremony at the Capitol was brief. As dusk dropped on the city the train left Union Station and headed for Marion. All through the night, time after time, the locomotive slowed down and we heard the people singing. It was the next afternoon when the President finally reached home. He was taken to the house of his father, Dr. George T. Harding, on Center Street. There his old friends went to see him. They were quiet. They did not weep. Their feeling was too deep for tears.

No one had ever held such a place in their hearts. They did not know what to do, now that they had lost him.

The next day, on the tenth of August, the funeral was held. A green carpet had been laid over the steps of the house. Over it the bearers took the flag-covered coffin. The procession wound through the streets of Marion, passing the office of the *Star*, where the President had been so happy, and where his wife, as his assistant, had in other years set off daily on her bicycle. It was a place they should never have left, I felt. Every step away from it had brought them closer to the tragedy of this day.

At the cemetery we walked to the tomb. Its iron gates had been opened. Inside flowers were piled. On a catafalque in front of the entrance the coffin was placed, and the mourners stood by it. The new President, Mr. Coolidge, stood next to a man who had been President a dozen years before, Chief Justice Taft.

Again we heard the voices, singing "Lead Kindly Light." A man began to pray. Another man sobbed. It was Doctor Harding. Then it was over. The coffin was carried from the catafalque. A bugler played taps. Mrs. Harding stepped into the tomb. The seconds ticked away. The President, the Chief Justice, and the others waited.

She came out. She was not weeping. Her face was lifted, and her eyes shone with a light I had not seen in them before. She walked away, and the others followed her.

When they had all gone the gates were swung shut, and Jervis and I, our new black hats still clutched in our hands, went slowly after them.

★☆★

CHAPTER FOURTEEN

The Little Fellow

WHEN WE LEFT the cemetery at Marion, Jervis and I were, temporarily, free men. Our duty to President Harding had ended, our duty to President Coolidge had not begun. Other members of the Detail were watching him. On the ride back to Washington we relaxed, and when we arrived there I went to my room and slept the clock around. I was completely exhausted, and did not report for duty for another day. Then, at a quarter of six in the morning, I went to the Willard Hotel and waited outside the President's suite on the third floor. I had heard that he was an early riser. At a quarter after six the door opened and he stepped out, dressed to go for a walk. He recognized me and said:

"Good morning, Colonel Starling, I've been wanting to see you. I want you to stay with me during my administration."

I had no hesitancy in answering him. He was a Congregationalist from the hills of Vermont; I was a Presbyterian from the hills of Kentucky. Though between such people there is a multitude of differences, the basis of their character is alike. This small but well-built man with reddish hair, soft brown eyes, and a determined chin, was easy for me to read in general outline. He was honest, brave, religious, and stubborn. With such a man I could get along.

"I will be most happy to remain with you," I said. "I will consider it an honor to serve you in any way."

Instead of answering he walked to the stairway. I followed him. We descended three flights of stairs and went out to F Street, walking toward the Washington Hotel. A few newspaper photographers, al-

ready versed in the new President's habits, were waiting. He posed for
them; then we continued, following the lines of the Washington Hotel
around to Pennsylvania Avenue, turning into E Street and walking
east to Twelfth, where we crossed and stopped in front of the Martha
Washington candy shop. Here the President spoke for the first time
since greeting me. I had presumed he was busy with deep thoughts
and had not bothered him.

"Do they make good candy here?" he said.

Before I could pull myself together and reply he answered himself:
"They must. My wife likes it."

We did some more window shopping, then walked back to the hotel.
There was no further conversation. At the door of his suite I left him
and went to get my breakfast. That afternoon we took another walk.
Crossing Fourteenth and F Streets he yanked my coattail.

"Better be careful," he said. "That was a woman in a Ford, and
that's a bad combination. One of them struck me in Northampton and
bruised my hip."

Next morning we strolled again before breakfast, and I realized it
was going to be habitual. At that time I was living at Thirteenth and
Kenyon Streets, and in order to get to the Willard on time I found I
would have to get up at four o'clock. While I was pondering what to
do about such a predicament the President one day made a suggestion.
We were in front of the Willard.

"You ought to move in here," he said. "It's a good place."

So I did, and remained there throughout his two terms of office,
eventually getting a private telephone wire installed between my room
and the White House.

The Coolidges remained at the Willard while Mrs. Harding packed
up and prepared to move. One day she sent for me and asked me to
select a set of golf clubs from her husband's collection.

"Take whichever set you like," she said. "I know Warren would want
you to have them."

I put these clubs with those which Mrs. Wilson had given me from
her husband's collection. I particularly liked to use them when at home

on vacation, playing over a beautiful course which neither President had enjoyed, and with a peace and contentment which neither had ever known.

At the White House I waited outside each morning for President Coolidge, going into the lobby if the weather was bad. By a simple procedure, without saying a word, he showed that he had chosen me for his walking companion. When I was not on duty early in the morning he did not go out.

A few days after he moved into the White House we struck out at the usual early hour, just as a gang of laborers was going to work in front of the Executive Offices, where they were tearing up the street, a favorite occupation in Washington. The Irish foreman, seeing us, said to one of the Detail who was standing nearby:

"What a fine looking man our new President is! So tall and straight! Who's the little fellow with him?"

He was told that the little fellow was the President.

"Glory be to God!" he said. "Now ain't it a grand country when a wee man like that can get to be the grandest of them all!"

From that time on President Coolidge was to us and all the members of the White House staff, the "little fellow."

I was distressed to find that he took no other exercise except walking. He did not play golf, ride horseback, fish, hunt, swim, bowl or even play billiards. He had no hobbies, not even stamp collecting. Moreover, he walked with his head thrust forward, his hands clasped behind him, his shoulders hunched, and his chest sagging. I finally got up enough courage to tell him that since he walked for a healthful purpose he should not defeat that purpose by his posture.

"It will do you so much more good," I said, "if you will keep your head up and your shoulders back, with your arms swinging. The important thing is to stimulate circulation in the chest."

He paid no attention to me, and for a week continued to walk as before. Then one day he suddenly struck out with his head stuck up in the air and his arms flailing, so that I had to walk at least three feet from him. I said nothing. After a while his arms fell into a normal swing. He never walked again with them behind him.

He liked to go to F Street and window shop. To get there we passed the Treasury building. The walk in front of it at that time was in wretched condition. The flagstones had lost their uniformity of level and formed pockets which filled with rain whenever there was a shower.

One day I noticed a young lady whose stockings were wet half way to her knees with water splashed from these puddles. I called the President's attention to her and commented on the state of the pavement.

"Yes," he said, "the Treasury Department ought to fix it. If they don't, some day my Secretary, ol' Andy Mellon, will come walking along here counting his coupons and stub his toe."

Everybody was "ol'" to him. I was "ol' Colonel Starling," Frank Stearns was "ol' man Stearns," Rudolph Forster was "ol' man Forster," and his Cabinet members were "ol' man Mellon," "ol' man Denby," etc. In the same way they were all "my": "my Secretary of the Treasury," "my Secretary of the Navy," "my Secret Service man." All the material trappings of the Presidency were likewise "my": "my car," "my house," "my lawn," "my garden," etc.

This feeling of ownership was a part of his attitude which puzzled me. He was not particularly proud of being President; he hated arrogance and conceit in all their forms. It was as if he were a small boy whose daydream of being king had suddenly been made real by the stroke of a magic wand. He would almost tiptoe around, touching things and half smiling to himself. In his high shoes and his great galluses he was an odd sight in the White House corridors.

On awakening in the morning he would walk across the upstairs hallway to the Lincoln room in his long nightgown and slippers. There he would peek out the window to see whether I was on the lawn. I stood there each morning taking my setting up exercises while waiting for him. If he did not see me he would have Brooks telephone downstairs to ask if I were in the building.

When he was satisfied that I was waiting he would dress and come down stairs. Sometimes he would tell the elevator operator to take him to the basement. Then he would try to sneak out the East or the West entrance, just to fool me. Everyone on the staff cooperated with me and tipped me off, so I was always able to catch him. One day I turned the tables on him and hid in the police box on the East side. He came out of the engine room, up the East steps, and passed right by me. I fell into position behind him. When he reached the gate he turned around with a look of glee on his face, thinking he had at last eluded me.

"Good morning, Mr. President," I said.

He turned and headed for F Street without saying a word.

"Guess you wonder why I like to window shop," he said one day. "It takes me away from my work and rests my mind."

His appetite for pranks was insatiable. In the afternoon we sometimes left for our walk from the Executive Offices. If the mood suited him he would press the buzzer which notified everyone that he was on his way to the White House. Then, while ushers, policemen, doormen, and elevator operators were rushing about getting things ready and snapping to attention, we would stroll out West Executive Avenue and leave them. One day he saw John Fitzgerald, the Beau Brummel of the Detail, go in the tradesmen's entrance. Fitzgerald, who was assigned to Mrs. Coolidge, went a little heavy on the talcum powder and toilet water. The President walked up to Sergeant Gibbons, the White House policeman on duty there, and began to sniff the air. Then he said to Gibbons:

"Who was that woman who went in here just now?"

Gibbons' face turned red. "There was no woman," he said.

The President looked him right in the eye and began sniffing again. Gibbons' face grew redder and redder. Finally he blurted out, "It was Mr. Fitzgerald."

He never smiled when he was telling a joke or making a witty remark. The first time I heard him laugh was one afternoon as we set out for our walk. He was smoking a cigar, and as we approached the gate he took it from his mouth and flipped it to the lawn—he never smoked while walking outside the White House grounds. The cigar struck the ground in a shower of sparks just in front of a squirrel, who jumped straight up in the air. He turned before he hit the ground. In a moment he was up a tree and out on a limb, where he sat staring at us in surprise and disappointment. His look of disillusionment was almost human. The President laughed until he had to hold his sides.

The serious side of his job he performed so ably that the staff in the Executive Offices soon relaxed. Rudolph Forster was able to lead a normal life again. He had been busy all through the Harding years, for Harding had trouble with details and paper work, and Rudolph had to work overtime.

"The little fellow wades into it like Wilson," he said. "He knows what he is doing and what he wants to do. He doesn't do anyone else's work either. He'll be all right at this job. He does a lot of thinking, and he looks a long way ahead."

It was true that he didn't do anyone else's job. One day his personal secretary, Ted Clark, came to the office and asked if he could show the President a file of papers which Secretary of Labor Davis wanted him to read.

"He would like to know whether you agree with his decision," Clark said.

"I am not going to read them," the President said. "You tell ol' man Davis I hired him as Secretary of Labor and if he can't do the job I'll get a new Secretary of Labor."

One evening as we came home at dusk I noticed a light burning in the office of the Secretary of Navy, Mr. Denby. I remarked that Denby was a hard worker, frequently staying in his office until late at night.

"He must be an excellent man for the job," I said.

"I wouldn't say that," the President replied. "I don't work at night. If a man can't finish his job in the day time he's not smart."

A few months later the newspapers were proclaiming that the only thing of which Denby was guilty in connection with the oil scandals was stupidity.

His uncanny judgment of people, and the things he knew about them, always amazed me. Once I described a certain man as stingy, and the President immediately reeled off a list of important contributions to charity which the man had made, and added that he had just sent a young fellow to Colorado for his health and was taking care of his family, which consisted of a wife and four small children.

He was so different from President Wilson that it was hard to realize the two were fundamentally alike. For both of them life was largely a mental experience, but whereas in Wilson this was obvious, in Coolidge it was not. I could never figure out, as we walked along silently, whether his mind was busy with great affairs of state or trivialities. In the end I decided that most of the time he let his worries drop back to the subconscious and enjoyed himself like a small town boy strolling down Main Street on Saturday night. The things he said to me might have been said in Northampton, Hopkinsville, or Lexington, Virginia. Passing a large department store one morning he said, "If you ever get married don't let your wife buy anything in there. My wife goes in there and it costs me a lot of money."

One afternoon we walked up Sixteenth Street to Scott Circle. Traffic was heavy and I had a difficult time piloting him safely across the street. As we continued west on Rhode Island Avenue he suddenly asked, "Who was the lady in the limousine wearing a red hat?"

"I didn't notice," I said, "but it might have been either Mrs. Alice Roosevelt Longworth, who lives on Massachusetts Avenue, or Mrs. Frank B. Kellogg, who lives up the way on Eighteenth Street. They both wear red hats."

We continued in silence, turning into Connecticut Avenue and walking south to the Mayflower Hotel, where we window-shopped one of the exclusive little stores.

"Think they're making any money?" he asked.

Nothing more was said until we reached the White House and he was in the elevator. Turning to bid me goodbye he said:

"Guess that was ol' lady Kellogg."

Mrs. Coolidge had occasion now and then to visit Northampton. Her mother was ill, and she herself found the climate of Washington difficult to bear. She was bothered with sinus trouble, and the Capital weather seemed to make it worse. One morning when she was away the President said to me as we returned from our walk, "Want to have supper with me?"

"I would be delighted," I said, wondering what time dinner would be served.

"Come on then," he said, walking into the elevator.

We went upstairs and into his bedroom, where he telephoned for two breakfasts. He didn't ask me what I wanted; he just told the cook to make his order double. It was served in the room, and consisted of fruit, oatmeal, bacon and eggs, coffee, toast and marmalade. Every morning thereafter when Mrs. Coolidge was away I shared this "supper" with him (every meal to him, I discovered, was "supper").

Whenever a letter was expected from Mrs. Coolidge we ended our walk at the Executive Offices, where he cut the twine on the stacks of his personal mail and looked through it until he found an envelope addressed in her handwriting. He would stuff it into his pocket and walk quickly to the White House. I would go up with him on the elevator but remain outside his room until he sent for me. He would lock the door, and it was often as much as half an hour before he opened it again and asked me in.

He loved his wife deeply. He was, of course, a very sentimental man, and a very shy one. He loved a few people a great deal, and he was embarrassed about showing it. Gradually, as time went by, I found him to be so human and thoughtful that I came to the conclusion his outward reticence and aloofness were part of a protective shell.

On summer nights when Mrs. Coolidge was away we sat on the back porch together and smoked and talked—he made me smoke his big, black cigars and they nearly knocked me out. Often then he spoke at length of his boyhood in Plymouth, of his deep affection for his mother, of her fair-haired beauty, of her love for flowers, of her understanding of him, and of the help she gave him in the problems he faced from day to day. He seemed to remember every day he had spent with her. She died when he was young, and he nourished his memories so that now they were living things, as real to him as the days he now was living. He communed with her, talked with her, and took every problem to her.

"I wish I could really speak to her," he said one night. "I wish that often."

He clung to the habits of his boyhood as well as the memories. When we returned from our afternoon walks he would take me to the butler's pantry and make two sandwiches of Vermont cheese, one for himself and one for me. He cut the cheese carefully, measured the sandwiches one against the other, and if they were not equal would shave off a little more cheese to make the balance. Then he would give one to me and we would sit down and eat them. The cheese was as strong as a billygoat. One day he said to me, "I'll bet no other President of the United States ever made cheese sandwiches for you."

"No," I said. "It is a great honor."

He added gloomily: "I have to furnish the cheese too."

He would go upstairs to his bedroom and eat crackers covered with preserves. He always kept a supply in his room. He ate nuts and peanuts too, and the peanuts were unparched. It was amazing that he never got fat.

One day as we passed the stand of the White House peanut vendor he sniffed at the roasting chestnuts, stopped, and put his hand into his pocket. It came out empty and he turned to me.

"Colonel," he said, "can you lend me ten?"

"Ten dollars?" I said, reaching for my wallet.

"No," he said, "Ten cents."

I gave him a dime and he bought the chestnuts. Some time after our return to the White House the elevator operator brought me an envelope. Inside it was a dime.

Later I became his banker on our walks, furnishing him with dimes and nickels for peanuts, magazines, and newspapers. I kept an account of my advances in my notebook, and every once in a while he gave me fifty cents to clear up the debt. When I was not on duty he took his afternoon walks with other members of the Detail. He took me up to his room one afternoon and while he changed his clothes I looked through the new *Collier's* we had just bought.

"I gave somebody a dime one afternoon to buy a *Collier's* and I didn't get my nickel back," he said.

"It wasn't I," I said.

"I don't know who it was," he said, "but somebody owes me a nickel."

"I don't owe you a nickel," I said.

"I didn't say you did," he said. "I don't know who he was, but he didn't give me back my nickel."

"Well," I said, "it wasn't I."

"Well," he said, "I'm not going to do anything about it. But he kept my nickel. He didn't give it back to me."

Not long after he entered the White House I saw evidence of his irascibility for the first time. He appeared one afternoon with a lock of sandy-colored hair showing from under his hat and the tip of his nose red. We walked rapidly toward Connecticut Avenue. At Jackson Place he said in a low, surly tone:

"I'm not going."

I didn't say anything. A few blocks later he said:

"I'm not going, and I'm not going to let that wife of mine go."

Some sort of comment was called for, I thought, so I said, "You certainly ought to follow your own judgment."

After a few more blocks he said:

"When I lived at the Willard and was Vice President they didn't know I was in town. Now that I'm President they want to drag me up to their house for one of their suppers and show me off to a lot of people, and I'm not going."

I remembered the invitation now. It was from the current Washington social queen.

"I'm not going, and I'm not going to let that wife of mine go," he repeated.

He didn't, either.

In time I grew to expect anything of him, and he never failed me. One morning we were having "supper" in his room and I heard someone pacing up and down in front of the door. I was seated with my back to it and I looked nervously around several times as the pacing continued. The President noticed it.

"That's just ol' man Stearns," he said. "He wants to come in and have some of our supper, but I'm not going to let him. He's eaten enough of my food already this morning."

Stearns, I discovered, had a habit of rising early and eating breakfast by himself. He then smoked a cigar and took his exercise by walking up and down the corridor.

One Sunday morning about a year after I had moved into the Willard, I was half way through shaving at six-thirty when the telephone rang. It was the night clerk. He was greatly excited. President Coolidge, he said, had just walked into the lobby on the Pennsylvania Avenue side and wanted to know if I could come down immediately.

I washed the lather off my face, leaving half of it unshaved, put on my shirt, tucked my coat and vest under my arm, and ran for the steps, knotting my tie as I fled down the hallway. I went down the steps three at a time to the main floor level on the F Street side of the building. As soon as I hit bottom I began wriggling into my coat and vest, when a voice just over my shoulder said:

"I thought you'd come down this side."

He had walked through Peacock Alley to meet me, and was chuckling at his shrewdness in having correctly guessed which way I would descend.

While he watched I buttoned my vest and coat, straightened my tie, and set my hat straight on my head. Then we went out for our walk.

★★

CHAPTER FIFTEEN

The Oil Scandal

SENATOR THOMAS J. WALSH's committee investigating leases of naval oil lands began public hearings on October 25, 1923. The results of these hearings were still being worked out eight years later, but the charges were made and the guilt fixed during that winter of 1923–1924. By spring the "Teapot Dome" scandal had smeared prominent people all over the land, some innocent, some guilty. Senator Walsh, who had spent eighteen months preparing his evidence, put on a three ring circus for the American public. He put everyone and everybody on the stand, including most of the male citizens of Oklahoma, Pat Mc-Kenna, Doc Smithers, and me.

The story had a simple beginning and a simple ending: Secretary of the Interior Fall made a crooked deal and was found out and punished. In between these two events there was a welter of confusion and mud-slinging which gave most of the nation a notion that the Harding administration was a combination of Nero fiddling at Rome and Cleopatra sailing down the Nile. What happened was this:

The Navy Department owned certain oil lands, which were being held in reserve for periods of crisis, particularly wars. Private companies sunk wells along the boundaries of these reserves, and, oil being an inconstant liquid, there was danger that the navy's underground riches would be drained off. It was suggested that the navy lease portions of its reserves to private companies for development. In 1920 a law was passed granting this permission. It was then that Franklin K. Lane, Secretary of the Interior under Wilson, quarreled with his chief over the matter and resigned. Secretary of the Navy Daniels made a few small leases, after asking for public bids.

Secretary Denby, who admitted that he knew nothing about oil, gave the matter completely into the hands of Secretary Fall. Fall leased the whole of a Wyoming hill, nicknamed "Teapot Dome," to a company controlled by Harry F. Sinclair. He also leased the Elk Hills reserve in California to a company controlled by Edward L. Doheny. The business was conducted secretly. No public bids were asked. A citizen of Wyoming, wondering about it, wrote to his Senator, John B. Kendrick. Kendrick, a Democrat, gladly asked Fall for an explanation. After a delay his department said the leases had been made because the oil was being drained from the reserves in large quantities. Fall finally said that the business had been conducted secretly because of such things as naval preparedness and the safety of the country. He wanted no questions asked.

Senator Robert M. LaFollette wanted to ask questions. He suggested a committee of investigation and the Senate obligingly named one, with Walsh, a Democrat from Montana, as chairman. Walsh found out a lot of things, including the fact that Fall had become suddenly prosperous about the time the leases were made. Fall was called as the committee's first witness. He denied that there was anything irregular about the leasing of the lands, and said he had received no compensation for anything at any time from Sinclair or from Doheny, who was an old friend of his. Doheny and Sinclair backed him up.

But Walsh kept plugging away. He turned up embarrassing records, showing expenditures of $175,000 by Fall on his New Mexico ranch. The committee asked Fall to explain. That was where I came in, by indirection. Fall said Ned McLean had given him a loan of $100,000. McLean, in Palm Beach, said it was so, and immediately began to pull all the wires within his reach to keep from appearing before the committee. Finally Walsh went to Palm Beach. McLean was rattled. He was trying to back up Fall, but Walsh tricked him into admitting that he had given Fall no actual money. Meanwhile agents of the committee were collecting all McLean's telegrams and there was a big hullabaloo when it was discovered that they were in code—in three codes, in fact. The testimony began to sound like the second act of an old time melodrama. The committee got an expert code-breaker, who went to work on such things as: JAGUAR BAPTISTICAL STOWAGE BEADLE 1235 HUFF, which turned out to be, WALSH LEAVES COAST LINE TONIGHT 12:35.

Nothing about the $100,000 was discovered in the code messages, and it was decided that there must be a fourth code, concealed in those telegrams which seemed to be written in straight English. Among them was my telegram to Guy asking him to get hold of Wilkins and send him on to Palm Beach. This, the experts decided, was the key message. If only it could be decoded!

One morning a New York newspaperman came to my room. He said he was a friend of Senator Walsh's and that if I would tell him all I knew about the oil scandal he would go to the Senator and pass it on, gaining immunity for me. Particularly he wanted me to tell him about the telegram to Guy. I thanked him for his offer but said I could not help him, since I knew nothing whatever of the matter. The poor fellow who had been hired to decode the telegrams came to me in a pitiful state. He was a mental and physical wreck, having spent days and nights trying to discover the code in my message. He had told the committee that he did not think it was coded, and they had ordered him to keep working, insisting that it was the key to the rendezvous at which the $100,000 was delivered.

At last my day arrived. Pat McKenna and Doc Smithers accompanied me to the Capitol. Doc was being called because he had worked at night on the Washington *Post,* McLean's newspaper, to add to his $2,500 a year White House salary. Pat was called because the committee wanted to connect the White House to the scandal by way of the back door. Pat was stationed at the front door. He might know something.

Walsh and the committee were going hog wild. So was everyone else. Even the Hopkinsville *New Era* blocked out the story of my alleged connection with the scandal and printed it on the front page.

People I had considered my friends wrote me letters expressing their surprise and disillusionment that I was mixed up with such a crooked gang. I was glad to know how much faith they had in me. For two weeks Pat and Doc and I walked down to the Capitol every day, waiting to be called. Finally I was put on the stand.

Walsh was the interlocutor. With his long moustaches pointing straight up on each side of his nose he did his best to give me the evil eye. I assumed the innocence of a babe.

"How long have you been on the White House Detail of the Secret Service?" he asked.

He must have expected me to say that I came in with Harding. He was poised for the kill.

"Since the second year of the Wilson administration," I said.

Slowly the moustaches descended. The evil eye softened. Walsh was an old Wilson man. He went on with the questioning in a gentle, friendly voice. I told him the story of Wilkins and McLean, and my part in it. I explained that McLean did not have Wilkins' address and had been told to wire me if he wanted to get in touch with him. Soon I was dismissed. I went to the White House, took a hot shower, and put on fresh linen. I felt that I had been in an unclean atmosphere. The Senators were rising to the same old bait—public crusaders sometimes win Presidential nominations.

The McLean story blew up when Doheny voluntarily revealed that he had given Fall $100,000 in cash on a promissory note. He produced the note, and McLean explained that he had merely "gone down the line" for Fall in an effort to help him out.

Eventually Fall went to jail for taking the bribe, the first Cabinet member in history to be so disgraced. Eventually, too, Forbes of the Veterans' Bureau and Colonel Miller, Alien Property Custodian, went to jail for similar misdemeanors. Jess Smith, it was discovered, got $50,000 from the Miller deal.

None of these money scandals reached Harding. He was incorruptibly honest, and it was so proved. His memory was smeared by the Nan Britton book, *The President's Daughter,* and by the fantastic web of lies in Gaston B. Means' book, *The Strange Death of President Harding*. Means turned the investigation of Daugherty into a vaudeville act, with himself as the star. Roxie Stinson, Jess Smith's divorced wife, testified and then retracted her testimony. Daugherty, who had been harassed from the day of his appointment by newspapers and senators, was not convicted of faithlessness to his office, but he resigned, and with him disappeared the remnants of the "Ohio Gang." They brought dishonor to themselves and shame to the memory of their leader, a man who had done no wrong except in trusting them.

While I was waiting to be called by the committee ex-President Wilson died, on February 3. I could not keep bitter thoughts from my mind as I stood in the S Street house talking of old times with Mr. and Mrs. Daniels.

The Coolidges made their formal bow as White House host and hostess that winter and were amazingly successful, being gracious and friendly without ostentation or flurry. I had only to coach the President on one point. Being basically bored with the whole idea of the receiving line, he had a tendency to pull people past him as he shook their hands. He would grasp a man's hand and draw it in such a way that the man had either to keep walking or pull back. It made them mad, and I explained this to him. He promised to do better, and he did. But he had his revenge on snobbery in another way. Whenever he spotted a particularly bejewelled dowager down the line, or a social leader of rank and distinction, he would nudge me and say, "Colonel, stop the line at that lady there. I've got to rest." Then, while the lady waited, he would go and sit down for five or ten minutes.

Mrs. Coolidge was the personification of charm. She more than made up for her husband's taciturnity. Everyone liked her, and she carried off the difficult role of First Lady beautifully. Without her the little fellow would have had a difficult time at the dinners, receptions, and balls which custom forced him to attend.

Two of the guests present at all formal receptions were ex-President, now Chief Justice, Taft and Mrs. Taft. One night Mrs. Taft wore a dress with a long train. Walking behind her in the line, the Chief

Justice stepped on it. She remonstrated with him. He apologized. A few minutes later he stepped on it again.

"William!" she said, fixing him with a cold eye.

The Chief Justice was disgusted.

"Oh, Mother," he said. "Drat the old thing!"

What a spring that was! Denby resigned, Daugherty resigned, the Soldier's Bonus bill for $2,000,000,000 was passed by Congress and vetoed by the President, Senator Greene of Vermont was accidentally shot as an innocent bystander in a pistol fight between prohibition agents and bootleggers on a downtown Washington street, the Senate refused to continue the "gentlemen's agreement" on Japanese immigration and paved the way for legal restrictions, Henry Ford made his ten millionth automobile, Gaston B. Means was sent to prison for taking bribes to obtain whiskey withdrawal permits, and an American automobile travelled the route of the Exodus over the Sinai Desert in four hours. It took the Israelites forty years.

"Maybe there weren't any damned fools on the road this time," the President said to me while we were taking our afternoon walk.

He was referring to a joke I had told him about John Calvin. One day Calvin was driving a horse and buggy along a road. At a narrow fill he met another horse and buggy, driven by an enemy. The enemy did not pull to the side of the road but drove straight at Calvin, forcing him to drive to the side and wait. As he passed the enemy sneered and said, "I never turn out of the road for a damned fool!" Calvin smiled, raised his hat, and said, "I do."

At Cleveland in June the President was nominated by the Republican National Convention, and Charles G. Dawes was named to run with him. The Democrats, at New York, were deadlocked over McAdoo, Wilson's Secretary of the Treasury, and Governor Alfred E. Smith of New York. They finally compromised on John W. Davis, formerly Ambassador to Great Britain, and Charles W. Bryan, Governor of Nebraska, brother of William Jennings Bryan, who had tried unsuccessfully to win the Presidency three times before turning over the job to Wilson in 1912.

The family planned to spend most of the summer at the White House, taking occasional trips on the *Mayflower*. The President loved the boat; it was one of the things he liked to refer to as "my." As soon as he walked up the gangplank he put his yachtsman's cap on. It was the symbol of his supremacy of the boat. A look of satisfaction would settle on his face, and he would prowl about the decks, inspecting things and touching them.

The boys, John and Calvin junior, returned from school in June. John had just been graduated from Mercersburg Academy. A few weeks later young Calvin, who liked to play tennis on the White House court, got a blister on his foot. Blood poisoning developed, and he became seriously ill. The President was a stricken man, going about as if in a dream. One day he went out and caught one of the many rabbits that live on the White House grounds. I watched him take the little animal in his arms and carry it inside to show to Calvin. He would have carried him the whole of the White House grounds, a handful at a time, if it would have done any good. There were no sulfa drugs in 1924. On July 7 young Calvin died. In his *Autobiography*, years later, the President wrote: "When he went, the power and the glory of the Presidency went with him."

We took the body to Plymouth for burial, and there Mrs. Coolidge put on his coffin the bible she had given him when he was very small. From there we went to Swampscott, Massachusetts, and then to Washington, but soon we were back in Plymouth. No other place could soothe the melancholy of the President. Young Calvin had been so much like him—in looks, in manner, and in reticence. The father had adored the son, and the son had worshipped the father.

Plymouth was too small a place to hold all of the Presidential party. It is a tiny town in a cut in the hills called the Notch. There is a store, a church, and a little cheese factory. The Coolidge house and Uncle Ben Wilder's house are the only other buildings at the crossroads, except for John Coolidge's blacksmith shop, directly across from his house. The President was born in an adjunct of the village store, which his father was running at the time.

The newspapermen, telegraphers, etc., could stay in such nearby towns as Ludlow, but they spent all day at Plymouth, and something had to be done to increase certain living facilities. We finally built, down behind Uncle Ben Wilder's barn, a magnificent three-holer. Never was so simple an architectural job accorded such scrupulous supervision. The newspapermen were mostly small town boys, and each had his ideas about the way to construct the building. Some leaned toward the classical, others were modernistic. Chief designer, by self-appointment, was Mark Sullivan of the New York *Herald Tribune*. The building was a great success, and thereafter when we had to round up the newspapermen for some special occasion we always sent a messenger to the three-holer. A few of them were bound to be out there, reading, smoking, and thinking.

I was housed in Ludlow, in an apartment over the garage of John Garibaldi Sargent, the town's leading lawyer and a life-long friend of the President's. Sargent was a great, shambling fellow, careless in his dress and manner but amazing in the breadth of his knowledge and wisdom. He had a tremendous library—thousands of volumes lined the walls. It was strange in a time when all talent seemed to gravitate to the city, to find such a man living in so isolated a place. My little apartment was beautifully furnished, and it overlooked a prize vegetable garden. Every morning I carried to Plymouth a batch of produce freshly picked from the rich beds.

One morning my basket contained some yellow wax beans with brown spots on them. About noontime, walking to the President's cottage, I saw John Mays, our colored porter and barber, engaged in a curious task. He had the wax beans in a bucket of water and with a wet cloth was carefully rubbing the rust spots. He looked very discouraged.

"Who told you to do that?" I asked.

"The little fellow," he said. "He told me to fill a bucket half full of water and put the beans in it, and then get a rag and rub the brown spots off."

"How are you doing?" I asked.

"Not a single spot has come off," he said dolefully.

He looked so forlorn that I told him he was being kidded, and that the only way to get the spots off was to use a knife.

Just then I heard the screen door open. The President came out and tiptoed up to John.

"How are you doing, John?" he said.

"Colonel Starling says the only way to get these spots off is to use a knife," John said.

The President looked at me with disgust for spoiling his joke. But I was happy to know that he was up to his old pranks. That meant he was feeling better, and overcoming his sorrow at Calvin's death.

He slipped back into the life at Plymouth as easily as if he had never left there. He would walk over to the cheese factory and eat whey. He made me get a list of all the participants in the Sunday church services so he could identify them and know whose daughter was playing the organ and whose son was passing the plate. He liked to sit out under the sugar maples and look at the hills.

One day I was lounging in the maple grove with Mr. Sargent, who was whittling. Looking up at the hills he began to tell me about life in the Notch during his boyhood.

It was a rough, simple life, entirely removed from the industrial civilization of the towns and cities. During the spring, summer and fall they worked on their farms. In the winter they were snowbound, cut off completely from the outside world, receiving no news or litera- ture of any kind.

"To break the monotony," Mr. Sargent said, " we formed a debating society. Every member was to have a vote and in case of a tie the pre- siding officer was to make the decision.

"Our first subject was Capital and Labor. After all the arguments had been put forward a vote was taken and ended in a tie. The presid- ing officer was a cousin of the Coolidges. He got up to announce the vote that was to break the tie.

" 'Well,' he said, 'all I got to say is that Capital and Labor are like the two sides of a sawhorse. Can't either side do without t'other.' "

We returned to Washington in August for a flurry of social functions, which included a visit by the Prince of Wales. He was a nervous young fellow, very ill at ease, and I was pleased to see that the President, noticing this, did a lot of talking and made the boy feel at home.

Very early one morning when I came to the White House I saw a small boy standing at the fence, his face pressed against the iron railings. I asked him what he was doing up so early. He looked up at me, his eyes large and round and sad.

"I thought I might see the President," he said. "I heard that he gets up early and takes a walk. I wanted to tell him how sorry I am that his little boy died."

"Come with me, I'll take you to the President," I said.

He took my hand and we walked into the grounds. In a few minutes the President came out and I presented the boy to him. The youngster was overwhelmed with awe and could not deliver his message, so I did it for him.

The President had a difficult time controlling his emotions. When the lad had gone and we were walking through Lafayette Park he said to me:

"Colonel, whenever a boy wants to see me always bring him in. Never turn one away or make him wait."

There was not much to his Presidential campaign. He delivered a few speeches, issued no charges or promises, and showed no worry about the outcome. He was, in fact, more serene during that autumn than at any time in the years I knew him. Calvin's death had forced him to look for a spiritual peace, and he seemed to have found it.

My mother often asked me what the President and I talked about on our walks. She had an idea that these conversations were interesting, or concerned things of importance. Returning from my vacation in late October I promised to send her a verbatim account of one of the talks, to prove to her that they were inconsequential.

This is what I sent her on October 30:

"Good morning, Mr. President."

"Good morning, Colonel. High fog this morning. Looks as if we will have a good day. Do you have any fogs in Kentucky?"

"We have fogs in the valleys of the mountains, but generally speaking we have few of them in the state. I first noticed fogs while in New Jersey. Ground fogs were prevalent there. As you say the fog this morning is high, indicating a light atmosphere and a clear day."

"Have you ever been at Cumberland Pass, Kentucky?"

"Yes, I have a very vivid memory of Cumberland Pass, for it was there the Louisville and Nashville Railroad and the Southern Railroad fought to beat each other for the right of way through the gap."

"Did they have to fight each other?"

"The tactics pursued in those days by competing railroads were pretty rough. I was sent from Birmingham once to stop the Southern Railroad from building a track across our Huntsville Branch number two at Ensley, Alabama. I was to do whatever was necessary and the boss would back me up. I had a long talk with their gang foreman and finally he and his men withdrew without making any trouble."

"How is the land in Kentucky? What kind of soil have you there?"

"We have three different soils in the state. There is the black section or pennyroyal, which is good for wheat, tobacco, corn and hay. There is the bluegrass section for grazing and stock raising, and in the last few years a great deal of this land has been converted into growing burley tobacco. Then there is the mountain section where coal is mined, and where some farming and stock raising are carried on."

Here the conversation lapsed for a few minutes. I began it again:

"Did Jervis tell you what happened at the Metropolitan Methodist Episcopal Church the other night when we attended the Roosevelt Memorial Navy Day exercises?"

"No. What was it?"

"An old man and his wife were seated in one of the rear pews in the church. The old fellow was hard of hearing and sat on the edge of his seat with his hand cupped over his ear, trying to hear what the speakers were saying. After the speeches were over the collection plate was passed, and when it reached the old gentleman he asked the man who was passing it a question. In a loud voice he said, 'Has President Coolidge spoken yet?'

"In a low voice the usher said, 'No, sir.' The old fellow said, 'Is he going to speak?' Again the usher said, 'No, sir.' Then the old fellow said, still in a loud voice, 'Well, I am not going to give a cent!'"

On November 4 Coolidge and Dawes were elected by the largest Republican plurality in history.

★★★

Coolidge Days

THE INAUGURATION of Calvin Coolidge on the fourth of March, 1925, had one outstanding feature. It was the first time the Inaugural Address was broadcast. For days preceding the ceremony I worked with engineers and sound men, setting up the various pieces of apparatus and figuring out where to lay the lines and plug in the connections. Radio was in its infancy, and was still regarded by most people as a toy. I called three successive Sunday evenings at the home of certain friends without gaining admittance. They were sitting at the radio, each wearing a set of earphones, and did not hear the doorbell.

The President was not greatly perturbed about the inauguration. A few days before it happened I found him in the basement putting a black cat in a crate with a rooster, just to see what would happen. About this time also he was carrying on a running joke with Brooks. I had told him how Brooks' finer sensibilities were offended by Susie, Mrs. Wilson's maid. Susie was the simple type of negress with enormous flat feet and a fundamental, uncomplicated approach to life. Brooks suffered when he had to share his table with her.

The President thought this over for a few days, then sent for Brooks and told him that Mrs. Coolidge's maid was not well and was to be sent away for a rest, being replaced in the meanwhile by Susie. Every day thereafter he made some remark about it, until the valet in desperation came to me and asked me to do something to keep Susie from reappearing.

One thing which did worry him during these weeks was the possibility of a defeat at the hands of the Senate. Since the first of the year there had been many changes in the administration personnel. The President's secretary, Bascom Slemp, resigned in January, and was replaced in March by Everett Sanders, former Republican Congressman from Indiana. Secretary Hughes had resigned and been replaced by Frank D. Kellogg. Secretary Wallace had died and been replaced by William J. Jardine. Curtis D. Wilbur had replaced Denby.

Harlan F. Stone had replaced Daugherty as Attorney-General. Now he was named to the Supreme Court, and to replace him the President sent to the Senate the name of Charles B. Warren of Detroit, a prominent Republican who had been Ambassador to Japan. At first it seemed there would be no trouble; then the Progressives and Democrats brought out the fact that Warren, a lawyer by profession, had acted as counsel for a large sugar company. He was accused of violating the anti-trust laws. The President issued a statement defending him, but it was apparent that the nomination would be difficult to confirm. No Cabinet appointee of the President had been rejected by the Senate since the administration of Andrew Johnson, and the President did not want such ignominy attached to his record. He was urged to withdraw Warren's name but he refused.

A few days before the vote was taken in the Senate I was tipped off that Warren stood little chance of being confirmed. I so informed the President on one of our walks. He was irritated. He did not believe me. I stuck to my story.

"Well," he said, "you're such a great Secret Service man I guess you know more than anybody else. You know everything. Maybe you can tell me just how everyone is going to vote."

"I will write out a report for you tonight," I said.

Warren had been brought to Washington and hidden away at the Willard without being registered as a guest. He seemed a little apprehensive, for when I carried messages to him I always found him in bed with the covers pulled over his head. In the same hotel on the day the vote was taken the Vice President, presiding officer of the Senate, was taking a nap. He had been assured that it was safe to leave the Capitol, but it wasn't. There was a tie, and although a special messenger was sent to fetch him, he arrived too late and Warren was rejected.

The President resubmitted Warren's name, and on March 16 another vote was taken. This time the rejection was decisive, 46 to 39. The next morning I was called into the President's office. He was in conference with Rush Holland, Assistant Attorney-General. The President excused himself to Holland and took me into the small anteroom between his office and the Cabinet room. He walked over to the window and took hold of the curtain cord, twisting it and tying it into knots. For several minutes he looked out the window, saying nothing. Then abruptly he asked me a question:

"Colonel, do you think your friend John Garibaldi Sargent would make a good Attorney-General?"

My friend?

"So far as I know I do not think you could make a wiser choice," I said. "I have learned to love and to respect Mr. Sargent. I know he is completely loyal to you, and I think he would be a credit to your administration."

Then there was another silence. More knots were tied in the window cord. Then:

"Do you think you can locate him?"

"Yes, I heard from his son-in-law, Sam Pearson, just a few days ago. He said Mr. Sargent was in Montpelier and would be there for several weeks."

"Well, you'd better telephone him to get his grip packed and be ready to catch that midnight train out of White River Junction any day now to come down here and visit you."

I went to my office and got Mr. Sargent on the telephone. He was staying at the Pavilion Hotel.

"What's it all about?" he said. "Why do you want me to come down there?"

"I can't tell you," I said. "Just get that grip packed and don't tell anybody, even your wife. I'll call you again today or tomorrow."

That afternoon I was at the Treasury Department talking with Chief

Moran when the White House operator called and said the President wanted me. When I got to the White House he was waiting for me.

"You'd better telephone your friend Sargent to catch that train to-night," he said. "He'll reach here tomorrow afternoon at 2:15. You take my car and chauffeur and meet him. You'd better take him up to 2400 Sixteenth Street and get him a room. Dress him up and take him to the Department of Justice and have him sworn in. Be sure he has on black shoes. Don't let him talk to the newspapermen. You talk for him. Then bring him over to me and I'll tend to him."

Sargent's name had been submitted to the Senate that day at noon. It had been immediately and unanimously confirmed, probably because everybody felt a little sheepish about the bitter fight over Warren. Next day when I got to Union Station a few newspapermen and photographers were there.

"Who the hell is John Garibaldi Sargent?" they all wanted to know.

I told them that Sargent was a "good guy" and that the President would give out his own story of the matter from the White House. They promised to refrain from questions until then.

When the new Attorney-General stepped off the train he had an old bulldog pipe in his mouth and a pair of enormous rubber overshoes strapped to the single small suitcase he was carrying. He was an odd figure, standing six feet four inches and weighing about two hundred and fifty pounds. Instantly all cameras were focused on the enormous pair of rubbers.

"Hello, Colonel," he said. "I'm here. Now what in tarnation is this all about?"

On the way uptown I explained. After getting him a room I produced a black string bow tie, helped him put it on and knotted it. His size 14 shoes were brown. We blacked them. Then I telephoned the Department of Justice that we were on our way down. After the formalities I took him to the White House and brought him to the President's office.

"Hello," the President said. "How'd you leave the folks at home?"

Another episode of this period amused the President immensely. Dr. William A. Mann, director of the National Zoölogical Park, and an accomplished zoölogist, was anxious to have a special grant of funds given his institution for research purposes. He and his subordinates expected to meet strong opposition from General Lord, the director of the budget, and some of the younger men cooked up an ingenious scheme. They took a luridly spectacular bird called the Malayan starling, a bird of bright yellow plumage with a black cape, and spent their lunch hours teaching him to ejaculate; "General Lord! What about that appropriation?" The bird had a rich baritone voice of peculiarly piercing quality. It presently became expert. About this time a meeting of the government officials concerned with budgetary problems was arranged in the main building of the Smithsonian Institution. Vice President Dawes, General Lord, Senator Morrow, and the heads of some of the departments were there; so was President Coolidge—and so was this gorgeous Malayan starling. The bird was hung in a handsome wooden cage at a carefully chosen and most strategic point; just the point where General Lord was being introduced to the guests. After the general's name had been repeated several times, the bird suddenly burst out in its ringing baritone voice:

"General Lord! What about that appropriation?"

The President shook with laughter. General Lord, who thought he was being made a butt, was at first irritated, but when the situation was explained, he laughed, too—and the National Zoölogical Park got its appropriation.

His stubbornness suffered another defeat that winter. Shortly after the election he made a trip to Chicago. Nothing would induce him to use a special train and he rejected the idea of a special car when he found that he would have to pay a fee plus all the fares normally received from the car's occupants. He ended up by engaging a drawing room. This left him entirely at the mercy of the other passengers, for it was too warm in the car to keep the door of the room shut and everyone on the train walked by to get a look. He never tried it again.

In this connection Coolidge has been credited with devising the plan of running the Presidential special as a second section of a regular train. In this way the expense of a special train is avoided, and the first section acts as a pilot. Those on the second section, including newspapermen and Secret Service operators, buy regular tickets. The expense to the President is relatively low and the privacy, safety, and comforts are comparatively high. Thus the Presidential allowance of $25,000 a year for traveling expenses is able to provide many more trips than formerly. But the railroad executives thought up the scheme, not the President.

He liked to eat in the dining car and always ordered a steak. He watched the steward examine each dish as the waiters brought them past. One day he found some muffins with currants in them. Carefully picking out a currant he placed it on the side of his plate.

"Look, Mama, what I found in my food," he said to Mrs. Coolidge.

The steward, thinking it was a dead fly, turned pale and went into a flurry of apologies. Then he began changing things on the table and shouting orders. When the President left the dining car the steward was in a state of collapse.

"One more trip like this and they can put me in my grave," he said.

Once I went through with what I thought was a Coolidge prank, only to find it wasn't. On the *Mayflower* one morning I was told that the President wanted me to join him at breakfast. I went to the dining saloon, where the family and guests were seated at a large table, and told the President that I had eaten already.

"Eat some more," he said, pointing to an empty place between himself and Mrs. Coolidge. I sat down and was served a large portion of bacon and eggs. I saw Mrs. Coolidge and young John stealing glances at me and smiling. Having nothing else to do I absently counted the number of guests. Suddenly I realized that without me there would be thirteen at table. I was being used as a jinx-breaker. Later I asked Mrs. Coolidge if this were true and she said it was.

I had not known that the President was superstitious. Perhaps he was aware that Wilson landed at Brest, France, twice on the thirteenth, one of them a Friday, and that Harding landed in Alaska on Friday the thirteenth. Anyhow, he took no chances.

That year a summer White House was established for the first time since 1916, when Wilson went to Shadow Lawn. The little fellow chose

Swampscott, where he would be near many of his friends. He wanted also to be fairly close to Plymouth. His father, Colonel John C. Coolidge, was not well, and was operated upon for prostate trouble soon after we got to Swampscott. The old man was now eighty-one, and Doctor James C. Coupal, the President's physician, was of the opinion that he would not live long. During the vacation months we went to Plymouth several times, and the two men, father and son, sat and talked. They were shy with each other, but the deep bond of affection between them was apparent.

That was the year when young men wore bell-bottom trousers, and young John, home from Amherst, had a pair wide enough to get two sets of legs into. One day at Plymouth he and his father were sawing some dead branches from a tree. The President was being careful not to soil his suit, a new one.

"That's a nice suit you have, Father," John said. "Where did you get it?"

"It's a piece of cloth from Bridgewater," the President said. "Ol' Colonel Brooks took it down to a tailor in Washington and had him make the suit."

"It's beautifully cut," John said, "I wish I had one like it."

"If you'd take some of the cloth out of those baggy-legged pants you'd have enough for a suit," his father said.

The President was a good judge of cloth and our problem of getting him into tailor-made clothes was solved when the first bolt of suiting was sent to him as a gift from the Vermont mills. When he saw what the tailor was able to do with it he gave up ready made clothes. He liked to look well, and he had a good build, without any fat. Yet under his trim suits he wore underwear three sizes too large for him, and held up his trousers with enormous suspenders. I remember how amazed I was the first time I discovered these habits. He sent for me and Brooks ushered me in just as he was climbing into his britches. I thought the oversize underwear and galluses were well-intentioned gifts, or a mistake. But they continued for all the years he was in the White House.

When young John was in Washington I was sent out with him to superintend his purchases of clothes. We had to bring the suits back for the President's approval. In order to get him to select what John wanted we tried switching tags, thinking he would be governed by price. But it was no use: he inspected the cloth, rubbed it between his fingers, and invariably chose the best piece of material, which often was not what John wanted, since he was at times swayed by style and pattern.

At Swampscott the President saw a great deal of his friends, Mr. and Mrs. Frank W. Stearns. Mr. Stearns, the owner of a large department store in Boston, was a loyal Coolidge man, and he helped me out a great deal in the early days of the administration by telling me what he knew of the President's likes and dislikes, eccentricities and prejudices. He was the first to tell me that in all things Mrs. Coolidge came first— something I found to be true without exception.

Another friend of the President's, Clarence Barron, publisher of the *Wall Street Journal*, had a large place above Swampscott. One day we went there to inspect his dairy herd and see his thirty-thousand-dollar bull. The President soon got fed up with the smell of cows and cow-barns and was not enthusiastic about going to see the bull. When I told him the barn containing the great animal was on our way back to the house he consented to look in. He peeped over the lower half of the stall door at the enormous animal while Mr. Barron reeled off the frightening number of calves sired by his prize, and told how all of his children who grew to be cows gave such rich milk that it could pass for cream. After about five minutes of this the President walked away from the stall and headed up the path toward the house. As he walked out of the barn he said in a low voice. "Some bull!"

Russ Young, now a city commissioner of the District of Columbia, then covering the President for the *Evening Star*, heard him. When we got back to Swampscott he wrote the story and sent it to his paper. Later he decided to kill it, but it was too late. The *Star* published it.

One morning after our return to Washington the President and I went to the Executive offices after our walk. We heard a typewriter going at full tilt in the press room and asked Captain Dalrymple of the White House police who was working so early. He said it was Russ Young. The President walked into the press room and said "Good morning. Are you writing a powerful piece, Mr. Young?"

"No sir," Russ said. "It is just a little human interest story about the White House. Would you like to see it?"

He took the sheet out of the typewriter and handed it to the President. The little fellow read it, handed it back, and as he walked away said, "Some bull."

Chief Justice Taft, who had been appointed to his post by Harding, used to come to the White House a good deal to call on the President. Sometimes his errand was to suggest appointments in the judiciary or the Department of Justice; sometimes, we supposed, it was to offer general advice. Certain conservative leaders in the party thought it well that Taft should keep in touch, so that he might influence Coolidge at critical points. But there were other men whom Coolidge trusted more. Once he remarked to me very seriously and gravely, "The longer I stay in the White House, the more I am convinced that to be a real success I must consult the practical politicians." By "practical politicians" he of course did not mean the coarse variety of political boss—he despised him; he meant such practical, hardheaded, farsighted men as Murray Crane of Massachusetts, who had done so much to guide him all the way up the political ladder.

I was still not getting anywhere in my efforts to induce the President to take up some form of exercise other than walking. All his physical tendencies were toward inertia. One of the best examples of this occurred when Jimmy Reynolds, former treasurer of the Republican National Committee, was elected vice president of a Washington bank. He came to see the President and told him all about his good fortune, sitting on the edge of a chair in the Executive Office while the little fellow sat with his feet on the desk, slowly puffing at a cigar.

"Mr. President," Jimmy said, "you know the success I had in securing funds for the Republican party. I did not ask for any recognition or thanks at the time and I do not ask for any now. But it would do me an enormous amount of good and be a feather in my cap if you would become a depositor in my bank. Will you do it?"

The President continued to puff at his cigar, watching the toe-tips of his shoes as he tapped them together. Finally, after several minutes of silence, he said:

"Couldn't you make me an honorary depositor?"

Returning from Omaha that November, after attending the American Legion Convention, our train stopped for coal and water at a small town on the way to St. Louis. Such a large crowd had gathered to greet the President that I went into his private car to tell him. He was seated on a big lounge, a table in front of him. His elbows were on the table, his hands were cupped about his chin. He was fast asleep. I tapped him on the shoulder and said, "Mr. President, there are about twenty-five hundred people waiting outside to see you."

Without a word he got up, smoothed his hair, straightened his jacket, and followed me to the observation platform. He gave the people his official smile and they applauded. Then Mrs. Coolidge appeared and was given an even greater ovation.

This was too much for the leading local citizen, who had apparently organized the reception. He was a typical small town big shot, self-appointed master of ceremonies at wakes, weddings, and dedications. Stepping up on one of the rails, with a hand on someone's shoulder to steady himself, he shouted:

"Now, you folks keep quiet. I want absolute silence. The President is going to address us."

Silence ensued. With a gesture of sacrifice and charity the big shot turned to the little fellow and said:

"All right, Mr. President, you may speak now."

Just then the train began to move away. There was a hiss of air as brakes were released. Gently we rolled out of the station.

The President, still smiling, raised his hand to the crowd and said: "Goodbye."

This I believe to be the shortest Presidential speech ever made.

My plan for a long time had been to rouse his interest in fishing and hunting. To do this I talked a great deal on our walks about the outdoors. He seemed to think he knew all there was to know about nature lore, and apparently was of the opinion that it was a boyhood fancy which men got over when they grew up. My project had tough sledding. One day he asked me the name of a certain tree and I told him it was a sycamore. I then recounted how as a boy I would climb out on a sycamore limb to get the eggs from an oriole's nest. He asked me what an oriole looked like. I told him it was a rather small bird, golden yellow and black in color.

"Oh yes," he said. "We have lots of them in Vermont. We call them bobolinks."

"That is not the same bird," I said.

"Yes, it is," he said.

So on our return I went to the dictionary and copied the definitions: oriole, golden yellow and black; bobolink, brown, sometimes called reed bird or rill bird. I then read the notes to him and he admitted that he was wrong. I was wearing him down, but it was slow work.

One day a friend sent me two rock bass, still alive, which he had caught on a fishing trip to Gunston Pass down the Potomac. I sent them up to the President by Brooks, thinking it would stir his interest. I expected him to send them to the kitchen to have them served for supper. The next morning he said to me:

"I put my little fishes in my bathtub and they swam around all night. One of them hopped out while I was asleep and Mrs. Coolidge had to come and pick him up in a newspaper and put him back."

I was pretty sure that he was not asleep when the fish awakened Mrs. Coolidge with its flip-flopping. He probably opened the door between their rooms so she could hear it and then played possum.

I got some unexpected help in the matter of exercise when an electric horse was sent to the President. He knew nothing about it until he returned to his bedroom one day and found me riding it, while A. M. "Blondy" Thomas, chief electrician for the White House, pushed the buttons. He was fascinated, and laughed so hard he had to sit down when I imitated a cowboy on a bucking broncho. I made more racket than the White House had heard since the days of Teddy Roosevelt; so much so that Mrs. Coolidge came to see what was going on. The President insisted that I entertain her also, and he pushed the buttons.

He would not get on himself, but the next morning he tried it out secretly and that afternoon took me up to his bedroom to show me his prowess. He insisted on keeping his hat on. I told him to hold tight while I pressed some more of the buttons. I got a good grip on his coat then pushed the buttons. The horse jumped, the President lost his hat, and almost lost his seat. I stopped the horse and he got off and spent about ten minutes trying to find out what made the thing jump. After that we rode every day, playing cowboy like a couple of kids.

His father was now very ill. In January a direct telephone line was installed between the White House and the homestead in Plymouth. Doctor Coupal promised he would tell the President when the end was approaching, so that he could reach home before it came.

Father and son had said goodbye in the fall. Both the President and Mrs. Coolidge had urged Colonel John to come to Washington, where he could be comfortable and have their company. But the old gentleman wanted to die in his own home, among his own people.

The President talked with him two or three times a day on the private telephone. He worried about him, fearing he would not be able to reach Plymouth in time when the last stage came. He almost became ill himself; his appetite waned and he was bothered with indigestion.

When Doctor Coupal gave the word for him to go, three feet of snow blanketed Vermont. I sat in the President's office talking to the proprietor of the Woodstock Inn, while the President walked nervously back and forth, asking questions, making suggestions, and figuring out schedules. He was nervous; he did not want me to leave him. He listened while I dictated final instructions to Woodstock:

"Our train will reach there at 6:30 tomorrow morning. Not less than six closed seven passenger automobiles are to be at the depot. All wheels on all cars are to be equipped with new chains. We will need four fur coats and two heavy lap robes.

"Test the brakes on each car and for chauffeurs have men who are not younger than forty and who are used to driving automobiles in Vermont.

"The point at which we are to change from automobiles to sleighs must be at someone's house. See that a good hot fire is burning there. The sleigh for the President must be thoroughly inspected—springs, body bolts, tongue, etc. It must be supplied with plenty of hot bricks. The horses which draw it must be strong, exceedingly gentle, and driven by either the owner or a man who is used to driving them. The automobiles must wait at the transfer point until released."

Everything went according to schedule. The snow was cleared for the sleighs, and pockets were cut in the side at regular intervals to provide for traffic in the other direction. No one was allowed to come against our procession except doctors and midwives, but for these we made provision. At Plymouth the snow had been shoveled away from the house, and as we arrived men were making a path to the church and to the cemetery. We were too late. Colonel John died on the eighteenth of March without seeing the face of his son for the last time.

With his father gone the President did not care to return to Plymouth for the summer. He sent me out to find a suitable spot for his vacation, stressing the fact that he wanted a climate which would aid Mrs. Coolidge's health. A pine forest in the mountains was the best possible place for her, and I finally settled on White Pine Camp, fourteen miles from Saranac Lake in the Adirondacks. It was offered by its owner, Irwin R. Kirkwood, a newspaper publisher at Kansas City. The place was deep in the forest, yet equipped with every modern convenience and most of the luxuries. It was on Lake Osgood, a beautiful stretch of water inhabited by Northern pike and pickerel.

One day in June, Doctor Jason Noble Pierce of the First Congregational Church, which the Coolidges attended, called me and told me that several large pieces of plaster had fallen from the ceiling of the church. I made an investigation and decided it would be unwise to have the President attend services until repairs were made. Doctor Pierce closed the church and the congregation met temporarily in the Metropolitan Theatre. On the first Sunday after his return from Amherst, John asked his father if they would attend church.

"No," the President said. "Ol' Colonel Starling shut up the church and won't let me in. We go to services in some theatre."

Not that he objected to the theatre. He liked to go occasionally, and he thoroughly enjoyed a good show. I remember once when I heartily wished he disliked the theatre. We were walking along in front of the Treasury Building when he asked me if there were any good shows in town. I reminded him that it was Lent and that the bills at the various houses were not up to their usual standard. I painted as pessimistic a picture of them as I dared: I had two dates that night, dinner with a very good looking young lady and an engagement later on with a ravishing creature who was coming down by train from New York. It was no night, in my opinion, for the President to go to a show, for if he went I would have to go with him.

"What's at the National?" he asked. I could feel the stubbornness rising in his voice.

"I don't think the National would interest you," I said. "I took Mr. Sargent there last night. It's just an ordinary leg show."

"I'd better not take my wife there," he said, "and you'd better not let the folks up in Vermont know that John Sargent is going to leg shows."

He then asked me about Poli's. I told him it was dark.

"What about the Belasco?"

"It is rented for this week to the Ku Klux Klan."

"Well, we won't go there. That's worse than a leg show."

There was a pause. Hope rose within me.

"You'd better get me tickets for Keith's tonight," he said finally. I was sunk.

When we reached the White House I made a last desperate effort to save myself. I suggested that I talk to the manager of Keith's and ask him whether the bill was any good. The President agreed that this might be a wise precaution. I went to the theatre and spoke to Roland Robbins.

"You probably got a pretty poor bill this week, haven't you?" I asked hopefully.

"No," he said. "As a matter of fact this is the best show we've had all season."

I groaned. "Make the usual arrangements," I said. "The President will be here tonight."

I lost both girls.

We went to Lake Osgood in July, and I immediately set to work on the final stage of my campaign to convert the President into a fisherman. I proceeded carefully, for I had made bets with most of the White House staff and some of the Cabinet members, and I did not want to lose. They said I would never get him into a boat or get a fishing rod into his hand.

He would stand on the dock at the boathouse or on the bridge across the bay leading to the residence, and I would get into a guide boat and stand up to cast, demonstrating that the craft was safe and steady and in no danger of turning over. After I hooked a few fish he showed interest. I would put them on a line and show them to him when I came in. Finally, when I almost had begun to lose hope, he said to me one morning, "I'd like to fish this afternoon."

It was not a particularly good day—breezy, with ripples on the lake and a little bright. I had to decide between giving him a nickel-plated Colorado spinner or a copper spinner. I finally decided to let him use a copper spinner, giving it a rub on the sleeve of my hunting coat to make it brighter. Oscar Otis, the superintendent of the estate, handled the boat. The President sat on the middle seat. I was forward. We proceeded along the shore about fifteen feet from the bank.

Nothing happened for the first half hour. Then the President's spinner began to move along near the bank. His line went tight. It was a good-sized fish.

"What'll I do with it?" he yelled at me.

"Keep a taut line with the rod tip up and let him stay in the water," I said.

I motioned to Otis to pull the boat out into open water, away from the shore, so there would be no interruption in the battle. The President followed my instructions and in about twenty minutes he had his fish alongside the boat. By this time he was wild with excitement.

"Get him in the boat! Get him in the boat!" he shouted to me.

"He's still your fish," I said, handing him the gaff. "Lift him into the boat with this."

He did, but not as I meant. Instead of aiming for one of the gills he hooked the fish dead center and with a tremendous heave jerked him into the boat. I covered my eyes with my hands. When I was able to look I saw a beautiful Northern pike flopping on the bottom of the boat. The little fellow was sitting down, shaking all over. I winked at Otis and motioned him to head back to the boathouse.

The pike, which weighed six pounds, I put on a fish string. When we landed I turned it over to the President, who took it in both hands and hurried up the path to the house. As he approached the cabin he called loudly for Mrs. Coolidge. She came out on the porch to see what was up. Waving the fish at her the little fellow cried:

"Mama! Mama! Look what I've caught!"

Thereafter we fished every day, rain or shine. The conversion was complete. The little fellow became one of the most ardent fishermen I have ever known, and I collected all my bets.

On our last day at the camp I had a private mission to perform. I told Jervis that I knew where there were at least four ten- or twelve-pound pike, and I was going after them. Everett Sanders had arranged for the newspaper photographers to take some pictures of the President, Mrs. Coolidge, and John, so I would be free to go alone.

Late in the afternoon I returned to the boathouse with two of the pike on my string, each weighing twelve pounds. Jervis and the President were on the dock, waiting for me. Jervis came forward to hold the boat steady while I got out with my tackle and fish, and as he leaned over he whispered, "Don't get mad. The little fellow is going to send you to Amherst with John."

Just then the President came forward and said, "What have you got?"

I showed him the fish and he took them. Then he asked me to come to the house to talk with him.

"I'll put the fish in the icebox," he said.

He did, and I never saw them again. Then we talked about John.

The boy had now finished two years at Amherst, and the President was worried about his progress. He thought his marks were unnecessarily low, and he was concerned about all of the younger generation. The jazz age was then at its height. We were smack in the middle of the Roaring Twenties, with hip flasks, joy rides, and bathtub gin parties setting the social standards. The President was the antithesis of all this and he despised it. He was enough a student of history to realize it was a temporary phase, but he wondered whether it would have a lasting effect on the members of John's generation. Later, in other conversations, I found that he foresaw clearly at this time the crash that was ahead of us. He wanted to know what kind of people we would have to pit against it.

"These boys are not Communists," he said. "They are Americans. But I want to know what kind of Americans they are. People are like apples. They can spoil."

I disagreed with his contention that I could find out anything or ride herd on John, and I told him so. I might have saved my breath. He had slept on the problem, weighed it, considered it from every angle, and now all hell could not alter his decision. At the tender age of fifty I was going to college.

Next morning John and I started off in one of the White House automobiles with Boots Miller, Mrs. Coolidge's chauffeur, driving. John was embarrassed and so was I. He was a thoroughly decent chap, however, and he inherited his father's sense of humor. He decided to make the best of it and I made him realize that I had no intention of sticking his nose into a book and holding it there.

There was no need for such tactics anyhow. As soon as we got to Amherst and settled down, the solution to the situation appeared. She was a pretty redhead named Florence Trumbull, daughter of the Governor of Connecticut. Every Saturday night we would take the trolley to Mt. Holyoke College, and while the courting went on I found some way of killing time. I slept in the same room with John and every morning we dressed to the tune of "Alice Blue Gown," played on the portable phonograph.

We roomed with Mr. and Mrs. Lindsey, two dear old people who took pity on my predicament and helped me fill out my course of study from their private curriculum. With their help I was able to map out some walks of from twelve to fifteen miles. I took long automobile rides with the Postmaster. I visited with Ray Stannard Baker, who was with us at the Peace Conference in Paris, and made friends with some of the Amherst faculty—Tip Tyler, the mathematics professor, President Olds, Doctor Richard Morton, and others. For my seminar work I undertook a complete study of the New England apple pie, which I found extremely suitable for a Ph.D. thesis—I could taste innumerable samples without being forced to any definite conclusion.

The newspapermen hounded me constantly during the first few weeks, but it was not my place to talk and I referred them to the President, who would make no statement. The boys made all kinds of guesses. They said John's life had been threatened and they tried to tie the whole thing up with the Sacco-Vanzetti case, which was then reaching its climax in Boston. After a while they took pity on me and let me alone.

My most prized souvenirs from those college days are a letter from the President and a verse copied from a tombstone in a Massachusetts cemetery. The letter says in part:

We have not heard much from John since he arrived at Amherst, so we suppose he is getting on all right. It seems to me it would be a good plan for him to get up about six o'clock or so and take a walk. He did not tell me what subjects he was going to take this year. I wish he would write me fully about that, and I should like to see what schedule he has laid out for studying and recitations. He ought to work out a set schedule for each day and then stick to it.

The epitaph reads:

WARREN GIBBS
DIED OF ARSENIC POISON
MARCH 23RD 1860
THINK MY FRIENDS, WHEN THIS YOU SEE
HOW MY WIFE HATH DEALT BY ME
SHE IN SOME OYSTERS, DID PREPARE
SOME POISON FOR MY LOT AND SHARE
THAT OF THE SAME I DID PARTAKE
AND NATURE YIELDED TO ITS FATE
BEFORE SHE, MY WIFE, BECAME
MARY FELTON WAS HER NAME

ERECTED BY HIS BROTHER WILLIAM GIBBS.

At Christmas John and I went to Washington for the holidays. The President was so glad to see me that he listened sympathetically to my plea for deliverance. I told him the younger generation was in danger from nothing more serious than love and a little laziness. He decided to let me stay in Washington.

★★★

CHAPTER SEVENTEEN

He Does Not Choose to Run

THE BIG QUESTION that winter was where we would spend the summer. The President was so anxious to get back to fishing that he scarcely talked of anything else—at least with me. A good fishing spot was not the only consideration, however. He wanted a climate which would favor Mrs. Coolidge, and he thought it would be nice to set up head-quarters in a part of the country which would be helped in a business way by such a move. Somewhere in the West, he thought, there must be a region which satisfied all these conditions. Senator Peter Norbeck of South Dakota gave him a sales talk on the Black Hills.

"You'd better go out there and look it over," he said to me, "and go to some other places too. Make sure about the rattlesnakes."

He had a deathly fear of snakes, and I knew that if one was so much as seen around the camp he would get on a train and go back immediately to Washington. It was going to be a job to keep them out of the way. None of the places on my list was free of them.

He was in high spirits after the holidays, in spite of the dismal weather. One rainy, foggy day when we did not leave the grounds during our walk, we spent most of the time hiding from each other in the policemen's boxes. Another day, when it was snowing, he saw Rob Roy, one of his dogs, being friendly with an old negro who was shovel-ling one of the paths. The negro was afraid of the dog.

"Will he bite?" he asked the President as we came by.

"Oh, yes," the little fellow said. "He's a very vicious dog. But he's a peculiar biter. He only bites lazy men. As long as you keep working he won't bother you."

When we got to the house he stood inside the door and gleefully spied on the negro, who shovelled furiously, while Rob Roy, who was interested in the procedure, sat on his haunches and watched.

One afternoon in the butler's pantry the President paused in the construction of our cheese sandwiches and said, "Do you think ol' man Forster would like one?"

"I'm sure he would," I said, "but tonight he and I are going up to Jimmy Taylor's for a ham supper with apple pie, and Mr. Forster likes apple pie so much he probably wouldn't want to spoil his appetite for it."

It was an awkward situation. I did not want to eat the sandwich myself, considering the feast which lay ahead of me, and I knew poor Rudolph's appetite would be completely ruined if he had to put away one of the President's sandwiches. He was the weakest member of our supper club, hardly ever lasting until the dessert. I groped for a solution.

"But that gives me an idea," I said. "There's nothing better with apple pie than cheese, and this cheese is so good I'll bet it would add just the right flavor to the pie."

That pleased him. "You take some along," he said, "and take some for ol' man Forster's pie too."

I did, but I neglected to tell Rudolph all the details of the transaction, and the next day he was flabbergasted when the President called him in for dictation and began by saying:

"I understand you are very fond of apple pie."

"No, sir," said Rudolph politely. "I don't care much for it. I find it rather heavy."

"You do so like it," the President said. "You can't fool me. Ol' Colonel Starling says you can eat a half a pie without stopping."

Rudolph blinked his eyes, then blushed to the ends of his ears. When he came out of the office he was so mad at me that he wouldn't speak. It took me two days to find out what had happened.

In the spring I went West and inspected various vacation spots. The State Game Lodge in the Black Hills of South Dakota seemed the best bet. There in Custer State Park were one hundred thousand acres of pine-covered mountains and valleys, with innumerable trout streams. The Game Lodge, admirably equipped, was thirty-two miles from Rapid City, which could be used as a headquarters for the administration. The area was rich in scenery and opportunities for recreation. The only problem was completing eleven miles of the road from Rapid City to the Game Lodge. That and the rattlesnakes. The local committee promised that the road would be gravelled, and at the Lodge a rattler extermination hunt was ordered.

Back in Washington I urged the President to approve the Black Hills. We walked down Connecticut Avenue discussing it.

"You can fish all day," I said. "You'll sleep well at night, and you can ride into the Executive Offices at Rapid City three or four times a week. You'll come back to Washington a new man."

"I'm not worried about myself," he said. "It's Mrs. Coolidge's health that bothers me. I don't think she can stand much more of this Washington climate and this official life."

"I'm getting mighty tired of it myself," I said. "I'm going to leave the Detail when you finish and go out West, where I can catch trout as long as my arm and shoot Chinese pheasants. I think I'll buy a small ranch near the Black Hills and put some cattle on it. I like that country."

"Can't you come with me?" he asked. "We can take a nice long trip across the country as soon as my term is over, and do all the hunting and fishing we want to without anybody bothering us. Then you can stay with me. Maybe I can get a job somewhere."

My reaction to the meaning of his words was slow. First I thought of his humility—an ex-President thinking there would be trouble about getting a job. Then I had a warm feeling all over at the realization that his affection for me was so genuine. He had made me his friend—why, I did not know, unless it was that we were both country boys who loved our mothers—and he wanted that friendship to endure, with its daily companionship, after he left the White House.

Then it struck me that he was definitely saying he would not run for a third term. I decided to make sure.

"I'm ready to go any time you say," I said.

"Well, we haven't much longer to wait now," he said.

It was a natural and logical decision so far as I was concerned. The novelty of being President had worn off; the glory of it had gone with Calvin's death; there was no great national crisis which demanded a continuation of his leadership. From now on the office was more a burden than anything else. The steady grind of work was wearing him down, and the duties of First Lady, plus Washington's weather, were weakening Mrs. Coolidge's health.

He had another reason too, a very practical one, quite in character with his longheaded thinking. But I did not find that out for many months.

I told no one of our conversation, naturally. The newspapers were speculating on a third term. The President's popularity was at its height, and since he had succeeded to the office from the Vice Presidency it was not considered that the two-term tradition was involved.

The Black Hills won his approbation, and early in June I returned to Rapid City, to remain there until the Presidential party arrived. To my surprise I discovered that nothing had been done to the road. The highway commission did not seem to realize the seriousness of the situation. I called the committee together and informed them that unless I was assured the road would be finished by the fifteenth I would wire the President to defer his trip. Next day the Governor called me and said he would come to Rapid City. He arrived next day and soon thereafter trucks and horses were on their way to the Black Hills. The trucks got stuck in the mud and a special train had to be used to transport them. After putting up the gravelling plant the foreman of the gang told me the gravel bed was not big enough for the job. So the whole plant had to be moved to another point. Things looked bad, but by four o'clock on the morning of the fifteenth, an hour and a half before the arrival of the Presidential train, it was reported to me that the road was ready.

In the meanwhile I had been busy selecting rooms for the newspapermen and their wives. They would wire me for a room and bath, then change their minds and decide they wanted a private apartment. First so and so was coming. Then I would be advised that he was not coming. Mr. Sanders would wire me that he wanted a house and servants. Mr. Clark would write me for a parlor, bedroom, and bath. In addition to this I was:

Going out to the Lodge to oversee its refurnishing, supervising the erection of seven canvas houses, and looking after such things as cleaning out the garage, putting in the gasoline tanks and pumps, testing the water supply, selecting a camp site for the soldiers, putting in additional electric power, building quarters for the negro servants, calling on the church people in the surrounding towns to inquire about their services, riding over the park and surrounding country to become acquainted with the region, moving furniture out of the Rapid City High School and putting in suitable desks, typewriters, telephone and telegraph wires, so it could be used for the Executive Offices; also inspecting the fire apparatus at the lodge, having the chemical tanks recharged, selecting the reception committee, schooling the housekeeper in marketing and purchasing for the Presidential family, and buying two days' provisions for the entire party.

Everything went off smoothly on the day of arrival. Soon the President was out back of the lodge pulling Lochleven and Rainbow trout out of Rhodes Creek, never suspecting that I had put the fish in there in the dead of night only a few days before, and that they were prevented from getting away from the area he was fishing by steel mesh nets sunk across the stream above and below the lodge, with logs on top to conceal them and complete the watergap. One of the first things he did was admit to the newspapermen that he used worms to catch trout. This precipitated a hullabaloo, with all the fly fishermen in the region shouting that to use worms was unsportsmanlike. The controversy was silly—any fisherman will use worms rather than go home with an empty creel. But I planned to convert the President to flies if I could.

A few days later he was fishing the same stream with a guide. I was behind him about a quarter of a mile, trying my luck with a Royal Coachman. He went for me.

"There's an ol' fish here that won't bite," he said. "He keeps taking my bait."

"What are you using?" I asked.

He showed me his hook. On it he had a salmon egg and a grasshopper.

"No wonder he won't bite," I said. "The bait is too big for him to swallow. There isn't a fish in the stream who could get all that in his mouth."

He ignored my criticism. "Suppose you try your dry fly," he said.

I made a few casts with my Royal Coachman. The fish played with it but wouldn't bite. Then I changed to an old, dilapidated Black Gnat. I put it on the grassy bank then pulled it back into the stream. Immediately it was sucked into the current, and the trout, with a mighty lunge, took it as if he had been waiting for it all his life.

The little fellow got so excited that he tangled his own line up in his rubber boots. He called to me, "Don't lose him! Don't lose him!" He told me how to play him. Finally, unable to stand the excitement any longer, he grabbed the landing net and waded into the water above his boot tops. With a quick thrust he got the trout, then carried it ashore, where the guide removed the hook from its mouth. Without a word he carried the fish to the automobile, and that was the last I saw of it. But my purpose was accomplished. Thereafter he fished with flies.

There were several churches in the region, each of them small and holding services only twice a month. I had visited them all and I described them to the President. On the first Sunday after his arrival he decided to worship at Hermosa, a nearby town. I went ahead to make arrangements, and found the preacher at the church. He was a young fellow, a college student who had taken the job for the summer. His name, he told me, was Rolf Lium. He was twenty-two years old.

I told him the President and Mrs. Coolidge were coming, and began to discuss the order of service. As I talked a change came over him. His face reflected the first symptoms of seasickness. We went into the little wooden chapel and wrote out the program. I made a copy for myself and one for him. He looked more and more ill. His forehead broke out in a sweat.

"Excuse me," he said. "I think I'll go home and get a clean handkerchief."

I smiled and reached into my pocket.

"Here is a clean handkerchief," I said. "You won't have to go home. I have two or three more."

Then I patted him on the shoulder. "You don't need a clean handkerchief," I said. "What you need is a little bucking up, a little courage and Christian fortitude. There isn't anything to be afraid of—the President is just a country boy like the rest of us. He came from a town like this. You ought to see the size of the church he goes to up there in Vermont. It's smaller than this.

"You don't have to do much preaching anyhow. He doesn't care for too much of that. He sits in church and mostly thinks about his mother.

"You've got a mother, haven't you? I thought so. Think how proud she will be to know that you conducted services for the President— and think how ashamed she would be if she heard that you ran out on the job.

"We're going to have services here, anyhow, you know, even if I have to go up on your rostrum and read from the bible myself.

"Didn't you say that you had a good organist and choir? Well, let them carry the burden. We'll have some fine singing. Everybody likes that."

I kept talking to him until the Presidential party arrived. Gradually he regained his courage, and he did a fine job, so much so that the President and Mrs. Coolidge came back each time during the summer that services were held.

On the twenty-eighth of June an unfortunate thing happened. Jim Haley, of the Detail, was assigned to Mrs. Coolidge, and that morning they took a long hike in the hills. They did not return in time for lunch, and the President grew worried. Eventually he became almost frantic, pacing the floor of the lodge and registering all the symptoms of intense suffering. He was sure something had happened to them. Most of all he feared that a rattlesnake had bitten Mrs. Coolidge. Searching parties were sent out, and they met the couple on the way. Due to the fact that Haley was a city boy and knew nothing of the woods they had gotten lost.

I was away that day, making arrangements for our visit to the Belle Fourche rodeo, and when I returned the President had already ordered Haley relieved of his assignment and put Mrs. Coolidge in my care. I was sorry for Haley. Some of the newspapermen tried to insinuate all sorts of things into the incident, and the foolish story has persisted into some of the Coolidge biographies. Haley was a clean, honest boy. I had myself recommended that he be appointed to the Detail, after rooming with him in Vancouver during the Harding trip to Alaska. Every night he got down on his knees and said his prayers before going to bed. At the time of the incident he was engaged to be married, and every day he wrote to his girl. Had I been there I might have staved off the President's wrath, but as it was I found myself in a fine fix. Mrs. Coolidge could not go walking unless I went with her. But if the President wanted me to go fishing I had to go with him and she had to stay home. She took it in good spirit and told me that she hoped I would not leave them as long as they remained in the White House.

Apparently he had not informed her of his invitation to me, to join him after his term was finished. He had not, I discovered later, even discussed his decision against a third term with her. When it was announced she laughed and said she was glad that after so many years of marriage her husband was still individual enough to make his decisions without consulting her. When I asked her what she thought of his refusal to run again she said, "I have such faith in Mr. Coolidge's judgment that if he told me I would die tomorrow morning at ten o'clock, I would believe him."

We had a fine time at the rodeo. The President, in fact, was having the best time of his life. He was given a ten gallon hat, and he wore it as proudly as if he had been a boy. When some of his Eastern friends told him they thought he should not be photographed while wearing it, since it would expose him to ridicule, he looked at them with amazement. He could not understand such a snobbish attitude. "They gave it to me," he said. "They want me to wear it, don't they?"

He was also given a cowboy outfit, which he wore, and he was made an Indian chief. If he had fallen asleep over a Buffalo Bill dime novel at the age of twelve and it had all come true, he could not have been more tickled. I had the impression all the time that he was living a boyhood that had been put off for forty years.

We made many trips—to Deadwood, Mt. Rushmore, Yellowstone Park, and the Bad Lands. The Bad Lands were a revelation to me. On the advance trip I went there by myself, and stood in awe at the strange, crescent-shaped span of gullies and mountains, devoid of vegetation, made of a chalk-like earth, impassable for man or beast. At its edge for hundreds of miles was an irregular wall or ridge. I was told that in a blizzard during the winter of 1905 the storm drove more than twenty thousand head of cattle over the wall and to their death. As late as the following July, Indians were hauling the carcasses away, finding those at the bottom still frozen.

At Yellowstone the President had one of his stubborn streaks. Near the lodge where he stayed, and not far from the geyser Old Faithful, was a stream which held very little hope for a fisherman. The water was tepid, and I and the park superintendent both advised him against trying it. So he said he would, the next day. I decided to save his face publicly and at the same time teach him a lesson privately. I telephoned Sam Eagle, postmaster of West Yellowstone, formerly superintendent of service at the Willard Hotel. I asked him to come over to the lodge the next day about noon and bring with him a creel of fresh trout. He was to keep them in his car and tell no one about them.

The next day Sam appeared at the appointed time. I told him to follow our party to the creek and wait there until I could come to him alone. After I had gotten the others started I took Sam to a hidden spot and there transferred the fish from his creel to mine, putting in some fresh grass. Then I stepped into the water and ducked my creel three or four times, wetting it thoroughly. I then said goodbye to Sam and fished along about a quarter of a mile behind the others. The trout in my creel were beauties—about two dozen of them, taken that morning from a mountain stream.

We fished for several hours. I caught one little fellow about four inches long. I held him up and made the rod dance, so that from a distance it looked as if I had something worthwhile. The President, looking back, saw that I had been successful and sent two of his party back to check up. When they arrived the little fish was out of sight and I was getting ready to cast again. They asked me what luck I was having.

"I'm doing pretty well," I said. "What have you fellows caught?"

"Not a damned thing," they said.

When the President decided to quit I caught up with them. We were on the wrong side of the stream for the automobiles and had to cross it to reach them. The President was wearing my hip boots, which came up to his crotch. I was wearing a pair made for a man smaller even than the President. So was the guide, who was also a big fellow. Crossing the stream we kept the President between us and let him walk on a small sand bar which kept him safe and dry. Both of us went in above our boot tops and the water poured down our legs. The President began to laugh in his curious way—gulping the air in instead of thrusting it out. This curious kind of mirth affected his diaphragm. When we reached shore he had the hiccoughs and had to sit down. When he was all right again we went to the car and I began to dismantle the rods. He wouldn't let me finish.

"Let me see what you have in your creel," he said.

I lifted the cover and showed him. He got so mad he jumped into the car and insisted that we go right back to the hotel. He would not wait for me to take the rods apart and I had to hold them out from the automobile as we bounced along. At the hotel he walked through the crowd in the lobby without speaking or looking to left or right, got into the elevator, and went up to his room. The people watched him until he disappeared, then turned to me.

"Here's Colonel Starling with the fish," one of the newspapermen said. "Can we see them, Colonel?"

I showed them the trout, and they oh'd and ah'd. The reporters made notes and the photographers took pictures. The President's reputation as an angler went up several notches.

Among the gifts to the President that summer was a horse, a saddle and bridle. The horse was a little mare, and after the presentation ceremonies at the Game Lodge I took her to the stable and asked two of my friends to try her out and let me know whether or not she was safe for the President. He had not been on a horse since his boyhood. The two friends, Cecil Gideon, lessee of the Custer State Park rights, and Clyde Jones, one of the finest broncho busters in the Dakotas, both put the horse through her paces. Meanwhile I went fishing with the President. When I returned they informed me that the mare was unsafe for any but an expert rider. She was high strung and foolish, and shied at everything that moved. I tried her out myself and agreed with them. If the President decided to ride her I would have trouble.

The next afternoon he appeared in his riding clothes, plus the ten gallon hat. He sat on the front porch and puffed at a cigar. Mrs. Coolidge sat near him, knitting a pair of socks for John. When I walked up on the porch he said, "Good afternoon, Colonel. I want my horse saddled. I am going to take a ride."

"You mean the little mare that was given to you yesterday?" I asked innocently.

"Yes, and I want you and Clyde Jones to go with me."

I smiled amiably. "Well, I don't know about the little mare. Clyde and Mr. Gideon and I have all tested her, and she is hardly safe for anyone. It would be much too dangerous for you to ride her."

His lips tightened. Stubbornness rose in him like mercury in a thermometer on a hot August day. There was a long, embarrassing silence. Mrs. Coolidge continued knitting. Finally she said:

"Father, if Colonel Starling thinks the mare isn't safe, I think you should accept his judgment. I shall be very uneasy while you're away if you go against his opinion and the warnings of Mr. Gideon and Mr. Jones."

"Well, what am I going to do?" he asked petulantly. "Just sit here on the front porch and ride back and forth to Rapid City?"

"No," I said. "I selected a wonderful horse for you some time ago in case you decided to ride. This animal is probably the best known horse in the Black Hills. They use him when they round up buffalo. He's sure-footed and intelligent and he knows every trail in this part of the world."

I had invented this story in the hope that it would save the situation. In the stable was a strawberry roan named Mistletoe, who was safe for anyone to ride. I wanted to make him desirable to the President. I could see what he was thinking—just because he was President of the United States he believed he could get on a horse and miraculously be able to ride. (They all do. They think the title of President is a magic wand which changes them into great horsemen, great fishermen, great hunters, etc.)

"Why didn't you tell me you had picked him for me?" he said.

There was another silence, then he said, in a more friendly tone, "Well, I won't go riding today, but I want my horse ready for me tomorrow afternoon."

There was a subtle difference in the way he said "my" which indicated to me that he was willing to accept Mistletoe, so I went to the stable and saddled him. They were still on the porch when I rode into the yard. When I was in a spot where he could not fail to see me I put on an exhibition. I rode straddle and sidewise. I got behind the saddle, turned around, and slid over and off Mistletoe's rump. I walked alongside and mounted him as he moved ahead; I stopped him, stooped, and walked under his belly; I mounted him from the wrong side; I made him trot, gallop and pace. Then I rode back to the stable.

The next morning before leaving Rapid City the President insisted upon going to the stable to visit Mistletoe. He fed him candy, patted him and made a date with him for that afternoon. The ride was successful, and thereafter Mistletoe was one of the Presidential pets.

I was glad these rides had been taken when I went to Mt. Rushmore a few weeks later to make arrangements for the President's visit. Rushmore is the mountain on whose face Gutzon Borglum, the sculptor, carved the heads of four American Presidents—Washington, Jefferson,

Lincoln, and Teddy Roosevelt. At the time of our visit only Washington's head was finished.

The road to the mountain was so bad that I at first decided the services attendant upon the President's visit would have to be held in the nearby town of Keystone. On second thought it occurred to me that I might get Clyde Jones to bring over Mistletoe and some other saddle horses. This was done, and the President, Senator Norbeck, Jones and I rode in cowboy style to the top of the peak. It was the first time in a good many years that a President had travelled on horseback to make a speech. He didn't think much of the idea at first, nor did Senator Norbeck. They watched some of the spectators negotiating the road in automobiles and seemed to think we could have done the same thing. Before we got to the end of the ride the President said to me, "Well, I guess our automobiles could not have made the grade." The cars of the spectators were everywhere along the road, and they had all walked the last stretch.

Senator Norbeck, who also admitted my judgment was right, pointed to the valley below the peak—a dell of virgin forest lying like a prayer rug before the great shrine of Presidents.

"That spot is going to be officially named Starling Basin, in your honor," he said.

I was so overwhelmed I almost forgot the details of my job. I made a date with the Senator to return one day before I left and inspect the valley. A mountain had been named after the President, and a stream after Mrs. Coolidge, but neither was as beautiful to me as this lovely primeval forest.

On August 2 I rode to town with the President. It was the fourth anniversary of his accession to office. At the regular nine o'clock press conference he asked the reporters to return at noon for a special announcement. Meanwhile he wrote on a slip of paper: "I do not choose to run for President in nineteen twenty-eight." He gave this to Everett Sanders and told him to have a number of copies made. He cut the slips himself with a pair of scissors, and as the newspapermen walked by his desk he handed one to each. No one was allowed to leave the room until everyone had been served his portion. Then there was a mad scramble for the telephones.

The decision had been made a long time before. I knew that. I also knew that he meant exactly what he said. To a Vermont Yankee nothing is more emphatic than, "I do not choose." It means, "I ain't gonna do it and I don't give a dern what you think." Nothing is more sacred to a New England Yankee than his privilege as an individual to make up his own mind—his freedom of choice. That fall, when some Republican leaders came to the White House to persuade him to run, they found this out.

The sensation caused by his announcement tickled the President. He liked to do things which caused little and foolish men to scamper about and make a fuss. His mind was now free of any particular worry about the future, and he enjoyed every day of his stay at the Game Lodge. Toward the end of the summer he said to me one evening, "You were right about these Westerners. They are hospitable, and they don't expect anything in return for it. I have had a good time."

The trip had, in truth, been very successful. There had been no accidents, and no rattlesnakes had turned up. One was killed a few weeks after our arrival but the President did not hear about it. One of the boys put it in my tent, to scare me, but the older members of the Detail told him he was wasting his time.

"He's killed dozens of them," Jervis said. "He's not afraid of rattlers. Better try someone else."

They put it in Boots Miller's tent, with excellent results. The country around the lodge was not, we discovered, noted for snakes, and few had ever been seen there.

On September 6 I rode to Keystone and met Senator Norbeck. We drove to Rushmore in his car, left it there, and walked down into Starling Basin. Our descent was difficult at times, so much so that we had to sit down on several ocasions and proceed at a backward crawl. After about forty-five minutes we reached a table land upon which stood immense virgin yellow pine trees. Going down again we crossed a stream and entered a forest of breathtaking beauty.

No ax had ever touched a single tree, large or small, and not more than half a dozen men had walked through the valley. We followed the stream almost due west, gradually going downward until we were among red oaks and spruce. As the sun set we entered Grizzly Creek Canyon, and soon found ourselves climbing immense rocks and wading through water. Finally we were out, and after a walk of two miles reached the automobile which had been sent to wait for us. We rode back to Rushmore. Looking once more into the valley, now lying in darkness, I felt a grateful thrill that this magnificent place had been named for me.

★☆★

CHAPTER EIGHTEEN

A President Plays

WE RETURNED to Washington early in September. Immediately our exercise was cut down to the morning and afternoon walks. One day as we strolled along the street an old negro in a horse-drawn hack drove alongside and raised his battered stovepipe hat.

"Evenin', white folks," he said. "Would yo'all like to take a ride? I know all the places where the famous men lives, and I knows all about them. I can tell you what they does and how they carries on."

A twinkle came into the little fellow's eye. He turned to me and said, "Let's take a ride."

"It'll cost you three dollars," I said.

"We'll walk," he said.

He took me upstairs one afternoon to show me his new vibrator. He demonstrated it, in his underwear, and then made me try it. He noticed that I had a slightly inflamed eyelid and insisted that Doctor Coupal, who was also in the room, put some drops in it. While this was going on he said:

"Colonel, seems to me that a man with your responsible position would be more careful of his drinking."

"What do you mean?" I asked.

"You can't get away with it," he said. "It makes your eyes all red and I have to get my doctor to take care of them."

With all this horseplay he ended up ten minutes late for dinner. But it made no difference to him. He would miss a meal anytime to play a joke. One evening as we were walking around the White House grounds he saw a pretty girl sitting in a green car in front of the Executive Offices. He asked me who owned the car and who the girl was. I told him both were Jack Fitzgerald's, the girl being his intended. He took a second look. Fitz was one of his favorites; he liked to tease him about being a Beau Brummel.

"Are they going to be married soon?" he asked.

"I don't know," I said.

"How long have they been going together?"

"I don't know."

"Why haven't they been married before?"

"I don't know that either."

"Does she work for the government?"

"Yes, but I don't know in what department."

"Well, you see that they get married right away, and when they do you let me know and we won't let his wife work for the government any more and we can save the government her salary."

He had what I call a sense of play—something different and apart from a sense of humor. I think he liked me because I responded to this part of him, and would follow him instantly from a serious discussion to something frivolous. It was make-believe, of course. We pretended all sorts of things, such as the fantastic notion that I was a great and secret drinker. I never pretended to dislike a drink of good Bourbon, but neither, for that matter, did he. Our joke was an effort to relieve the gloomy, depressing atmosphere which surrounded the subject of liquor during those days. The little fellow did not believe in prohibition any more than did the rest of the sensible citizens, but he observed it strictly while in the White House because he considered it his duty to do so. His opinion of it was simple and forthright.

"Any law which inspires disrespect for the other laws—the good laws —is a bad law," he said to me.

It was strange that he, the most popular man in the country, was the direct opposite in every way of what the public was taking for its model. He not only disliked the things that were going on, he feared the results of them. During that fall there was a lot of talk in favor of nominating the Secretary of Commerce, Herbert Hoover, at the Republican Convention the following June. One of Hoover's supporters dubbed him a "superman." As we strolled through the streets one afternoon the President said to me, after a long silence:

"Well, they're going to elect that superman Hoover, and he's going to have some trouble. He's going to have to spend money. But he won't spend enough.

"Then the Democrats will come in and they'll spend money like water. But they don't know anything about money. Then they will want me to come back and save some money for them. But I won't do it."

He said "I won't do it" in his most stubborn manner, and I knew he meant it. I also knew, then, his practical reason for not running again. He saw economic disaster ahead. In the years that followed I was amazed at the absolute accuracy of his prediction. Truly, he was a long-headed thinker.

He had scotched all rumors that he might allow himself to be drafted for a third term in his address to Republican National Committeemen on December 6. The meeting was held in the East Room of the White House. Just before leaving to attend it Everett Sanders and I were with him in his office.

"I want you two to go with me," he said. "They're going to try to get me to run again, and I won't do it."

We walked over to the White House and I accompanied him upstairs to his room while Sanders waited in the Chief Usher's office. He did not stay long. He straightened his tie, adjusted his jacket, took the pages of his prepared speech from his pocket, and glanced through them. Then we went downstairs and entered the meeting.

While he read his speech Sanders stood on his left and I stood on his right. The text contained these words:

"My statement stands. No one should be led to suppose that I have modified it. My decision will be respected.

"After I had been eliminated, the party began, and should continue the serious task of selecting another candidate from among the numbers of distinguished men available."

That settled it. I saw tears in the eyes of some, particularly Charles D. Hilles of New York and Mrs. A. T. Hert, of Kentucky, Tobe's widow.

In January he went to Cuba to attend the Sixth International Conference of American States at Havana. On returning the party landed at Key West. Riding in the car with the Mayor of Key West the President was tired and more taciturn than usual. The Mayor was self-conscious and tried to keep the conversation going. After several unsuccessful attempts to enlist the little fellow's interest he launched into a peroration.

"Mr. President," he said, "I think your understanding of the problem of our Southern neighbors is amazing. I think your visit to Cuba and your address to the Pan-American delegates there assembled, will be acclaimed as one of the outstanding achievements of your splendid administration. I heartily concur in the program and I know the nation agrees with me in this opinion."

"Mr. Mayor," the President said, "have you got any good picture shows in town?"

The Mayor gulped and stuttered.

"Why, yes, Mr. President," he was finally able to say. "We have four or five picture shows in Key West at present. Two of them, I am told, are very good."

The President looked at him solemnly and said: "Do you get free passes?"

Before the poor, bewildered Mayor could reply he continued:

"They used to give me free passes when I was Mayor of Northampton."

The Mayor was licked. When we got to the special train all he could say was, "Goodbye."

That spring I bought a brown suit. On the day I wore it for the first time I selected a green tie as a fitting accessory. I noticed the President looking at me sharply several times during our morning walk, but he said nothing. I thought he was appraising the cloth in my suit. I expected him to tell me how much it cost, or to ask me what I paid for it and tell me that I had been cheated.

The afternoon schedule called for a visit to a specialist, to have the President's sinuses examined. As he came out to get into the car he stopped, looked sharply at me again, then turned and went back into the White House. He got into the elevator and went upstairs. The staff began to whisper among themselves. Nobody knew what was wrong.

"He sure looks mad," John Mays said.

When he returned he was composed. In his hand he carried a small brown paper bag. He handed it to me.

"Here," he said. "Take this."

I put it in my pocket and we went on with the business of the afternoon. Only after we had returned to the White House and I was on my way to supper did I take the bag from my pocket and find out what was in it.

It was a brown tie.

We had talked a great deal, of course, about where the summer vacation would be spent. I had coached the President during the winter in dry fly fishing, and he was anxious to try his skill. Mrs. Coolidge had again suffered from the Washington climate, so the considerations which governed the selection of a site the year before still obtained. I again made a trip through the West, and finally, through Senator Irvin B. Lenroot of Wisconsin, we selected the Pierce estate on the Brule River. It was an ideal spot. The air was soft and saturated with the odor of pine resin—perfect for Mrs. Coolidge. The main house was on an island in the middle of the river. Quarters for the rest of the party were on the mainland, and the temporary Executive Offices were in Superior, thirty-six miles away. Separated by four or five ridges of hills was Lake Superior. The Brule River, fed by springs, was cold and clear and full of wily trout. Nature could not have been improved upon, and every luxury of civilization was also available.

John Lambert, superintendent of the estate, told me that we were apt to have plenty of rain during the latter part of June and for the first few days of July. He had studied local weather for years, in connection with the fish hatchery on the estate. He was an accurate prophet. The Coolidges arrived on the eighteenth—delayed three days by Mrs. Coolidge's ill health—and ten days later we had a record of ten days of rain. The President had not been able to fish very much, and Mrs. Coolidge had not been able to take any walks. She was showing no improvement.

Doctor Coupal advised leaving the place and going to Yellowstone Park. I talked to Lambert about the weather. He said if I could keep the President there until the fourth of July he would guarantee me perfect weather thereafter. But Coupal was insistent. He did not like the Brule himself, and he held that it was bad for Mrs. Coolidge's condition.

On the evening of the twenty-eighth the President sent for me. It was after supper, and he and Mrs. Coolidge were sitting on the porch.

He went straight to the point. "Doctor Coupal has decided that this is not the climate for Mrs. Coolidge," he said. "He thinks she should go West to some drier climate and I am about of the same opinion. We have been here ten days and it has rained every day. We have to come to some decision soon and we want to know what you think of the idea. Your judgment has always been good and we will depend upon it now."

"I would like to stay here," Mrs. Coolidge said. "But if it keeps raining I will have to go somewhere else."

I spoke my piece.

"I will tell you plainly what I think," I said. "I too have been bothered about the rain. I wanted to see the sun shine for both your sakes. I have the facts from the Weather Bureau in Washington showing how much rain has fallen in this vicinity for the last ten years. There has never been much rain in July—some in June but not as much as we have had this June.

"I am assured that a day or two after July 1, ideal weather will set in and continue. I know all about Doctor Coupal's desires. He wants you to go to Yellowstone Park.

"I know too that your medicine cabinet, Mr. President, is too full of the wrong kind of thing. That is why I want you to get out and fish, so you will feel better and throw away all those bromides and pills. It has been a long stretch since last summer and it has tired you out.

"These people up here in Wisconsin are mostly poor, yet out of their love for you two they have raised money to make this place livable for you and your servants. If you left now you would give their country a black eye, and all kinds of rumors would be circulated.

"Imagine your privacy at Yellowstone Park! It would take a regiment of soldiers to keep the tourists away!

"I submit this plan. Give this place until July 4. If it is not raining on that day we stay. If it is raining we go at once to Yellowstone and you can blame me for the mistake.

"I would also like to make you a proposition about your medicine cabinet, Mr. President. If we have fished ten days by July 15 we will go strong on more fishing and slow on the pills and bromides."

They agreed to stay. July 4 dawned clear and warm. All day the sun shone and every day thereafter was perfect. We fished from early morning until long after dark. The pine trees bathed the air with their incense. Mrs. Coolidge grew healthier day by day. The President was so busy fishing he had no time to take any pills. He even took his city visitors out fishing at night, to their dismay and discomfort. One day he lost a fish he had been playing and I heard him say, "Damn!" Then he turned to me and with a shy smile said: "Guess I'm a real fisherman now. I cussed."

I had one more ambition to achieve with regard to his outdoor life. If we were to be together after his administration I wanted to convert him to hunting. So that summer I had a clay pigeon outfit installed. It was on the mainland, near our quarters. I ordered two guns. For the President I chose a Winchester pump with a 28-inch barrel and a modified choke. Mine was a full choke. I trained several of the boys in loading the birds and pulling the lever which released them. I then tested the trap and the guns, firing several dozen shots. As I expected, the President sent for me.

"Who's shooting on my place?" he asked.

"Well," I said, "the Secret Service has to keep in practice. I have had a clay pigeon outfit installed and I was trying it out. If the noise of the shooting bothers you I will have the trap moved."

Nothing more was said, but the next morning after breakfast he remarked, "I want to see where you were shooting yesterday." I took him to the trap, where we found Mr. Lambert. I had anticipated the situation and told the other boys to keep away. The President would be shy with them. He had grown accustomed to Lambert, who was a fine gentleman and an expert outdoors man.

Lambert loaded the trap and released the pigeons while I shot at them. When I had hit about a dozen the President said, "I want to shoot."

He was nervous, and at first I had to pump the shells into the chamber of the gun for him. He caught on quickly, however, and after using up a few boxes of shells he was breaking the pigeons pretty regularly. When he returned to the lodge he was tremendously excited and told Mrs. Coolidge about it.

"Mama," he said, "Colonel Starling was shooting those things they call clay pigeons and I took the gun away from him and broke a whole lot of them."

After that he shot every day, and Mrs. Coolidge had to come and see her Daniel Boone perform. I was delighted, and began to tell him about the joys of quail hunting and the art of the trained bird dog. He promised he would go hunting with me in the fall.

Hoover was campaigning that summer and came to visit the President. The little fellow was very sour about it. He told Sanders that he would see no one but Hoover. The others in the party, including Hoover's secretary George Akerson, he said would have to remain on the mainland. Sanders was disturbed, and so was I. We were both friends of Akerson's.

"Let's bring him over anyhow," I said. "I would rather face the little fellow than tell George he can't come."

He was irritated and stubborn when he saw what we had done. He sat on the front porch with Hoover while the photographers took pictures. He made no effort to converse with the nominee, and Hoover, a dreadfully shy and self-conscious man, could not keep things going. Finally the news cameramen asked the President to say something to Hoover.

"Let him talk," the little fellow said surlily. "He's going to be President."

It was a drearily unsuccessful meeting.

When we returned to Washington both he and Mrs. Coolidge were in excellent health. His medicine cabinet had been cleared of everything but fruit salts and aspirin. But he continued his strange eating habits and soon he was suffering again from indigestion. He would eat unparched peanuts and then have such severe gas pains that he would have to go and lie down to get relief. That Thanksgiving we were at the Swannanoa Country Club in the mountains near Waynesboro, Virginia. About three o'clock one morning Dowling, who had taken Brooks' place as valet, came to my cottage and said that the President wanted to know if I had any salts. I said I hadn't, but I could go to Waynesboro and get some.

I quickly dressed and went to the President's room. He was still suffering but would not hear of my going to Waynesboro. At six o'clock he dressed and we went for a walk. Doctor Coupal was at Atlantic City, where the President had asked him to go to take care of Mrs. Stearns. He had sent a young doctor with us to take his place.

"I looked in that young fellow's satchel," the President said, "and there were some knives and chisels and saws and pliers in there, but not one bottle of salts."

Later in the day I went to Waynesboro and loaded up on salts. When we returned to Washington Mr. Stearns told me that his wife had been cured by a joke, a joke I had told her husband. It was the story of a drunk who ran into a telephone pole on his way home at night. Three times he backed up, carefully turned, and walked smack into the pole. At last he gave up. "What a pity!" he said. "Lost in an impenetrable forest!"

In late December we got in our hunting. We went to Sapelo Island, Georgia, as the guests of Howard E. Coffin, the engineer. Quail and pheasant were both available, but the quail were too fast for the President, and he had to content himself with hitting pheasant. On our last day Mr. Coffin and his nephew, Alfred Jones, arranged a pheasant shoot for us on Little Sapelo. As we rode over on Mr. Coffin's yacht I suggested to the little fellow that since this was our final hunt, and since we wanted to return to Washington with as many pheasant as possible, that we shoot as two men in the field, not as the President and a Secret Service man. He agreed, and we had a grand time. I nosed him out by two.

His last shot was a masterpiece—in reverse. As we were walking through the long swamp grass a big cock pheasant came sailing toward him at about sixty miles an hour. He tried to get a bead on the bird but the pheasant was going too fast. He turned to get him after he had passed, but his feet tangled in the grass and as he shot he sat down solidly in the mud, his ten gallon hat tilted to one side. He looked at me and grinned.

"I missed him," he said.

"Yes," I replied, "by about fifty feet."

It was January when we returned to the White House. Hoover had been elected in November and in a few months now the Coolidges would move out. I was to remain on the Detail until the little fellow was settled and ready for me. Then we were to take our fishing and hunting trip to the West coast. I was as anxious for it as was he. Fifteen years in Washington had not succeeded in removing from me the constant yearning for a quiet, simple life, close to the outdoors.

During those last months of his administration the President consented to sit for a portrait which was to be hung in the famous Saddle and Sirloin Club of Chicago. The artist, who was commissioned by Arthur G. Leonard, President of the Chicago Union Stockyards and Transit Company, was Robert W. Grafton. He stayed at the Willard Hotel, and he told me his troubles. He made one attempt after another to get the President's likeness, to catch his personality, to divine his spirit. He failed utterly. The little fellow was too elusive. What he showed to the painter was not his real self. The intangible thing which formed his character would not come forth. Grafton was discouraged and nervous. He could not sleep at night. He became filled with despair. He was convinced that he could not execute the commission. He decided to make one last attempt and then give it up.

The sittings were being held in the northwest room on the second floor. It was a bright, clear, beautiful day when Grafton made his final effort. The President came in and went to the little dais on which his chair was set. He looked out the window at the sunshine and said to Grafton:

"Good morning. It might rain."

Grafton was so shaken that he upset a can of turpentine. As he watched it spread over the beautiful rug covering the floor, despair completely engulfed him.

"Oh, Mr. President, I am so sorry!" he said. "Please have the rug sent to the cleaners and I will gladly pay the bill."

The President looked at him and a twinkle came into his eyes.

"Now, don't you worry about the old rug," he said. "I'm going to move out of here in a few days."

Grafton stared, then relaxed and smiled. Without a word he seized his brushes and began to paint. The spell was broken, the problem was solved. Grafton finished his work in a short time and did a grand job. He caught the little fellow exactly—half owl, half elf.

My own estimate of him is just that: he looked wise and solemn— yet he was full of mischief and laughter. The two were blended in him more completely than in most people. The average person's serious and humorous aspects are separate. In President Coolidge they were mixed, so that the one interpenetrated the other. To me it seemed a step forward in evolution, for the serious side of life needs to be looked at with the tolerance and understanding which a sense of humor provides, and our laughter should be grounded in an understanding of the spiritual purpose of our existence.

President Coolidge accepted politics as the machinery by which gov-

ernment comes to be, and he took government as Jefferson took it
(Republican though he was) : the arrangement by which man exists on
earth with his fellowman while pursuing the business of his immortal
destiny. Thus he felt that the best government was that which, like a
watch, was most excellent in all its parts. He disliked intensely the
growing tendency in his time for the smaller governments to lean on
the larger ones, for state and local governments voluntarily to surrender functions to the federal government, for men of talent to seek
national fame instead of being content with selfless service in the bor-
oughs and townships of their birth. In his Message to Congress of
December, 1925, he said:

The functions which the Congress are to discharge are not those of
local government but of national government. The greatest solicitude
should be exercised to prevent any encroachment upon the rights of
the states or their various political subdivisions. Local self-government
is one of our most precious possessions. It is the greatest contributing
factor to the stability, strength, liberty, and progress of the nation. It
ought not to be infringed by assault or undermined by purchase. It ought
not to abdicate power through weakness or resign its authority through
favor. It does not at all follow that because abuses exist it is the concern
of the federal government to attempt their reform.

Calvin Coolidge may or may not have been a great President. That
is for history to decide. To me he was fundamentally and primarily
something which I treasure above all the things of earth: he was a good
man. He was thoughtful, he was intelligent, he was sentimental, he
was wise. There were times when he was irascible; there were occasions when I was glad to be away from him. But I found him in the
large and full portions of existence an admirable and a satisfying man,
a peaceful and pleasing and loyal friend. His feelings, like his thoughts,
ran deep and did not swerve. I liked him as a man; I loved him as a
friend.

★☆

A President Leaves the White House

WASHINGTON on the day of March 3, 1929, was pale and listless, sprawled in the sunlight without vigor or beauty.

The wind had gone somewhere else, except for the irritable gusts that picked up the little piles of dirt left by melted snow and pitched them in the faces of passersby. People huddled in their overcoats, blew into their handkerchiefs, and thought evil thoughts about the Capital's climate.

In the parks and squares and wherever land was uncovered, the earth rocked in labor with new life. Trees, so bare to the eye, were infernos of creation inside. All around the city, in the open country of Maryland and Virginia, fields and forests were awakening. Walking home to the Willard Hotel in late evening I thought I could feel beneath me the swamp bogs, once free to burgeon and foster, now clawing at the concrete and macadam that pressed them down. I wished myself home in Kentucky.

I was still a country boy, and to me it was spring. The brooks were filled, the marshes were singing, and I should have been in the woods that day, looking for Dutchman's breeches, listening for the first frog to cry, the first cardinal to call.

Instead I had met with the Senate Committee for the Inaugural next day. I had met with the Joint Committee of the House and Senate for the Inaugural. I had talked with the Clerk of the Senate about seating arrangements; I had talked to the doorkeepers of the Senate and the House of Representatives about admission to the galleries. I had checked

273

the arrangements for the Press. I had checked the routes to be taken by the Senators and Congressmen, the Press, and the President's party from the House chamber to the Inaugural platform on the steps of the Capitol.

Once again—and this time with more caution than ever—I had gone over the route of the Inaugural Procession from the White House to the Capitol. For two months, with hundreds of assistants, I had been examining that line of parade. Every family and every business in every building along the way had been investigated. New tenants had been particularly scrutinized. All the roof-tops were under surveillance. All the alleyways were watched. So far as human foresight and caution could make it, the long lane of Pennsylvania Avenue was safe.

Also that day I had checked the Inaugural plans at the White House, arranged for the new President's arrival there, and completed the plan for taking the little fellow to the train at Union Station. I had been to see Chief Moran, I had conferred with Dick Jervis, I had spoken to the President. I had talked to everyone in Washington, it seemed, but myself. I was tired.

In my room at the Willard I checked one last item. All my suits had to be pressed and ready; each pair of shoes had to be shined and waiting. If it rained the next day, heaven alone knew how many times I would have to change my clothes.

Finally, lying in a warm bath, with the water imploring me to relax, I ran over the scene again in my mind. Bits from the official program drifted through my thoughts. "All doors of the Rotunda will be closed and passageways leading thereto will be kept clear . . . the occupants of the East Galleries will be escorted down the east steps, by the painting of the Battle of Lake Erie . . . the occupants of the Diplomatic Gallery and the West Galleries will be escorted down the west steps, by the painting of the Battle of Chapultepec . . . when the President's party, reaches the south door of the Senate Chamber, the Supreme Court, headed by their Marshal and Clerk, will form in line and lead the procession. . . ."

The bath muddied. How marvellously dirty a man can get just sitting down in a room with a lot of other men! I ran a jet of cold, cleansing water through the tub, rinsed myself, and stepped out. It was 9:30.

"Now for a good long sleep," I said, speaking to myself for the first time that day.

I got into bed and picked up the book on the night table, a history of Kentucky. A friend had sent it to me because it contained something about my father.

The sleep I wanted wouldn't come. I was still reading when the telephone rang at 11 o'clock. It was the White House operator.

"Is that you Colonel Starling? The President wants to speak to you."

The instrument clicked into silence for a moment. Then I heard the familiar level voice, precise and calm-sounding, as always, as if it were being played on a Jew's harp.

"Colonel? Were you asleep?"

"No, I was lying in bed reading."

"What were you reading?"

"The history of Kentucky."

"Hmmm. I'm glad to know that your literary tastes have improved. How long will it take you to come to the White House?"

"Ten or fifteen minutes."

"All right. You come over."

As I put the receiver back on its hook fifteen years of habit took hold of my surprised body and hurled it out of bed. The clothes I had laid out for the morning were on me in five minutes. In ten minutes I was on the street, my legs still numb, my spine jarring the back of my head with the shock of my steps, unable to cushion them on such short notice. When I got to the northeast gate of the White House it was 11:20.

The doorman and the night usher were expecting me. The night usher took me to the second floor in the elevator. The door to the President's room was open. He was sitting beside the window in a straight armchair, his hands in his lap.

"Come in, Colonel, I've been waiting for you," he said. He pointed to a chair he had set for me on the opposite side of the window, facing him. "Sit down over here. I want to talk about our plans."

Sleep was the furthest thing from his mind, obviously. He was as bright as midday. His clothes looked as if he had just put them on— a neat blue double-breasted suit, a high stiff collar, a subdued tie, dark brown shoes with a high polish; low shoes, I was proud to notice. It had taken me five years to win him over to them.

"You're going to get the car for me?" he said when I was settled. "Don't forget that. Make sure it's in good shape, and have it delivered to me at Northampton. Find out how much I'll have to pay the Ford people."

"I've made a note to see Dick English about it," I said. "He's the local dealer."

The car in question was the Lincoln limousine which had been— and would be until tomorrow noon—the Presidential car. Such machines are leased by the government from the manufacturer and revert to him at the end of a President's occupancy of the White House. The new President gets a new car.

"Good. I want that car. Now let's plan our trip. But first tell me again—are you perfectly satisfied to leave the Secret Service and come with me?"

I leaned forward to give my assurance emphasis.

"Any plans you make for my future, whether they are the plans we've discussed or some others, will be all right with me. Whatever you decide, I'll be happier serving you as a private citizen than remaining here in the Secret Service."

He seemed unusually pleased, though his face did not tell it. He spoke with his eyes. I saw them grow warm and sparkle as he talked.

"That's fine. As soon as I'm settled and get a job we'll take that car and go on our fishing trip. When we get back we'll go to work.

"I suppose we'll be in New York a lot, but we can sort of commute from Northampton. Where shall we stay in New York?"

"At the Waldorf-Astoria," I said. "I've always stayed there. Mr. Boomer will fix us up. The new Waldorf is beautiful."

"That's good. We'll stay there." The shadow of a smile raced over his face. "You'll be my executive assistant."

He cut his eyes toward me.

"How about starting now? Let's get a map up here and mark out our trip."

Instantly I was rejuvenated. I telephoned the night usher and asked him to bring us a road map of the United States.

When it came we had difficulty finding a place on which to spread it out while we worked. The room had been emptied of everything but the large double bed, the chairs we were using, and a small, low table at the foot of the bed, covered with homemade jellies and preserves from my mother's cellar.

The only other article in sight was a dog carrier—a box-like contraption covered with wire and fitted to strap to the side of an automobile. It had been sent to him by an admirer. I took it and set it on end between our chairs. The little fellow looked at it absently while I unfolded the map.

"How's Palo?" he asked.

Palo Alto was a bird dog, given to the President as a gift, and given by him to me to be trained for use on our future hunting trips. He was then on my farm in Kentucky, a black and white English setter with an oversensitive nose.

"He smells too much," I said, "and he's a little too timid yet. He always finds the birds, but he stands them too far away. And sometimes his nose is so good that there aren't any birds there at all. He's just not bird-wise yet."

"He'll be all right?"

"Oh, yes. Palo is only two years old. It takes five years to train a bird dog properly."

The map was unfolded now, and I began to trace the automobile route from Northampton.

"The Brule River first, for trout," he said.

I sketched the trip quickly, glad that this time I would not have the responsibility of setting up a summer White House and easing the newspapermen out of the garage without hurting their feelings.

We both knew where to go next—the State Game Lodge in the Black Hills. I would have headed for there first, I think, had he not mentioned the Brule. I was anxious to see again the stark peaks, the precipitous, deep valleys, and the ice-cold streams full of game fish.

"Glacier National Park ought to be next," I said. "We'll go to Shelby, Montana, to get there. Then we can go from there to the salmon country in Washington and Oregon."

Only a real fisherman can appreciate how we felt at that prospect. The President was like a boy looking at a Christmas toy catalogue. So was I.

"I want to get some of those salmon," he said.

"Then we'll go down the Redwood Trail and up to Yosemite. They have rainbow trout up there as big as your leg."

We worked on, getting more and more excited, until we had swept through the whole west and southwest like a scourge, leaving empty streams wherever we went. I hardly noticed when the door between the two bedrooms opened and Mrs. Coolidge came in. Before I could rise she was looking over my shoulder at the map.

"That's going to be a wonderful trip," she said. "Promise you'll bring me back something."

"How about a stuffed trout from Grace Coolidge Creek?" I said, getting up.

"I'll be just as happy if you eat him and get the nourishment," she said.

She declined our invitation to remain.

"I just came in to say goodnight," she said. "I'm going to bed and get some rest. Tomorrow will be a full day."

She turned to me and smiled.

"You two can stay up and talk as long as you like."

Suddenly I realized that she was happy. Her face had a soft, almost ethereal loveliness. "She's glad to be getting out of here," I thought. "And so is he."

"Well, we won't tell you goodbye until the train tomorrow," she said.

In her left hand she held a number of letters. She lifted them toward the President as she turned to the door.

"I'll answer the rest of these notes in Northampton. Goodnight."

When I turned from the closing door the President was looking at me.

"You're going to the station with us aren't you?" he asked.

"Yes," I said, "I am."

We didn't discuss it further. A sudden wave of melancholy was rising in me. I knew he was glad to go, and I was happy to see him leave before something happened to him. He was getting away in good health, unworried and unburdened. I should rejoice for him. I fought back the sadness. We went back to the map.

"Then we'll come up to Reelfoot Lake in Tennessee," I said. "That's in the Memphis section. After that we can go by Hopkinsville for the quail shooting. We'll go out to the farm and give Palo a chance to show off."

"Guess we'd better get back to Northampton after that," he said. "For the holidays."

So it was planned. We sat back, looking at the map, choking into the future all the good things we were leaving behind us here. We spoke only in the future tense.

"You'll be able to see more of your mother," he said. "You can go home more often."

He was thinking then, I knew, of his own mother, the faraway, tender woman who had understood him when he was young, and who lived with him constantly in the strange, mystical union that seemed to comfort him so when he was troubled.

It was late. The quiet pulsed against my ear drums. I folded the map and put the dog carrier back by the table at the foot of the bed. He watched me.

"Well," he said, "you've beat me out of everything else in this room. You might as well have that too. You can give Palo a ride."

He had given me a set of golf clubs, a chamois jacket, a pair of hunting boots, a tapered fly line—all gifts to him from admirers. It wasn't a matter of accepting or rejecting them. It was a command performance.

"All right," I said, "but while we're settling up, you might as well be on the receiving end."

I took a notebook from my pocket and consulted it.

"According to my record," I said. "I owe you twenty-five cents."

He hesitated. Then he said, "You keep it."

"No," I said. "When I leave here tonight I want to be square with you."

I held the quarter out to him. Reluctantly he accepted it. From his trouser pocket he took his small leather change purse. Precisely, holding it between thumb and forefinger, he put the coin inside. Then he closed the purse and returned it to his pocket.

"Well, Colonel," he said. "I guess you'd better get some sleep."

I dared now to look at my watch. It was 2:30.

He reached out, took my hand, and shook it; a firm, honest grip.

I knew what he meant, but I was a Kentuckian. Somehow there had to be more, though I didn't know what. I let my left hand fall on his shoulder.

"I'm sorry to see you go," I said, "but our best days are ahead of us."

He didn't answer me and I didn't want him to. He wasn't any good at that sort of thing.

Suddenly he pointed to the jams and preserves on the small table.

"You bring those to the train tomorrow," he said. "I'm not going to leave them here. I'm going to eat them in Northampton."

I took out my notebook again.

"I'll make a note of it," I said.

He began to take off his coat. The broad bright suspenders came into view, tremendous galluses strong enough to hold up a chandelier. Next his underwear would appear, three sizes too big, as always.

"Goodnight," I said.

"Goodnight, Colonel," he answered.

As I reached the stairway in the hall I heard the door close and the lock click.

Outside the air had softened. It smelled of rain. Unaccountably there popped into my head the winter night in 1918 when President Wilson emerged from the Executive Offices.

"It's snowing, Starling," he had said. "That means more traffic stalled. More people without coal. More suffering."

I tried to shake off the melancholy, walking rapidly back to the Willard. That was a long time ago, I told myself, that night in 1918. Then the world was teetering on the edge of ruin. Now it was saved, happy and prosperous. There was nothing to be sad about. I was just tired.

★☆★★

CHAPTER TWENTY

Hoover—The Depression

HERBERT HOOVER began his administration under auspices more favorable than any which had prevailed during my stay at the White House. Throughout the country prosperity had risen like a spring tide. The old American adage that every man can be rich was coming true actually. As the President and the President-elect walked up the steps to the Capitol on March 4, 1929, the clouded skies above were not symbolic. The peace, the prosperity, and the contentment of the nation were unprecedented. The great crowds along the way were happy and easygoing. At Union Station cheering groups had gathered to bid farewell to the man they believed responsible for the good things of life they were then enjoying.

I saw the Coolidges off on the train to Northampton. Our goodbye was cheerful; we expected to see each other soon. My return to the White House was without excitement. I had known Mr. Hoover in his various governmental capacities since the days of the World War. He would not be very different as President—a shy, quiet man, given to efficiency in everything he did. Of course, there would be changes at the White House, but nothing of a drastic nature. Things would go along pretty much as before, and I would drop back into the anonymity of my post as a Secret Service man.

One change which I did not expect was the installation of three Presidential secretaries. Thus far the Presidents had been satisfied with one such assistant, and he had frequently found little to do. President Hoover's secretaries, however, were very busy. They carried work to their boss, and since three men can carry a lot more papers than one man, they kept him snowed under. Frequently at the week's end I would be waiting to take the President to his fishing camp at Rapidan. As the time approached for our departure each of the three secretaries would go in for a last-minute conference. Hours later the President would emerge, glassy-eyed, not knowing whether he was going to Rapidan or a hot dog roast. He would stare without recognizing me as I handed him his hat. Then he would shake his head and say, "Oh, yes, Colonel Starling. Are we ready to go?"

The secretaries were all nice fellows, and theoretically each had a particular function. George Akerson, who had been with the President in the Department of Commerce, and who had coined the term "superman," was in charge of appointments. George was a large, pleasant man, six feet tall and gray-haired. He was a former newspaperman. Walter B. Newton, a former Congressman from Minnesota, took care of the legislative end of things. The President was further removed from politics than Wilson, and Newton was a great help to him in his dealings with the Senate and House. Larry Richey, an old Secret Service man who had often worked for the President before his election, took care of the more personal items. His Secret Service training caused him naturally to remain in the background, but toward the end of the administration his ability and his loyalty to the President brought him forward a great deal. Later Ted Joslin, a Boston newspaperman, took Akerson's place.

The Rapidan fishing camp was one of the first projects I undertook for my new employer. I discovered that he did not ride horseback, play golf, swim, or hunt. He liked to fish, and wanted a place nearby, where he could go on weekends. After visiting various spots a place was chosen on the Rapidan River in Virginia, 109 miles from Washington, a three hour trip by automobile. The route was through Falls Church, Warrenton, and Culpeper, with a right turn at Madison Church, proceeding thence to Creiglersville. From there it was eight miles up a mountain to the camp, which was built by Marine and Army engineers. There was a community house and cabins for sleeping purposes. Filipinos from the yacht *Mayflower* comprised the domestic staff, and the Marines, who had a camp nearby, assisted in guarding the place and looked after the property.

The river was stocked with trout, but had to be restocked frequently because of eels. We set many eel traps but caught very few of them. The expense of building the camp was supposedly offset by turning back the *Mayflower* to the Navy and doing away with the White House stables, two master strokes of economy.

As a fisherman the President knew what he was doing when trolling from a boat or fishing downstream with a wet fly. When it came to casting upstream with a dry fly he was out of his class, but so was every other President I have seen attempt this difficult feat. As the years went by and the depression came, President Hoover grew nervous. His hands would tremble as he worked with his tackle. I have seen him catch a fishhook in his trousers, his coat, and then in his hat. It was odd to see this, for he looked like a man without a nerve in his body. He was sturdy, pudgy, long-waisted and short-legged. Almost he seemed an Oriental. Yet he was born in Cedar Rapids, Iowa, and went to Stanford University.

He would set the time for leaving at three o'clock Friday afternoon. Then he would get tangled up with his secretaries and it would be between four-thirty and six before we left. Always he wanted to make up the time by speeding, and he was annoyed that the Detail would not allow this. Consequently we would be late for dinner, and the week-end would be off to a bad start. Returning on Monday morning he insisted on leaving at six o'clock, so he could arrive at the White House at nine. He was never able to do this because he was just in time to hit the traffic of government clerks on their way to work. It began ten miles outside of the city and we were always right in the middle of it. He could have left at seven, planning to arrive at ten, and missed all this. But as I said, this administration was run by plan, so it would be efficient.

Efficiency began to permeate the entire White House staff. The people of Bangor, Maine, sent a fresh salmon to the President, entrusting it to one of their Congressmen. He sent it to the White House by messenger, intending to come by later to be photographed with the fish and the President. Meanwhile efficiency, working at a mad clip, shuttled the fish to the White House kitchen, where its head was removed and it was set aside to be prepared for cooking. All was chaos. The Congressman wondered what he would say to the folks back home. I felt so sorry for him that I decided to make an attempt at saving the situation. I got a needle and thread and sewed the head back on the fish's body. The picture was taken and Maine did not go Democratic for three years.

One day there were three groups of visitors out in the backyard waiting to be photographed with the President—everything was now being done in threes, it seemed. Dick Jervis was running around getting things lined up. The President asked him the identity of the groups. Dick reeled off two of them, then referred to the card in his hand to ascertain the profession of the third. He looked at the word I had scribbled for him—"Morticians."

"Five hundred bricklayers!" he said.

President Hoover himself was a man of tremendous ability, and surely he was as earnest and as honest as any man who ever held the office. He was handicapped, I felt, by certain habits he had acquired during his career as an engineer, and by the fact that he thought of humanity as an abstract quality instead of a collection of highly differentiated personalities. Thus he believed that all tasks could be accomplished by adequate planning and sufficiently expert supervision, and the American people could be served and aided without reducing them to individualized portions of creative expression. The three secretaries constituted an example of these ideas. I think President Hoover would have done better with a single secretary, a man with a genius for people, who would have served as an intermediary between the citizens and their Chief Executive, and who might have been able to show the President where to go to find the spirit of the people, which he needed to understand—at baseball games, musical comedies, country fairs, and church picnics.

He was a poor speaker. His addresses were well-prepared—he spent a lot of time on them—but he never looked up while reading, and he held the sheets at the height of his waist, so that his head was bent and his voice was almost lost to the microphones. To counteract this I devised a metal stand with a light attached, for holding the pages of the speech. It was set at the level of his eyes, and just to his left, so that while reading his head was held high and turned a little, giving the audience a fine half profile view of him, and making it possible for the microphones to pick up his voice without difficulty.

On July 24 ex-President Coolidge returned to the city to sign the Kellogg-Briand peace pact. I went to the station to meet him, along with Everett Sanders and George Akerson. It was curious to see him descend from the train alone, unguarded and unnoticed. He looked in excellent health, except that around his wrist he wore a bandage.

"I hurt it fishing," he said. "It's almost well now."

"Do you still rub anise seed oil on the bait?" I asked.

He grinned. "Yes," he said, "and they still bite."

We went to the Willard Hotel and I remained with him most of the day. When we were alone he told me that he was still looking for a job, but that every one which came along turned out to be, on investigation, something which he could not accept, either because it was related to the government or because in one way or another it would demand that he exercise his prestige as a former President.

His best bet was the presidency of a life insurance company, but a friend of his now held the position and the little fellow did not want to push himself into the spot. In good time his friend would retire and the job would be his if he wanted it. Meanwhile he was busying himself with the writing of his *Autobiography*.

Doctor Coupal came in during the day and examined him. "Hard as a rock," he said. We sat and talked of old times, and again laid plans for our fishing and hunting trip. The little fellow's enthusiasm for fishing was greater than ever. By now he was becoming really expert with a fly.

I was sorry to see him leave, and I returned reluctantly to my post, realizing how lonely it could be. I liked my new boss, but he held himself aloof. He took one walk with me, during the first few days of his administration. After that Mrs. Hoover came along, and I walked behind them. It has been said that he resented the supervision of the Secret Service. Perhaps he did, since there were times when we had to refuse his requests, particularly his orders to drive more rapidly over dangerous roads. He regarded us, it seemed to me, as a necessary evil, and once he made up his mind that we were thinking always of his welfare, we got along all right, though often he heartily wished we were elsewhere. When Ramsay MacDonald came to visit him the two sat on the banks of the Rapidan discussing international affairs. MacDonald glanced over his shoulder several times, watching me as I leaned against a tree. He seemed uneasy.

"That man can hear what we are saying," he said to the President. "Hadn't you better tell him to go away?"

"He won't go," the President said gloomily.

MacDonald became interested. "Who is he?" he asked.

"He's a Secret Service man," the President said. "They have to watch me."

MacDonald was so captivated by this idea that he later came and talked to me about it, inquiring the details of our work. He seemed to think it an admirable system, commenting that England's great men have no such protection.

In October, 1929, the crash came. On the twenty-fourth of the month, "Black Thursday," the stock market went into a tailspin. The following Tuesday, with recorded selling of more than sixteen million shares, it hit bottom. From then on things went from bad to worse. Less than a year later one out of every four factory workers had lost his job. So many people jumped from hotel windows that newspaper editors christened them "dry divers." Prices went down like a falling meteor. Salaries and wages were slashed unmercifully. Middle-aged employees who were earning good money were fired, and young men were engaged at slave wages to replace them. Apple salesmen appeared on street corners.

At first no one recognized it for what it was—the Deluge. It was a heavy shower, as even the administration admitted, but it would pass soon and there would be a chicken in every pot and two cars in every garage. It was fantastic to suppose that the waters could rise so high that only those on the highest peaks of prosperity would be saved. But by 1931 this had happened.

By 1931, too, the prohibition situation had come to a head. The people of the country had manifested clearly their complete disagreement with the W.C.T.U. In their determination to express their individual liberty, men who might never have taken a drink became devotees of bathtub gin and New Jersey Scotch. The unfortunate aspect of the whole thing was that liquor moved out of the saloon into the home. Women, who had been a sturdy seawall against the tides of alcohol, were as deeply submerged as men. The Wickersham Commission, which had been appointed to study the problem, announced its findings in January, 1931, and if any stalwart citizen had held out until that time against the urge to whip up a batch of home brew, he now gave in under the overwhelming weight of stupidity and chicanery which appeared in the Commission's report. Less than a majority of the members in their separate opinions favored continuation of the law, but their collective opinion was in favor of the "noble experiment." Such moral cowardice caused the entire nation to snicker.

The administration wrestled valiantly with the giant of unemployment. The things which were suggested and tried during these early years of the depression are forgotten now, for they did not work. President Hoover's notion of how to cope with the trouble was different from that of his successor. He said, "This is not an issue as to whether people shall go hungry or cold in the United States. It is solely a question of the best method by which hunger and cold shall be prevented." His idea was to give a dole where it was necessary, on the theory that outright charity would hurt the average man's pride, so that he would not accept it a moment longer than was absolutely necessary. If the man worked for the money, he reasoned, he would find little incentive to end the arrangement. So far as the dead calm in commodity buying was concerned, that would take care of itself when the things people owned began to wear out. The vacuum would create the breeze and the ship of trade would move on. It might have happened that way; we will never know. The election of November, 1932, intervened. The prescription was changed.

The effect of the depression on the Detail was acute. Our vigilance had to be doubled; the worries and problems which ordinarily beset us were multiplied. Crank letters, threats, and eccentric visitors reached a new high. Secret Service agents all over the country were busy checking on the people who felt an inclination to swell the White House mailbags.

Letters from people who want to tell the President how to run the country, who want to shoot him, who want to marry him, are weeded out of the day's mail carefully and turned over to the main office of the Service. If the writer signs his name or the letter is from a small town, checking up is an easy matter. The problem of an anonymous letter, mailed from a large city, is more complicated. None of these letters reaches the President, except now and then when a Chief Executive takes chances against our advice. On such occasions he is apt to find a threatening letter in the midst of his morning mail. It usually has the desired effect. Most of the letters are written by people of unsound mind, and in the majority of cases the author has no intention of taking action. But we can never be sure, so we must treat each one as if he were in dead earnest.

Those who bring their messages in person are treated as diplomatically as possible. We do not wish to embarrass them or frighten them. We try to win their confidence, and we stick with them until they are safely back in the hands of relatives or in an institution. Most of them react well to kind and friendly treatment.

One day a sweet little old lady came and sat in the reception room, refusing to tell her business to anyone but the President. She was dressed immaculately in a black silk dress, with white gloves and a little bonnet that framed her tiny, exquisite face. Her voice and manners were cultured; she was a real lady, of the old school. I talked with her for quite a while. She was from the South, and soon we discovered mutual friends and places we both knew and loved.

"You know," she said after a while, "I wasn't going to tell my secret to anyone but the President, but you have been so sweet—and you're practically a cousin—that I will confide in you. This is the situation:

"I am engaged to marry the Prince of Wales. The wedding will take place soon. I want the President to know about it so that he can invite me to all the social functions at the White House. Then I will be known to the proper people and when the announcement is made he can make me the guest of honor.

"If he does not do this the British Government will be embarrassed, and it may cause trouble between the two countries."

"My goodness," I said. "This is certainly a very delicate problem. I wish I had been able to get more sleep last night. I need to think clearly about this. Perhaps some fresh air will help me. Let's you and me go for a walk and talk this over."

We strolled around the White House grounds and pretty soon I learned that she had a son and a daughter, both living in Washington. Then we went back to the Executive Offices, and while she continued to wait for the President I called her children on the telephone and told them I was bringing their mother home. I then had the White House automobile sent around. When it was in front of the door I rushed out to the old lady and said:

"Gracious me! The President will soon be ready to receive you, and it just occurred to me that you are dressed informally. This will never do. I have the President's car waiting outside. We had better go to your home at once and you can change into the proper attire."

She was delighted. Off we went, to the home of her daughter, and I never saw her again. I could not help contrasting her with the big pock-marked blonde who strode into the lobby one day and told Pat McKenna to announce her presence to the President. She was heavily made up, and wore a fancy pink dress with slippers to match. Her eyes were blue and bold. Pat placed her in a far corner and asked me to take charge of her. "She's a hard one," he said. "You'd better send for a couple of hefty policewomen."

She was not at all coy about her business with the President. She was with child by him, she said, and had come to tell him about it. She talked in a loud voice and I asked her to speak more softly, lest we be overheard.

"Why should I?" she shouted. "I'm proud of it! I don't care who knows it!"

It was three hours before I was able to persuade her to leave. She would not reveal her name, but we found it out when she registered that night at a hotel. Immediately we got in touch with our agent in Kansas City, which she had given as her home. The next afternoon he telephoned me that she was a dangerous maniac, cunning and vile-mouthed. She was a member of a prominent family and had recently escaped from the institution to which she had been committed. A man was already enroute to Washington to get her.

The next morning we took her in charge. She kicked out two windows in the automobile, knocked the front seat off its base, and raised hell in general. When I saw the wrecked front seat I was reminded of another of our lady visitors.

This one came as a sightseer, entering at the East portico during the prescribed hours of 10 A.M. to 2 P.M. This brought her into the basement, whence she could proceed upstairs to the East Room and the other rooms on the ground floor. At the West end of the basement, guarding the President's private elevator and the route to the Executive Offices, sat Gene Davis, one of the White House staff. He was occupying an ancient swivel chair, so battered and dilapidated that even the boys in the Press Room had tossed it out. It was in danger of falling apart at any moment, but it suited Gene's figure and he enjoyed relaxing in it.

The lady visitor had six children in tow. Spotting Gene she bore down on him and began asking questions. She wanted to know the history of the White House, the story behind each room, the gossip about each President, the habits of the various First Ladies, the dimensions of the rooms, the style of furnishing used in each, etc., ad infinitum.

She poured out questions for a solid hour, then, satisfied that she was prepared for the great experience, she went upstairs, her six offspring trailing behind her. Scarcely had Gene relaxed and shaken the smoke from his brain when she was back.

"We've seen everything," she said. "But I want to be sure before we leave that we have not missed something of importance. Are you quite sure now, young man, that we have covered all that we should?"

Automatically Gene started to say yes, then caught himself. Revenge flickered in his tired mind.

"Well, there *is* one other thing," he said. "It's so special that we've stopped letting people see it. Something might happen to it.

"In fact it has been turned over to me to be personally guarded. I must make sure that no one puts a hand on it."

The lady was awed. She begged Gene to tell her what it was. Reluctantly, pretending he was submitting to her charm, he gave up the secret.

"It's this chair I am sitting in," he said. "It is the very chair which Columbus used as he looked for land from the prow of the *Santa Maria*. He was sitting in it when he discovered America!"

There was a moment of reverent silence. Then the woman, in a hushed tone, began to ask more questions. Her eyes lingered covetously on the chair. She didn't suppose anyone was ever allowed to *sit* in the chair except Gene himself. No, that was Gene's job—to see that the sacred seat was not sullied by unconsecrated rear ends. There was another silence, then Gene spoke. Of course, where it concerned a friend. . . .

The lady sat in the seat. The children sat in it, one by one. They whirled around in it, yelling and howling, imitating Columbus. Then they all left, happy and satisfied.

Except in wartime the business of guarding the White House and its grounds is done so unobtrusively that few people realize there is any surveillance at all. The White House police do not display themselves to the public. They are not outlandishly garbed and placed about like ornaments, as are the guardians of the great in other countries. They do their work without fanfare, and they do it well. In all the years of my service on the Detail only one letter of complaint against these men was received, and that was unjustified and was withdrawn when the facts were explained. The White House police pistol team has consistently defeated every group against which it has competed. But it doesn't do its shooting where the public can see it. Its deadly accuracy is kept for that emergency which the Detail and the police have to guard against twenty-four hours a day.

★☆★

The Bonus Army

ON THE SIXTEENTH of June, 1931, we went to Marion, Ohio, for the dedication of the Harding Memorial. Many prominent Republicans were afraid to go; by that time Harding's memory had been so smeared that people who guided their lives by what other people thought were disavowing any connection with him. Not so the President and the ex-President. Mr. Coolidge was glad to go, and brought his wife with him. He was still waiting for his job, and still enthusiastic about our trip. He looked in splendid health and seemed very glad to see me. The President, in his speech, faced the Harding issue squarely and stated the facts. He said:

"We came to know that there was a man whose soul was being seared by a great disillusionment. We saw him gradually weaken not only from physical exhaustion but from mental anxiety. Warren Harding had a dim realization that he had been betrayed by a few of the men he had trusted, by men he had believed were his devoted friends. It was later proved in the courts of the land that these men had betrayed not alone the friendship and trust of their stanch and loyal friend but they had betrayed their country. That was the tragedy of the life of Warren Harding."

By 1932 the depression had so deepened that despair reached out to everyone. There seemed to be no bottom to it. The most certain thing was that the Democrats would win the next election. Everything the Republicans had sponsored since they defeated the League of Nations was on the skids—prohibition, prosperity, isolation. All over America factories were idle and speakeasies were busy. All over Europe armies were preparing to march again.

In the spring of the year I went to Hopkinsville to visit my mother. She was now 86 years old, and she felt, with that certainty of intuition which comes to the very old, that her end was near. She asked me not to return when she was dead, but to remember her as she was during this, my last visit. She had remained so youthful in spirit that I had never had a realization of her advancing years. Her letters were like those of an eighteen-year-old girl. The house always was thronged with young people, who came to see her because she somehow managed to be their contemporary, while at the same time dispensing a wisdom which they needed and desired. She had always been everything to me. I promised her that I would not see her dead, that to me she would always be the person who sat before me now, smiling and talking and being busy with her hands.

A new class of people was now rising in the country—the economic experts. Each had a solution to the depression; as soon as he got it worked out on paper he got on a train and came to Washington. It was hard to believe that some of them were not on leave from an asylum. The administration, of course, was considering all sorts of devices and cures; the Reconstruction Finance Corporation, for instance, had been organized and was in operation.

One notion which was put forth seriously that spring might have been of political benefit to the Republicans had it been put into effect, as it later was by the Democrats. On June 21 Colonel George E. Ijams, of the Veterans' Administration, submitted a memorandum to Walter Newton in which he outlined what later became the Civilian Conservation Corps. In almost all its details the plan was identical with that adopted by President Roosevelt. Ijams did not claim it as his brain child. He said many people had spoken to him of some such organization as a means of combating unemployment.

Newton turned the memorandum over to Fred C. Croxton, Assistant Director of the President's Organization on Unemployment Relief.

Croxton and his colleagues turned the idea down. In his reply to Newton, Croxton said:

". . . we have not believed that the organization of a peace time army was the best approach to the present situation.

"We have felt that it was a very much better policy for the local communities to assume responsibility. . . ."

In July the Bonus Army arrived in Washington. Congress had approved a bonus for 1945; the veterans wanted it paid now. They drifted in from north, east, south, and west, bringing their families in some cases, all in dire want, often begging along the way. Our agents were among them, keeping us informed of the number of radicals in every group, and checking on the influence they had with the men. Generally speaking there were few Communists, and they had little effect on the men's thinking. The veterans were Americans, down on their luck but by no means ready to overthrow their government.

Once they got to town they were the problem of the Metropolitan Police. It was our opinion that camps should be provided for them, in isolated spots where adequate living facilities were available. They should be fed and housed, we thought, and separated into small groups so that no concerted action could be planned and carried out. Instead they were allowed to camp between the White House and the Capitol, on Pennsylvania Avenue—the most conspicuous spot in America. Others were just across the Potomac River, on the Anacostia flats. They built themselves shanty towns, of the type that was springing up all over the country under the general name of Hooverville.

They were orderly enough. They picketed the Capitol, but when the Senate, knowing they were outside, voted No to the bill for immediate payment, they quietly dispersed. Then came the July 28. The government ordered the Metropolitan Police to clear the area in front of the Capitol. The land was part of a new government building project. All the lots had to be vacated.

The Metropolitan Police said they would need help. The President ordered the army to assist. The soldiers marched up Pennsylvania Avenue, sent by their Chief of Staff, Douglas MacArthur. I was in the

Executive Offices when I heard the news. I went to Larry Richey.

"There are women and children in that camp," I said. "They should be gotten out before those boys move in."

"I think so too," Richey said. The President was conferring with Secretary of War Patrick Hurley. Richey went into the office and told them what I had said. They agreed with me—both were tired and harassed, and had overlooked the item. Hurley left immediately, to issue an order holding the troops until the families were removed.

He was too late. Already the soldiers were in the camp, and tear gas bombs were being hurled. The veterans retreated across the bridge into Anacostia. The soldiers followed, and fired the huts and shacks there. That night the sky of the city was red with flames. It was a shameful sight. Twenty-three years before I had eaten dinner with some of those boys in France. I almost wished that I had taken the job Hoover had offered me a few years before.

It was early in the Hoover administration. Larry Richey came to me and said:

"The President wants you to take the job of Superintendent of the Metropolitan Police. He wants you to clean up Washington. The pay will be raised from $6,000 a year to $9,000. What do you think about it?"

"I don't want it," I said. "The biggest crooks in Washington aren't the kind you can put in jail. Why should I chase gamblers and bootleggers? That's like swatting flies. Let the administration look in its own eye, lest there be a mote therein."

"Think it over for a few days," Richey said. "Then see the President about it."

My mind hadn't changed when the interview took place. The President outlined his plan: he wanted the city to be a model of law enforcement; he knew I could make it that; he would back me up.

"I have but one question to ask," I said. "Do you want me to leave the Detail? Is this a way of getting me out of the White House through the front door?"

"No," the President said. "You can stay on the Detail as long as you like. It is because of my regard for your ability that I want you to take this assignment."

"Thank you for your trust and confidence in me," I said. "I sincerely appreciate it. My desire is to remain with the Detail.

"The City of Washington is governed by three Commissioners, politically appointed. I would have to work under them. One might be a former businessman, one might be an ex-lawyer, one might be a schoolteacher. They would know nothing about police work, yet I would have to work under them. That is something I will not do—take orders from political appointees who know nothing about my work."

He was obviously disappointed, and a little irritated. I hastened to add that I could recommend a man who was more fitted for the position than I. That seemed to please him, and he accepted my suggestion that Henry Pratt, of Fredericksburg, Virginia, be given the post. Pratt proved an able man in the job, but at the time of the Bonus army he had resigned and the position was held by Colonel Pelham Glassford.

On a September night in that year, while at the Rapidan Camp, I received a long distance call from my brother Guy. Our mother, he told me, had but a few hours to live. It was impossible for me to get away—Jervis was gone and two of the men were sick—and I could not have arrived there for two days and nights. So I kept the promise I had made to her in the spring. In utter loneliness I stood in the early autumn night. Then the loneliness passed away and a different feeling passed me. Now for the first time the world and the whole of the universe held a personal meaning for me. My mother had become a part of it. For thirty years I had written to her every day. Now every day she would answer me, if I would listen.

The President did not learn of my bereavement. He was not that intimate with me, or with any of the Detail, and he was beset during that time by personal troubles. He had planned to conduct his campaign as he had in 1928, by ignoring the Democratic candidate. But now there was no able spokesman for the Republicans, and when Maine went Democratic some of his supporters were panic-stricken. He was urged to make a speaking tour of the country, and he decided to do so. Then we of the Detail were panic-stricken. With fear and trembling we set about constructing the most elaborate safeguards ever devised.

His first two speeches, in Des Moines and Cleveland, went off without incident. The third, scheduled for the twenty-second of October in Detroit, had us really worried. The city was in an ugly mood, and it was a four-mile run from the railroad station to the Olympic arena, where the President was to speak. I chose a route with as many wide streets and as few sharp turns as possible. I had every building along the line checked. I had plainclothesmen at all the points I considered dangerous. Squads of detectives in automobiles and armored cars were to cruise up and down the line of parade. I heard that admission tickets to the arena were being counterfeited. We were handpicking our audiences, of necessity, for there was obviously an attempt to get troublemakers into the hall for the purpose of demonstrating against the President. I had every printing press in the city under surveillance, and found one where an unauthorized order for tickets had been given.

The area around the railroad station was cleared, but across the street a large crowd gathered. I decided to keep the President on the train until the motor cavalcade was ready to start. I would then put him in his car and emerge from the cover of the station at a fast clip, taking the crowd by surprise and getting past it before a demonstration could be staged. I had trouble persuading the members of the official party to get into their cars and to move into their place in the line. Despite their protests I held the President until they had done as I asked. Then, with a pilot car leading the way, we swung out of the station.

The crowd recognized the President. There were cheers. There were also other sounds. For the first time in my long experience on the Detail I heard the President of the United States booed. All along the line there were bad spots, where we heard jeers and saw signs reading: DOWN WITH HOOVER; HOOVER—BALONEY AND APPLESAUCE. The President looked bewildered and stricken.

At the arena the crowd was friendly and listened appreciatively to a speech that lasted an hour. In the course of it I was startled to hear the President mention Franklin D. Roosevelt, the man he intended to ignore. He read a letter written by Roosevelt, which said:

"I believe in the inherent right of every citizen to employment at a living wage and I pledge my support to whatever measures I may deem necessary for inaugurating self-liquidating public works—to provide employment for all surplus labor at all times."

"This letter," the President said, "was published with the approval of Governor Roosevelt. It is a hope held out to the ten million men and women now unemployed and suffering, that they will be given jobs by the government. It is a promise no government could fulfill. I ask you whether or not such frivolous promises and dreams should be held out to suffering unemployed people. Is this the 'New Deal?' "

We got back to the train all right, and the President was cheered by the congratulations he received on his speech. But on our next appearance, in St. Paul, he was booed again by the crowds in the street, and just before the train reached Beloit a man was caught pulling up spikes from the tracks. In the St. Paul speech the President, referring to a Democratic prediction that mob rule would follow a Republican victory said:

"Thank God, we still have a government in Washington that knows how to deal with a mob."

A ripple went through the audience and I broke into a cold sweat. After the speech a prominent Republican took me aside and said, "Why don't they make him quit? He's not doing himself or the party any good. It's turning into a farce. He is tired physically and mentally."

The next speech was in Salt Lake City. From there the special train headed for the coast, and the President went to his home in Palo Alto to vote and await the election returns. When the train stopped at a small town along the way a friendly crowd gathered around the private car and called loudly for the President. Secretary of the Interior Hubert Work volunteered to pinch hit. He stepped out on the observation platform and spoke to the assemblage.

"The President was up very late last night," he said, "and he is still asleep. I bring you his greetings, and while I am here I cannot miss the opportunity to say a few words for myself. I am myself from the West, and I have spent many delightful hours in your beautiful little city. In fact I see several faces out there that I know. It is a very genuine pleasure to find myself back here . . ."

He stopped suddenly and turned to Jervis, who was standing beside him. Out of the side of his mouth he growled:

"Where the hell are we?"

Unfortunately an employee of the local broadcasting company was holding a microphone against the rear of the platform, and the Secretary's question was perfectly reproduced. Everyone within an area of a quarter of a mile heard it, and with typical Western humor the crowd roared with laughter.

When his defeat was announced, the President returned to Washington to complete his term. For relaxation he went to Florida to do some sailfishing. After a successful trip the party boarded its special train at West Palm Beach. The President stepped out on the observation platform while waiting for the train to start. Among the crowd which had gathered was a negro string orchestra, playing for whatever fees its listeners offered. Its leader, a roly-poly fellow, took off his hat and made a sweeping bow. The President, embarrassed by the gesture, reacted in his usual shy manner. He worked his right shoulder up and down and rattled the keys in his left trouser pocket. Just then the train began to move. The orchestra leader turned to the musicians and raised his hand. Instantly they came to attention and broke into the strains of a familiar melody—"Happy Days Are Here Again," the Roosevelt theme song.

On the morning of the fourth of January the clerk at the Willard Hotel handed me a letter postmarked "Northampton, Massachusetts, January 2, 8:30 P. M., 1933." It was from Mr. Coolidge. He had written it in longhand on the afternoon of the second. I noticed that the writing was less firm than usual. The letter read:

Dear Colonel Starling:

We have heard you were in Kentucky. I suppose it is your annual visit. No doubt you found it was very lovely.

Nevertheless I venture to offer the greetings of the season and hope the change did you good.

A card came from someone I suppose was the lame paper boy at the corner. Please thank him. I do not have his address. I find I am more and more worn out. I am sorry for anyone in office these days.

Yours,
Calvin Coolidge

The next afternoon the papers carried headlines of his death. I left the following morning for Northampton. When I arrived at the Coolidge residence, The Beeches, I met Ted Clark, the little fellow's private secretary, and Frank Stearns. I told them I had come as a friend, not as advance man for the President. As we were talking Mrs. Coolidge called downstairs and said, "Don't I hear Colonel Starling's voice?" Clark answered her, saying I had just arrived.

"Please tell him to come upstairs," she said.

She met me with arms outstretched. Putting her head on my shoulder she wept.

"Oh, why didn't I write you to come and live with us?" she said. "I shall never forgive myself for not writing and letting you know how much he needed you. He wanted you so much, but he always said, 'The President comes first. I am only a private citizen.' But if I had written to you and you had come this would not have happened."

Now all my earthly plans were ended. My mother, with whom my life had been bound up, was gone. The little fellow, with whom I had planned to end my career, was also gone. In deep melancholy I rode in the long funeral procession from the Edwards Congregational Church in Northampton to the cemetery in Plymouth. There I watched the scene which one newspaperman described as follows.*

Plymouth, Vt., Jan. 7—

Calvin Coolidge was buried here in Plymouth Cemetery late this afternoon as a driving wind and hail storm beat a rhythmic requiem on the improvised canopy over the family gravestone and swept the

* Thomas Sugrue in the New York *Herald Tribune*.

words of a brief benediction into the shadows of Salt Ash Mountain.

It seemed that nature and the Green Mountains, during the hundred-mile drive to Plymouth, were intent on revealing themselves in all the phases in which Mr. Coolidge had known and loved them. At Brattleboro, Vt., the light rain ceased and a bright sun turned the fields and hills into a reminder of a late October picture. The water that had paused in its journey down the hillsides to become ice again took up its journey, moving slowly under the wheels of the cars, and the gray mist of the mountains turned to blue and finally lifted. Thousands of white birches gleamed in the light, bare of leaves and looking like porcupine quills on the backs of sleeping monsters.

When the cars turned up the steep hill to the cemetery the rain had stopped again, and a pale light made everything visible and unusually clear. The honorary pallbearers took up their station above and behind the open grave, and Mr. Penner [the minister], wearing the same scholastic gown in which he had officiated in the morning, stood under the canopy at the right of the grave, in the midst of the floral tributes that had been sent from Northampton.

The first words rang sharp and clear on the still air, but just as he began the phrase, "Him that cometh to Me I will in no wise cast out," the hail began to fall, rising to blinding speed and strength as the words "None of us liveth to himself, and none of us dieth to himself" struggled to carry their message to the listeners.

Somebody opened an umbrella for Mrs. Coolidge, but the others remained immobile. "Wherefore my heart is glad, and my heart rejoiceth," Mr. Penner recited. The rest was lost in the noise of the hail.

The storm lightened somewhat as Mr. Penner read a few lines of scripture and the words of a brief poem penetrated through the white, stinging maze.

> *Warm summer sun shine kindly here,*
> *Warm south wind pass softly here,*
> *Green sod above lie light.*
> *Good night, dear heart, good night, good night.*

The storm descended again, cloaking the burst of tears that Mrs. Coolidge could no longer restrain. The last words of benediction, which

Mr. Penner pronounced with his right hand raised and pointing over the grave, were lost to all but the small group nearest him.

The windlass was turned, creaking slightly, and the coffin descended into the brown earth. It rested in its destined place and the mourners stood transfixed for a moment, staring at it. Then Mrs. Coolidge hurried toward the car and the others hurried after her. Four national guardsmen of Company B, Ludlow, Vt., took their places at the corners of the grave and began the vigil that will last until midnight Monday. The green license plate bearing the number 6779 flashed past the onlookers and Mrs. Coolidge, taking a white handkerchief from her eyes, threw a brief look back at the mound of fresh earth.

When only the guardsmen were left a stooped figure moved toward the grave and called to some laborers who had been standing high on the hill. To Ezro Johnson, sexton of the cemetery, had fallen the task of superintending the digging of the grave and the more difficult task, for him, of replacing the earth.

Silently the men worked, and silently Mr. Johnson looked at the casket which five hours before had stood in state before the nation's great. Quickly the earth covered it, while the guardsmen chatted and tried to joke about the bitter wind that had followed the sudden surcease of hail. Thirty minutes after it was lowered to its resting place it was covered with six feet of dirt, and only the sod remained to be replaced.

The train which carried me back to Washington seemed to beat out the requiem of my own life. I had nothing to look forward to but another fourth of March, another President, another administration with its hopes and plans, and the disillusions and tragedies which inevitably would be its fate.

★☆★★☆★

CHAPTER TWENTY-TWO

Roosevelt–The New Deal

DURING THE winter months of 1933 Steve Early, who was to be one of the new President's secretaries, came to see me several times about details of installing the new administration in the White House. One of the things we discussed was Mr. Roosevelt's physical condition, which would be a constant problem to the Detail. He suffered from the effects of infantile paralysis in both legs from the hip down. This necessitated the use of steel braces, which were locked at the knee when he stood. With the aid of a cane in his right hand and a person on his left, against whom he could lean, he was able to walk. It was, however, a tiresome process, and for all but brief distances he used a wheelchair. We would have to build a set of ramps, some permanent, some portable, and devise a routine for his movements from place to place, particularly when they involved public appearances.

My experience in the last year of the Wilson regime proved helpful to me in preparing routes and building approaches at the White House and the Capitol. For the inauguration I made an arrangement which was to be used by the same man four times, though of course I had no idea of that at the time. We drove up to the Capitol and went under the main stairway leading to the rotunda. At the lower door two ramps allowed us to reach a small elevator, which landed us at the entrance to the office of the Sergeant-at-Arms of the Senate. There Mr. Roosevelt waited until the Inaugural Committee brought word that it was ready. Still in his wheelchair he followed the committee to the rotunda, where I had built a wall of boards, making a private passageway against the wall. At the east door he rose from the chair and walked to the In-augural Stand, a distance of thirty-five yards. There he made a speech, which, if it be measured by its effect on the country, was one of the most powerful ever delivered. His statement that, "The only thing we have to fear is fear itself," was like an injection of adrenalin in the veins of public morale. The confidence, the courage, the boundless vitality of the new President, reached out and infected the whole country with hope. So far as the spirit of the thing was concerned, the depression ended right there.

According to custom, I accompanied the outgoing President to the railroad station. About a month before George Akerson had asked me to go with Mr. Hoover as far as New York, where he was to stay for a while before returning to California. I told him I could do it only if so ordered by Chief Moran. Moran, of course, refused the request. Then somebody said we were playing favorites, that I had gone to Northampton with the Coolidges. This was not true, but I could understand the anxiety among members of Hoover's staff. The depression was at its worst, and although the people were good-natured and tranquil, they might erupt at any moment.

Going through Union Station the crowd pressed closely against us. Larry Richey, nervous and excited, said to me:

"Bill, I am instructing you now to go with the chief to New York. You must do it."

"I am sorry, Larry," I said, "but you are now a private citizen with no authority to order anyone to do anything. Don't worry. There are four hand-picked special agents of the railroad on your train. They have worked with us many times. These railroad people know almost as much about looking after a President as we do. The depot in New York will be cleared and guarded. You will have plainclothesmen, railroad officials, and a motorcycle escort to look after you. Goodbye and good luck."

After bidding the Hoovers farewell I returned to the White House, which had been transformed during my absence into a gay place, full of people who oozed confidence and seemed unaware that anything was wrong with the United States. The President was the most happy and confident of them all.

"Well," I said as I shook hands with him, "you never can tell who's going to turn up in the White House."

He laughed. "I'm glad to see you, Ed," he said. "I hope you will stay with me while I am here."

"I'll be glad to," I said rashly.

On that day in 1933 I realized he had overcome more than a physical illness. He had somehow acquired a vigor, an optimism, a feeling of sureness in himself which he never before had possessed. The country was feeling it also. That night he closed the banks, and the next day skeptical newspaper reporters discovered that they could get checks cashed in almost any place of business where there was money in the till. The battle had been won.

The next afternoon the President took a ride. He insisted on circling the Speedway, which was jammed with cars. He got stuck in the traffic, naturally.

"Pull out and drive on the grass," the President said. "You won't hurt it."

A few days later he broke a long-standing tradition that the President does not make social calls on private citizens, by going to the home of former Supreme Court Justice Oliver Wendell Holmes, to congratulate the old gentleman on the occasion of his birthday. It was obvious that we were in for some changes in Presidential customs and manners.

The White House itself was undergoing changes. A swimming pool, paid for by popular subscription, was built in the basement. The Executive Offices, which had been damaged by fire during the Hoover administration, were expanded and rebuilt, with a concealed third story, a new office for the President, additional offices for the various secretaries, and a larger lobby. Later the kitchens were overhauled and modernized.

The system of three secretaries was continued: Louis McHenry Howe, Marvin McIntyre, and Steve Early moved in. One day Pat McKenna, the doorkeeper, told me that Early and McIntyre wanted to see me. I called on them and they said they were certain that someone in the telegraph and telephone room was drunk; would I please go and investigate? I said I wouldn't, since Doc Smithers was in charge of that office, and it was none of my business anyhow. Later I found Jervis and we went to see the two secretaries together. We told them flatly that our job was to protect the President, not to report on the conduct of White House employees. They complained to Louis Howe. Howe carried the tale to Chief Moran. Moran, of course, backed us up, in no uncertain terms.

By summer the New Deal was well begun. Then the President scared the wits out of us by announcing that he was going to spend his vacation sailing up the coast of New England in a yawl. Paul D. Rust, Jr., of Marblehead, Massachusetts, placed at his disposal the *Amberjack II,* a trim forty-four footer which would sleep five persons comfortably. No one of the five would be a Secret Service man. We could like it or lump it, but that was the way it was going to be. Three of the President's sons would be with him—James, John, and Franklin. I went to Marion, just below Quincy, Massachusetts, where the boat was anchored, and to Boston, where I talked with Jimmy, who was to be first mate. He promised me that no gasoline or oil would be left on the floor of the boat, and that no cigarette butts would be thrown anywhere but overboard. I was worried about fire, and possible explosion of the bilge, into which gasoline fumes might seep, causing a backfire.

The boat itself I trusted. It was sturdy and well-made, and trim as a young girl at a dance. Love at first sight was reflected in the President's face when he reached the dock at Marion and saw her for the first time, her brass shining, her hull gleaming and rolling coquettishly. He could hardly wait to get aboard. Once there the little boat moved out into Buzzards Bay and anchored for the night, while our patrol of speedboats circled about disconsolately.

The destination of the cruise was the Roosevelt summer home at Campobello Island, off Eastport, Maine, and just over the Canadian line. Our fleet consisted, in addition to the *Amberjack,* of the Coast Guard cutter *Cuyahoga,* loaded with the Detail; two destroyers assigned by the Navy—the *Bernadou* and the *Ellis*—the power boat *Comanche* and the ketch *Mary Alice,* full of newspapermen; and an ancient Gloucester fishing boat, *Old Glory,* gunwales down with photographers. I was on shore with a fast automobile. By telephone I could find out from Washington where the boat was anchored for the night—the destroyers having wirelessed the position to Arlington—and proceed to the nearest point of land. There I could get transportation and go out to the *Amberjack,* bringing mail, telegrams, and supplies. With me I took a Western Union man.

The President led the rest of the fleet a merry chase. He knew the coast thoroughly, and he put his small, fast craft into places where the bigger boats could not follow. Thus he maintained the privacy he desired; the photographers seldom got within shooting distance. They were busy fighting bedbugs on the *Old Glory.*

The *Amberjack* was a pretty sight, with all her canvas drawing and her rail down to the water, driving along the rockbound coast of Maine. The President lost little time, and when anchor was dropped one night off Rogue's Bluff he told the boys they would make Campobello by the next sunset. In the morning he awoke to find a pea-soup fog in charge of the situation. He could not move. The boat was anchored in shallow water, among rocks, beyond hail of the other boats in the fleet.

On shore in Machias I received wireless reports from the destroyers saying they had lost touch with the *Amberjack,* and that the fog showed no signs of lifting. The Western Union man had important telegrams to deliver; I, naturally, was worried about the situation on the boat. We decided to try and reach her.

We drove to Rogue's Bluff, our car creeping along a road we could not see. At the bluff I was told that the speedboat I had hoped to borrow was tied up at its wharf on an island ten miles off shore. The fog was like a dark gray wall; it seemed impossible that any boat could penetrate it safely. I asked if there was a man who would try.

"Find Henry Wallace," I was told. "He can find anything, fog or no fog. He can trace a broken lobster pot that's drifted ten miles from its anchor."

We located the Wallace home. Henry was fishing. We waited until he returned, then explained our predicament.

"I guess I can find it," Henry said laconically.

His boat was pulled up on the beach for repairs. We helped him get into the water. It was a flimsy thing, homemade, powered by a Ford engine that sounded definitely tubercular. The front part was covered by a tarpaulin sewed together from odds and ends by Mrs. Wallace. This was the only protection against breaking seas. The Western Union man took a long look and decided to stay ashore. He gave me the telegrams and Henry and I set out.

Henry stood erect, one hand on the hand-whittled tiller, the other on a stick which controlled the speed of the engine. Between his feet he held an old brass compass. From time to time he glanced down at it. He seemed to know exactly what he was doing, and we rolled through the fog as nonchalantly as if we had broad daylight to guide us. After what seemed like a long run Henry shut off the motor and said, "Here's one of your navy boats."

We were alongside the *Ellis*. I asked them where the *Amberjack* was anchored.

"Just over those rocks, in a cove," they shouted, pointing into the fog.

Henry nodded and off we went. Soon a jagged rock loomed up. We rounded it and drifted up to the *Amberjack*. The President was loafing on deck, smoking a cigarette. His eyes widened when he saw Henry and me come alongside.

"Hello, Ed!" he said. "Where did you come from? I thought we'd lost you."

He was enjoying himself, and I don't think he cared particularly about having his reverie interrupted by the batch of telegrams I carried. But the boys were glad to see me. They were running out of cigarettes and fresh meat.

"How about bringing us out some thick, juicy steaks?" Franklin junior said.

"I endorse that suggestion," his father said.

"Are you all right otherwise?" I asked.

"Ed," he replied, "I am having a wonderful time. I don't care how long this fog lasts."

He was wearing an old gray sweater, a pair of dirty flannel trousers, and a dilapidated hat. His face sported three days' growth of beard. He looked completely content.

It was a good thing he was, for the fog lasted five days, during which time the *Amberjack* and her convoy were unable to move. Henry and I made numerous trips in the lobster boat, bringing food, mail and cigarettes. Henry always proceeded at top speed, and I was sure that every trip was our last, but he seemed to smell his way among the rocks and we never had so much as a close call. The sun finally came out and the trip was completed in less than a day.

The President had no objection to our surveillance, and he coöperated with us completely, but his absolute lack of fear made it difficult at times for him to understand the safeguards with which we surrounded him. He liked to feel completely free, and he saw no reason why he should not be. He never fretted because of our presence, however, and his sense of humor was stimulated by the care we took to dog his every move.

One afternoon at Hyde Park he ordered the small car which was fitted so that he could drive it, and with his secretaries Miss LeHand and Miss Tully, started out for a ride. He headed for the woods between the residence and the Hudson River. Members of the Detail were behind him in the big Secret Service car, and behind them were state troopers in one of their automobiles. I remained at the house to answer the telephone and take care of some callers who were scheduled for the afternoon.

When he was well into the woods the President decided to turn around and come back. He soon had his car facing the other way, but the road was narrow and the other two vehicles were temporarily stuck. Gleefully the President raced by them, and in a few minutes rolled up to the residence and called out to me.

"Ed," he said, looking very serious, "I have lost the Secret Service boys. I cannot find them anywhere. Do you know where they are?"

I kept a straight face and went to the telephone. Calling the front gate I left word for the boys that the President was waiting for them at the house. As I returned the state troopers' car came around the corner on two wheels. Behind it was the Secret Service car, also travelling at top speed. After telling them that he was sorry, and that he hoped they would not get lost again, the President drove off, a mischievous grin on his face.

He enjoyed himself at Hyde Park, and it was a pleasant place for the rest of us to be. I became very fond of his mother, Mrs. James Roosevelt. One day, after her son had been President about three years, she said to me:

"Colonel Starling, a photographer from New York wanted to come here and take some pictures of me. I told him it would be impossible this week. In fact I am of the opinion that people are getting tired of seeing so many pictures of the Roosevelt family. There have been too many of them."

She was a regular attendant at St. James Episcopal Church at Hyde Park, and the President always went with her to the services when he was at home. The rector was a fine gentleman named Doctor Frank Wilson. The photographers liked to snap pictures of him, and he was always very gracious about it. One summer he preached at Welch Pool, a small Maine town near Campobello. He was on the pier fishing, dressed in old clothes, on a day when the President was due to arrive on a cruiser. The photographers, waiting, walked out on the dock. One of them said:

"I wish Colonel Starling would finish telephoning and come out here and tell us where the ship will stop."

Doctor Wilson spoke up.

"Well, boys," he said, "I am almost positive she is going to stop near that buoy about a quarter of a mile from here. You ought to get a good picture when she turns and drops anchor."

The photographers turned to look at him. They did not recognize him. One of them said sarcastically:

"Thanks for the information, old man, but how do you think we are going to get out there—walk on the water like Jesus Christ?"

One day as we drove into the Hyde Park estate I noticed a sign which read: FRANKLIN D. ROOSEVELT MEMORIAL LIBRARY. When we stopped at the house I ran ahead and asked the President whether he had noticed it.

"No," he said, "but Miss LeHand did. What did it say?"

I told him. He looked at me gravely.

"I may be dead," he said, "but I haven't been officially notified yet. How long will it take to get that sign down?"

"About ten minutes," I said.

"Did the newspapermen see it?"

"I don't think so, but we'll soon hear about it if they did."

Apparently they hadn't, for although three cars filled with them passed the sign, none of them mentioned it or wrote anything about it. I had it taken down and put away immediately.

President Roosevelt broke all the travel records set by his predecessors. He kept me on the go from the day of his arrival at the White House, and since as advance man my mileage was three times his, I began to feel like a combination of Marco Polo and the Fuller brush man. The innumerable details attendant upon a Presidential visit to any part of the country became routine with me, though I could never ease up on a single one of them or take the most insignificant arrangement for granted. One of the things I had to look for wherever I went was a seven passenger open car for the President's use, and as the nineteen thirties progressed it became increasingly difficult to find them. (The President got into such a car by sliding to the jump seat and going from there to the rear seat.) In Los Angeles I finally borrowed one from Cecil B. De-Mille. In Dallas, Texas, after a futile search, some friends telephoned that they had found one. It arrived with a roar—blazing red, with DALLAS FIRE DEPARTMENT across its body in bold letters. We painted it black and used it.

On a Western trip in 1935 I received my greatest fright with regard to the President's safety. The fact that the danger was all over when I found out about it did not lessen my feelings. I had made the necessary arrangements for a trip to Boulder Dam and was in Los Angeles working on local reception plans when the newspapers called to ask about a rumor that the Presidential party had gotten lost on some mountain road near Las Vegas. I knew nothing of this. The committee at Boulder Dam had informed me by telephone that the party had left there on time. Officials of the Southern Pacific told me that the train had pulled out of Las Vegas late, but was now enroute to Los Angeles with everyone aboard.

At eight o'clock the next morning I met the train. The first man I saw was Henry Taggert, whom I had left in charge of the Detail.

"What happened at Las Vegas?" I asked.

He was so mad he spat out the words: "Key Pittman and Harry Hopkins got the President to drive up a narrow mountain road just to see a CCC Camp and the whole party got stuck and had to turn around on a dime. We had a mountain on one side and a drop of about a mile on the other."

Key Pittman was the Senator from Nevada. Harry Hopkins was then Federal Relief Administrator. Why they should interfere with the arrangements I had made, which were timed almost to the split second, I could not understand.

"Why did you let them change our plans?" I asked Taggert.

"I didn't," he said. "I went to Marvin McIntyre and told him we had made no arrangements for a side trip up Mount Charleston. I said it was foolish and unnecessary and a big risk.

"He went to the President's automobile and told him the Secret Service was against the trip. Before the President could answer Senator Pittman interrupted and said the road was perfectly safe. Hopkins butted in and said the trip ought to be made. So the President overruled me."

The road was of gravel, built by CCC boys. It wound around shoulders of rock on the edge of a precipice, with just enough room for a single car to pass. The grade was so steep that the wheels of the cars slipped in the gravel, and the water boiled in the radiators. One of the cars assigned to the newspapermen stalled, and had to turn back. Finally Taggert stopped the Secret Service car, which was in the lead, acting as pilot, and went back to tell the President that the road ahead was impassable. The camp was still several miles away. To his relief the President agreed that they should go back, and told his driver to turn around at the first suitable point.

This was not easy to find. When a spot was finally chosen it was necessary for the chauffeur to jockey the car back and forth on a narrow ledge. The President stayed in the car, and Marvin McIntyre was so frightened that whenever the rear wheels approached the edge of the precipice he gripped one of the back mudguards, prepared to hold it up by main strength if it slipped over. This was too much for the President's sense of humor—McIntyre weighed scarcely one hundred pounds—and he burst into laughter.

"We finally got turned around and came back down," Taggert said. "We were two hours late leaving Las Vegas."

I left him and went to the President's private car. McDuffie, the valet, stuck his head out when I knocked. The President, he said, was dressing. Behind him a voice called out:

"Come on in, Ed."

He was laughing when I entered. "Have you heard about our mountain adventure?" he asked.

"Yes," I said, "I have heard all about it. That's why I am here. I don't think you were fair to me or to the Secret Service or to the country to go up that mountain last night. You took an unnecessary chance. I know it is hard to realize that you have no right to endanger yourself, but you haven't. Your life isn't your own to give or to take now. It belongs to the people of the United States. That's why I am paid to look out for you. If anything had happened last night my whole life would have been ruined, not to mention what would have happened to the country."

He stopped smiling and a grave look came into his eyes. He was being bawled out but he was taking it like a man.

"I am sorry, Ed," he said. "You're right, and I will square you with the Secret Service. I'll wire Moran and assume personal responsibility for an unwise act."

Just then Mrs. Roosevelt, who had been in the adjoining apartment, appeared in the doorway.

"I couldn't help overhearing Colonel Starling's plain talk to you, Franklin," she said. "I endorse everything he said. I think it is only fair for you to promise him that you will adhere rigidly in the future to the itineraries he approves."

The President raised his eyebrows.

"Apparently the majority is against me," he said. "Very well, I'll promise."

I was surprised to receive help in the matter from Mrs. Roosevelt, who had steadfastly refused to allow the Secret Service to accompany her on her journeys. Since we are technically empowered only to guard the President, there was nothing we could do about it. As the years went by I wondered what might have happened had we been able to enforce our presence on her. Some of the boys would have seen little of home and hearth and much of the world. It may have been best for all concerned that she, who traveled fastest, traveled alone. I would not want the job of keeping up with her.

★★

Another War—The Circle Closes

THE HISTORY of the Roosevelt administration is a thing of the future—perhaps of the far future. What happened during the nineteen thirties cannot yet be assayed or judged. It is certain that by his optimism, vigor, and initiative, President Roosevelt got us through a bad economic depression with a minimum of scars to show for it. As for the debt—when you are as old as I am you realize that money in such quantities is purely theoretical, and may not be at all what it seems. We may not owe nearly as much money as we think we do; we may owe more. It depends on what happens to our economic system in the next generation.

My own admiration for Mr. Roosevelt is based more on his handling of foreign affairs than his treatment of domestic crises, for it was in the delicate matter of international diplomacy that I saw President Wilson defeated and the little people of the world betrayed. The spirit of Christ sat with the American President at his small desk in the Holy of Holies at the Quai d'Orsay, but the purpose for which he went to Paris was defeated and from the moment he put his name to the peace treaty in the Hall of Mirrors at Versailles, the Second World War was inevitable. Franklin D. Roosevelt knew this. From 1933 on he saw the shadow of the conflict drawing closer and closer. His task was to coax a pacifist, isolationist nation into a realization of danger and a willingness to prepare for it. This he did with consummate skill, and it will, I think, be considered as one of the deeds greatly to his credit. Once in the struggle, it was his job not only to run the war, but handle the delicate situation between himself and the heads of the other allied nations.

Here again I believe he also scored. He was never outsmarted or out-foxed, and his friendly relations with our allies certainly laid a firm foundation for the winning of the peace.

In the middle nineteen thirties I lost my batting eye so far as politics and public affairs are concerned. I was looking at something else. It happens to every man, but usually the dull, flat roar of the approaching hurricane is heard at an earlier age. When the storm broke over me and I began putting things in the wrong pockets, changing my tie three times before going out in the morning, and trying to smoke a cigarette with my ear, I didn't know what had happened, except that it happened most when I was with her. She was Ida Lee Bourne, of Kentucky, and I had met her when she came to Washington to visit former Governor and Mrs. E. P. Morrow, also of Kentucky. She was a beautiful woman, who looked straight at you when she laughed. When I discovered that I was in love I said, "Will you marry me?" and to my consternation she said, "Yes." So it happened on February 1, 1936, with Jimmy Taylor officiating and Ulric Bell, of the Louisville *Courier-Journal,* and Mrs. Bell, as attending couple. I was frightened at the notion of being so happy day after day—I was sure something was going to occur to throw me back into the same lonely groove I had occupied for so long. But it didn't.

Meanwhile the New Deal was coining three-letter monograms for its innumerable agencies, and people were convinced that the country was going to hell. The only difference between them was that some were enjoying the ride. Being of the opinion that progress is never efficient, since it has no idea where it is going except that the direction is forward, I was not one of the nail-biters and "Whither now?" people of that period; but seeing the odd assortment of visitors who called at the White House each day, and looking over some of the plans for salvation sent through the mail by self-styled geniuses, I could not but compare the state of the whole nation to the bewilderment of the negro preacher who said to his flock:

"An' lo, de Queen of Sheba, she went down into Jerus'lem a-sittin' on a mule; an' behole, de mule flung her, an' she fell among thieves, but dey passed by on de udder side. By an' by she come ter herself an' got again on de mule's back an' she seed dem a-comin' from a-fur off, an' five of dem wuz wise an' five wuz foolish; an' dey come forth ter meet her wid palm leaf fans, cryin' 'Great is Susanneth of de Ephesians!' an' dey waved dem palm leaves in dat mule's face. An' she rode down de street an' she looked up into de second store window an' cried out, 'Fling down Jezebel!' an' de answer come back, 'We ain't gwine ter fling down Jezebel,' an' she said unto dem a second time, 'Fling down Jezebel!' an' de answer come back again, 'We ain't gwine to fling down Jezebel.' An' she cried unto dem yit a third time, 'Fling down Jezebel,' an' den dey changed dair minds, an' flung her down seventy times seven, an' busted her unto pieces which could not be numbered, an' fed de multitude; an' dere was great weepin' an' wailin' an' snatchin' out of teeth; an' dey picked up her fragments an' filled twelve baskets full, an' five loaves an' two fishes was left over. An' I say unto you, brethren, on de Day of Judgment, whose wife am Jezebel gwine ter be?'"

Just before the war broke out in Europe the King and Queen of England made a brief but pleasant visit. They were properly under the care of the State Department while in this country, and I was delegated to act as liaison officer between the White House and Cordell Hull's special agents. This State Department force, though small, was efficient, and with the added help of Scotland Yard's representatives we gave Their Majesties adequate protection. By invitation Mrs. Starling and I attended the famous garden party. That night as we returned from the British Embassy the King came to me and said:

"Colonel Starling, I understand that you have been assigned to the White House for a quarter of a century, and that you came to England with President Wilson, and knew my father."

"Yes, sir," I said. "I had that honor, and if you do half as well as your daddy you will make a good king."

I don't know why I said it, except that he looked so young and so earnest that I felt fatherly toward him. His eyes filled with tears, and he stuttered. The Queen, smiling, patted his arm and said, "Wasn't that sweet?"

The President was interested in every detail of our arrangements. One day he sent for me and said:

"Here are my plans for the visit of the King and Queen to the World's Fair, and their motor trip to Hyde Park. We will leave here on the same train at night, and drop the King and Queen off along the New Jersey shore the next morning. A boat will take them to New York and on the way they can see the skyline. After visiting the Fair they will come to Hyde Park, where Mrs. Roosevelt and I will be waiting."

"That's fine," I said, "except for one thing. Let's not put all our eggs in one basket. At this point in history I don't think the heads of the two greatest nations on earth ought to be on the same train, with everybody in the world knowing about it. Suppose you let the King and Queen go on one train, and then, a little later, you and Mrs. Roosevelt leave on another one, over a different road. If anything happened to the King and Queen, England would never forgive us, and if anything happened to you I couldn't set foot in Kentucky again."

He smiled and cocked his cigarette holder at the ceiling. "You're probably right," he said. "We'll use two trains."

I accompanied the Presidential special to Hyde Park, and while my host sat on the front porch I gave him news every fifteen minutes of his guests, getting word by telephone from our agents in New York.

"They are fifteen minutes late leaving the World's Fair," I said.

"That's Grover Whalen," he said. "They're lucky to get away at all."

In September the Second World War began. Immediately my job became more arduous. Since Jervis' transfer to field service in 1935, I had been head of the Detail. Now, with an election and a war to complicate matters, I had on my hands the most high-spirited and incautious President since the days of his cousin Teddy. I remember how disturbed Daniel J. Tobin was when I went to make the arrangements at Constitution Hall for the President's address to the International Brotherhood of Teamsters. The speech was to be delivered on the evening of September 11, 1940, at the opening gun in the campaign for re-election. At the time Dan Tobin, president of the union, was one of the President's administrative assistants. It was largely as a favor to him that the speech was made.

The union, the largest in America, was holding its convention in the hall. I went to Dan and told him the meeting would have to adjourn at 3 P.M. instead of 5:30, to give me time to examine the building. He was so interested in our preparations that he followed me about as I led my men on a search into every corner and closet. I explained to Dan that in a place so large and equipped with so many entrances, there were innumerable opportunities for assassins to hide or conceal bombs. It was routine work with me but it began to affect Dan's imagination. He saw dynamite in every corner and a maniac in every closet. Finally he said to me:

"This is the first time in my life I have ever been frightened. I wish I had never asked the President to come."

I tried to reassure him, but he was an unhappy man until the President had come, delivered his speech, and been safely carried back to the White House.

We now were building an army, and instead of visiting public works projects our auto cavalcade rolled up to army camps and naval stations. We began seeing old friends—Major General Levin H. Campbell, Jr., now Chief of Ordnance; Lieutenant General Brehon Somervell, chief of the Army Service Forces; Major General Clinton L. Corbin, Quartermaster General; and my old colleague, General Henry H. "Hap" Arnold, now head of the Army Air Corps. I had met him first when, as a lieutenant, he had flown the mail to President Coolidge in the summer of 1927, when we were in the Black Hills. His smile, his friendliness, his lack of temperament, and the fact that he was always on time no matter what weather prevailed, had impressed all of us. We put him down as a young man who would go far, and he did.

It made my heart sick to see the unpreparedness of the nation, but as we visited the arsenals—the old faithfuls at Watertown, Massachusetts, and Frankford, Pennsylvania,—and the Aberdeen Proving Grounds, I took courage at the work which had been done at these places during the years of our careless isolationism. Blockbusters had been tried out as early as 1923, and our guns, as soon as they could be manufactured, were prepared to shoot heavier projectiles farther and with more accuracy than the enemy's. Nothing had been overlooked. When I gave Major General Thomas Hayes, General Campbell's assistant, a twist of tobacco from my Kentucky farm, he loyally tried it out and reported that it nearly killed him.

"Now I know why the Indians passed the peace pipe," he wrote me. "They used Kentucky tobacco, and after one whiff all that a brave could do was pass the pipe to the next fellow and collapse."

At noon on December 8, 1941, we rode to the Capitol. This time we drove past the East plaza to the end of the building, then turned and went to the southwest corner. By means of a ramp at the south entrance we rolled the wheelchair to the lower corridor. The elevator took us to the second floor and the President waited in the office of the Speaker of the House until the joint meeting was ready. Then he rolled part way to the door leading to the rostrum. Getting up, he walked through the door and up a ramp to the stand prepared for him. Above him sat Vice President Wallace. Just below Wallace, and to his left, I took up my position. Members of the Detail were scattered throughout the room. I signalled to them with innocent-looking movements of my hands and fingers. The President began to speak:

"Yesterday . . . a day that will live in infamy . . ."

So we started again on the long, tortuous road of war. It was twenty-four years and eight months since I had made the same journey for the same purpose. Then it was a gentle spring night, with rain falling. Twenty years before that date I had been a soldier myself, in another war. It made me feel old, sitting there listening to the birth of a third struggle—one that would dwarf all those which had gone before it. All our civilization was able to accomplish, it seemed, was bigger and better wars, with more refined and efficient ways of killing. It was time for a man of my age and temperament to go away to a quiet place and think. Everything else had been tried as a means of saving the world, and had failed.

In the almost half century in which I had dealt with men as a deputy sheriff, railroad special agent, and Secret Service operator, I had discovered enough about them to know that waging and winning the war would not make them capable of making and keeping the peace. Men are not made good by their actions, but by inner decisions reached in quiet, and carried out in the passive patterns of thought. Another armistice would be achieved, I knew, by our guns; but only our prayers and the lifting of our hearts above selfishness and greed could accomplish a durable peace.

We left the Capitol and returned to the White House. Again I witnessed the signing of a Declaration of War. In a few weeks we were at the air field meeting Winston Churchill. He arrived on the shortest day of the year, and the long night seemed to symbolize the darkness of the Allied cause at that hour. Through the months of 1942 we fought, along with Russia and England, an uphill battle. By 1943 we were on the offensive. Again it semed a matter of the peace—how it would be handled, and whether it could be made to stick.

I felt now that I could retire. I dared not wait longer. Rudolph Forster, my old friend, had stayed on the job past the age of retirement and had died in harness, not long after saying to me, in his gentle voice and with his characteristic smile, "This isn't an administration; it's a dynasty."

When I went to the President and told him I planned to retire he said he had hoped I would remain with him while he was in the White House.

"I know," I said. "But nobody knows how long that is going to be. Rudolph Forster was going to stay until you left, and he's gone. I don't want to die on the job. It wouldn't be becoming. And I'm not sure I can outlast you. I'm not going to try. I'm going fishing."

He laughed and said, "I wish I could go with you. Good luck, Ed. I'll miss you."

"I'd sort of like to be at the peace conference," I said, "and now that I'm leaving I'll tell you what I think about it. I don't think the treaty should be completed until three or four years after the war is ended. There should be time for hates and prejudices to simmer down. We should have a commission of smart and able men, and the commission should not be headed by the President of the United States. I'd like to see you there, but not as President. I don't think those European fellows can fool you."

He cocked an eyebrow and pointed his cigarette holder at the ceiling. "Some of them think they do," he said.

So I left the Detail, after thirty years of uninterrupted service during which I did not lose a day through illness or for any other cause, and in the course of which I traveled approximately 1,200,000 miles. I took with me the feeling that I had done my best with that which was entrusted to me, and memories that convinced me of my country's greatness and vigor and humanity. They were mixed, and they were largely inconsequential, but they proved, at least to me, that over the years democracy works, for the Presidents I knew were accurate reflections of the people who elected them.

Wilson was the American concerned with the perfection of his own country, and unaware of Europe as a factor in his destiny. When it forced itself upon his plans he dealt forthrightly with the problem, assuming that he was encountering reasonable men and reasonable situations. Harding was the American disillusioned of this hope, retreating in contempt and disgust from the chicanery of Continental diplomacy, taking pride again in his own country as the only worthwhile place on earth. His weakness was his ample trust in all other Americans—a belief that national virtue somehow brought about individual goodness. Coolidge was the apotheosis of the American's idea of himself—a canny fellow with a dry wit, a sharp mind, a trading instinct, and a solid backlog of morality. But while this solemn Sunday notion of himself was in the White House, the American was disporting himself in Saturday night abandon.

Hoover was the successful American, a man who by industry and intelligence had lifted himself to high office. He was efficient, honest and well-intentioned, but he no more than any other man could stem a tide of fate. He well exemplified the futility of man's perfecting himself in an earthly mold; only spirit could survive the inundation that began in 1929.

But the American bobbed up like a cork coming out of a whirlpool. Now he was Franklin D. Roosevelt, a man with a four-foot yardstick, as vigorous and as optimistic as the pioneers, but wise from a century of party politics and no longer naïve about Europe and her balance of power. The American, after a great many growing pains, had come of age.

Here in the Florida sunshine, where I have come to fish and relax and think, such thoughts are mixed with other and more trivial remembrances: Wilson dancing a jig, Harding cussing amiably at a golf ball, Coolidge sneaking into the East Room before a reception to steal and eat the choice cakes. The little fellow was an incurable nibbler. How he waited for me to bring preserves and country sausage from Hopkinsville! He served the sausage at his breakfasts for Senators and Congressmen. He would invite two or three of them, and they would go away wondering why he had sent for them, for he would talk of nothing of importance. He had no purpose except to see what they looked like, listen to them talk, and thus find out what sort of men they were. "Mama! Mama!" he cried one evening as he dressed for dinner, "I want some preserves for supper." "We haven't any, Father," Mrs. Coolidge said. "Oh, yes we have," he said gleefully. "Ol' Colonel Starling just brought me some and I am going to eat all I want!" One day I went to fetch him for a visit to the Capitol and found him in the State Dining Room, seated in his great chair at the head of the table, wearing his high silk hat, with a napkin tucked under his chin, sipping a bowl of soup.

There was the time Mrs. Hoover's Russian wolfhound was sick at Rapidan, and the doctor with the help of the Filipino cook, gave him a dose of castor oil. He disappeared for a week. When he finally came out of the woods the Filipino boy saw him and called to him. The hound took one look, turned, and ran blindly back to the forest. He was so scared he ran straight into a tree, and he was going so fast he knocked himself unconscious. There was the time Marvin McIntyre and his White House quartet sang over the radio, and President Roosevelt called up the station to see about signing them up for a commercial program. "Who the hell are you?" McIntyre said into the telephone after the President had led him on with descriptions of a juicy contract. "I'm the advertising manager for Cascarets," the President said, and hung up. There was the night Walter Huston tried in vain to convince the policeman at the White House gate that he knew me and should be allowed to enter. "I've seen you somewhere," the policeman said, "but not with Colonel Starling." After a long minute of thought he said, "Now I know. You're 'Gabriel Over the White House.' Go ahead, you live here."

Did I learn anything in all those years? Perhaps. I learned something on a day in 1899 when I called on a girl who said she had some information about a murderer I had arrested. She talked around the subject for half an hour. When I rose to leave she came toward me with a disarming smile. An instant too late I saw that her eyes were blazing with hate. She whipped a knife from the belt of her dress and buried the blade in my left shoulder. She was the murderer's sweetheart.

I learned to read men's characters by the signs in their faces—to look for a little quirk in the left side of the mouth, a slight cock to the right eye, a cleft in the chin, an odd formation of the lower lobe of the ear, hair growing low on the forehead. A weak mouth and a conical-shaped head, with ears close to the skull, told me of an intelligent and thrifty man, whose plans were well thought out but who would be useless in any crisis. A long face with strong jaws, medium forehead, ears close to the head, eyes close together and a strong mouth, told me of an intelligent and determined man, but one easily prejudiced, egotistical, and narrow-minded. He would be unable to hold friends.

If I had to do business with a man whose head was well shaped, whose eyes were large, gray, and prominent; who had a sensuous nose with large nostrils, a good strong chin, a full mouth, and large ears well shaped and well placed, I would invite him to dinner at the best restaurant in town and get a pretty girl for his partner. I would know him to be a ladies' man with a brute nature predominating, self-centered and susceptible to praise, with a weakness for gaiety and night life.

All this became part of my nature—this reading of character by countenance, feature and expression. From such particular observations I gradually formed general conclusions.

People do not become better individuals or progress toward a better communal life except by inspiration and example. Thus there is never a time when a lot of people are getting better just because it is their nature to do so, any more than there is ever a time when a lot of people are getting worse because it is their nature to do so. Always they follow their leaders, men who are strong and purposeful, and either spiritual and selfless or ambitious and egotistical. A little group of willful men, as Wilson said, can lead a nation to hell or salvation.

We Americans are a good people, and we are spiritual. But we have left our churches and put away our hymnals. We believe in religion, but we have ceased little by little to practice it; and we have ceased little by little to practice charity. We are, we say, Christians, but too often the word is given for the deed. We cannot endure in this way of life; we cannot prosper. Christianity is not a theory to be believed. It is a living force which must be active, else it will die; and if it dies everything which it has touched will perish with it. No thing has being except in the imagination of God; if He ceases for an instant to think of us, we no longer exist.

You will say that this is an old-fashioned sermon by an old-fashioned Presbyterian. That is true. But if I may be allowed one word of my own here in this book, let me say that all of us had better harken to the old-fashioned way. We had better be about our Father's business. He will not wait forever.

Index

About the Author

THOMAS SUGRUE *was born in Naugatuck, Connecticut, in 1907. He studied at Washington and Lee University, where he obtained a master's degree in English in 1930. In 1931 he went to work for the* New York Herald Tribune *as a reporter, leaving this position to work as a staff writer for the* American Magazine *in 1934. For several years he travelled abroad for the* American. *Since 1938 he has devoted himself to book reviewing and free-lance writing. His reviews have appeared in the* New York Times, *the* New York Herald Tribune, *and the* Saturday Review of Literature. *Among his books are a novel,* Such Is The Kingdom, *published in 1940; and a study of clairvoyance and extra-sensory perception,* There Is A River, *which appeared in 1943. He writes poetry and occasional articles for various magazines. At present he is a member of the staff of the* Saturday Review of Literature, *which he joined shortly after completing work on* Starling of the White House.